Cultivating Their Own

Rochester Studies in African History and the Diaspora

Toyin Falola, Series Editor
The Jacob and Frances Sanger Mossiker Chair in the Humanities
and University Distinguished Teaching Professor
University of Texas at Austin

Recent Titles

Race, Decolonization, and Global Citizenship in South Africa
Chielozona Eze

Plantation Slavery in the Sokoto Caliphate: A Historical and Comparative Study
Mohammed Bashir Salau

African Migration Narratives: Politics, Race, and Space
Edited by Cajetan Iheka and Jack Taylor

Ethics and Society in Nigeria: Identity, History, Political Theory
Nimi Wariboko

African Islands: Leading Edges of Empire and Globalization
Edited by Toyin Falola, R. Joseph Parrott, and Danielle Porter-Sanchez

Catholicism and the Making of Politics in Central Mozambique, 1940–1986
Eric Morier-Genoud

Liberated Africans and the Abolition of the Slave Trade, 1807–1896
Edited by Richard Anderson and Henry B. Lovejoy

The Other Abyssinians:
The Northern Oromo and the Creation of Modern Ethiopia, 1855–1913
Brian J. Yates

Nigeria's Digital Diaspora: Citizen Media, Democracy, and Participation
Farooq A. Kperogi

West African Masking Traditions: History, Memory, and Transnationalism
Raphael Chijioke Njoku

A complete list of titles in the Rochester Studies in African History and the Diaspora series may be found on our website, www.urpress.com.

Cultivating Their Own

Agriculture in Western Kenya during the "Development" Era

Muey C. Saeteurn

University of Rochester Press

The University of Rochester Press gratefully acknowledges the generous support of the Department of History and Critical Race and Ethnic Studies, the Center for the Humanities, and the School of Social Sciences, Humanities, and Arts at the University of California, Merced.

First published 2020

University of Rochester Press
668 Mt. Hope Avenue, Rochester, NY 14620, USA
www.urpress.com
and Boydell & Brewer Limited
PO Box 9, Woodbridge, Suffolk IP12 3DF, UK
www.boydellandbrewer.com

ISBN-13: 978-1-58046-979-1
ISSN: 1092-5228

Library of Congress Cataloging-in-Publication Data

Names: Saeteurn, Muey C, author.
Title: Cultivating their own : agriculture in western Kenya during the "development" era / Muey C Saeteurn.
Other titles: Rochester studies in African history and the diaspora, 1092-5228 ; 90.
Description: Rochester, NY, USA : University of Rochester Press, 2020. | Series: Rochester studies in African history and the diaspora, 1092-5228 ; 90 | Includes bibliographical references and index.
Identifiers: LCCN 2020004282 | ISBN 9781580469791 (hardback) | ISBN 9781787448650 (pdf)
Subjects: LCSH: Agriculture and state—Kenya. | Agriculture—Kenya. | Agriculture—Economic aspects—Kenya.
Classification: LCC HD2126.5 .S23 2020 | DDC 338.1096762/809045—dc23
LC record available at https://lccn.loc.gov/2020004282

This publication is printed on acid-free paper.
Printed in the United States of America.

To Mark David and Eleanor Ching

Contents

Acknowledgments

This project has its roots in a paper I wrote for a seminar on the social history of modern Kenya during my second year of graduate school. Through its metamorphosis, I have lived in seven cities on two separate continents all the while accruing debts to family, friends, and mentors who supported and believed in me (and this project) every step of the way. Here is my modest attempt to repay this large debt.

I am forever thankful to Timothy Parsons who continues to be an exceptional advisor. Without his excitement and genuine interest this project would never have been started and without his intellectual guidance would certainly never have been finished. I am also grateful to Jean Allman for her generous advice and encouragement throughout the years. Her knowledge of nationalism and decolonization strongly influenced the development of this project from its earliest stages.

I owe a great debt also to Sara Berry whose incisive comments and thoughtful questions improved the manuscript. Richard Roberts has graciously offered me sage advice over the years, and provided me with an intellectual base in the Bay Area. Jim McCann's guidance and insights on African agriculture have been invaluable. I must also thank Corrie Decker, Daniel Immerwahr, Rachel Jean-Baptiste, Robert Maxon, Derek Peterson, Nancy Reynolds, Gabe Rosenberg, Brett Shadle, and Martin Shanguhyia for providing useful commentary and research leads at various stages of writing. I am immensely thankful to Toyin Falola for his enthusiasm and for believing in the book.

I could not have started, let alone finished the project, without the assistance of many in Kenya. I would like to extend my deepest gratitude to the kindhearted *wazee* who trusted me with their stories and who never allowed me to leave their homes empty-handed. The staff at the National Archives in Nairobi, especially Richard Ambani, Peterson Kithuka, and Barbara, made sure that my visits were productive. Elijah Nyamberi, along with his staff at the Western Provincial archives in Kakamega, not only helped me locate valuable source material but provided me with delicious sandwiches and tea every time I dropped by. I would never have been able to explore Maragoliland's rich history (and its hilly terrain) without the help of my remarkable and resourceful Research Assistant, Nicholas Lagoswa and his family. Thank you for making my time in western Kenya so memorable. Richard Amwanyi, Victoria Mutheu, and Katia Nagarajan also provided me with a great deal of assistance. I am also indebted to Kathy Howitt and her parents, Joan and Rodney Morris, for allowing me access to the family's personal archives. I hope my writing captures the degree to which Joan and Rodney dedicated themselves to western Kenya and to building the local Friends community.

While in Kenya, I had the good fortune of befriending so many brilliant and generous individuals. I am especially grateful to Netlyn Bernard, Ana Crumling-Effinginer, Lynsey Farrell, Donald and Ruth Thomas, John Muhanji, Rose Afanda, the entire Grace family, and Rachelle Strawther for helping me find my bearings. My time in Kisumu was particularly enjoyable because of Mary Cooke who was always willing to explore the town with me. I cannot begin to express my gratitude to you and Simon Letherman for your friendship, generosity, and hospitality throughout the years.

The friends I made while in graduate school continue to inspire me. Thanks to David Chancellor, Jane and Nate Green, Sara Jay, Cree Johannsen, En Li, and Kevin Wooten for making time for our cohort dinners, especially during my daunting first year. I am also very appreciative of John Aerni-Flessner and Meghan Ference for leading the way, and to Keona Ervin, who not only helped me demystify graduate school but encouraged me to embrace my own process along the way. Waseem Kasim and Adwoa Opong made my return visits to Washington University in St. Louis memorable and enlightening. Margaret Williams and Sheryl Peltz helped me successfully navigate the bureaucracy of grad school. As a Chancellor's fellow, I could always count on Sheri Notaro, Rafia Zafar, and Amy Gassel for advice and moral support. I was also very fortunate to have known Maggie Garb both as a Professor and friend. I will always be grateful to her and Eva Garb for providing me with much needed distractions and perspective. The person most responsible for making sure I was well-cared for while in St. Louis was Courtney Berg. Thank you for your warmth and friendship.

My colleagues at Mississippi State University's history department made my transition from graduate student to faculty member smoother. Marsha Barrett and Andy Lang, in particular, made working at the office entertaining. Thank you both for your support and camaraderie. Davide Orsini helped me to improve my writing habit. Kathryn Barbier and Alix Hui continue to provide words of wisdom and encouragement from afar. Alan

Marcus ensured that I had the time and the funding to work on the project. Starkville felt a little more like home largely because of Martha, Henry, and Brandon Barton, Megan Bean, Courtney Carter, Nickoal Eichmann-Kalwara, Kate Fabel, Jim Kalwara, Kecia Johnson, and Karina Zelaya.

I continue to have good fortune when it comes to home institutions. I am grateful for my colleagues in the HIST/CRES Department at the University of California, Merced who have embraced me and made certain that I had the time to complete the book. I want to especially thank Kevin Dawson for his mentorship. David Torres-Rouff has been an incredibly kind and understanding Chair. I am lucky to call Sandie Ha and Patricia Vergara my colleagues and friends. The staff from the School of Social Sciences, Humanities, and Arts (SSHA) provided a great deal of assistance as I prepared the final manuscript. A grant from UC Merced's Center for the Humanities also enabled me to complete the project in a timely manner.

Even if some have yet to fully comprehend what I do for a living, my family and friends never wavered in their support. I am indebted to Jonathan and Debi Kerrick, who have been my biggest champions since the very start of this journey. Old Man, I would never have come this far without your reassuring presence and profound belief in me. I want to also thank Ernest Gonzales, Joanne Hotchkiss, Mary Pickering, Devika Singh, Charlie Thomas and Benjamin Uchiyama for continually reminding me of my potential. To Randi Bivona for your wit and dependable hospitality over the years. Grateful to Katie Henderson, Kara Moskowitz, Teresa Parish, and Chris Shu for holding me to my writing deadlines. My dear friend, Andreea Mihalache, never fails to amaze me with her intellect and thoughtfulness. I am so glad I knocked on your door, Neighbor!

My parents, Manh Fow and Lou Siew Saeteurn, along with my siblings—Nai, Kao, Nancy, and Carrie—have never questioned my stubborn persistence. Thank you for always reminding me of how loved I am no matter where I happen to be in this world. I am also very lucky to have Jeff, Sean, Charlotte, Avery, and Danny as members of my family. David, Jan, Kristin, Andrew, Carlie, John, and the entire Whitehouse clan have been encouraging over the years, and to Eleanor Ching Whitehouse who had no part in this project yet everything to do with my happiness this past year. I am in awe of you. Finally, I am grateful to Mark David Whitehouse for his humor, levelheadedness, and unfailing confidence in me. The very fact that this book exists is a testament of your love and dedication. Thank you for letting me be your *Little Wanderer*.

Acronyms and Abbreviations

ADC	African District Council
CCK	Christian Council of Kenya
CDC	Colonial Development Corporation
CD&W	Colonial Development and Welfare
CLB	Central Land Board
EAYM	East Africa Yearly Meeting
FAM	Friends Africa Mission
FTC	Farmers' Training Center
ICA	International Cooperation Administration
IDS	Institute of Development Studies
ILO	International Labour Organization
KADU	Kenya African Democratic Union
KANU	Kenya African National Union
KLFA	Kenya Land Freedom Army
KPU	Kenya People's Union
LDSB	Land Development and Settlement Board
LSWD	Land Settlement and Water Development
LSS	Lugari Settement Scheme
MAS	Million Acre Scheme
USAID	United States Agency for International Development

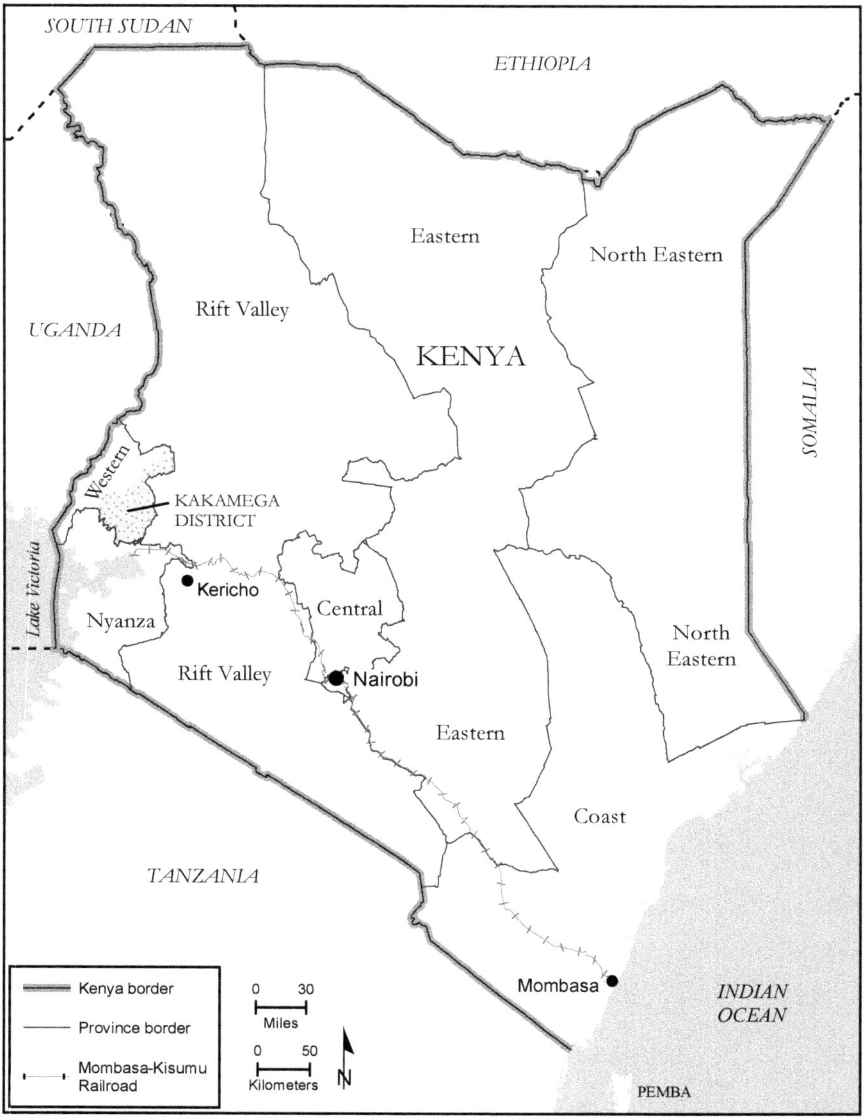

Figure I.1. Map of Kenya. Map by Brian Edward Balsley, GISP

Introduction

In a televised speech given on September 11, 1964, Jomo Kenyatta, then the Prime Minister of Kenya, emphasized to his fellow Kenyans that the greatest asset they possessed as citizens of a newly-independent nation-state was the land.[1] "In land lies our salvation and survival," he stated, "whatever our plans for the future, they must spring from a resolve to put to maximum production our land, however small the acreage we possess."[2] Having only assumed complete sovereignty from Britain on December 12, 1963, Kenyatta and his Kenya African National Union (KANU) government were hard at work building the new nation-state. Though KANU politicians disagreed as much among themselves as with members from the oppositional Kenya African Democratic Union (KADU) party about what type of Kenyan state would be built, they recognized the urgency of addressing the socioeconomic issues persisting from the colonial era. Specifically, the *uhuru* (independence) government focused on reducing the high unemployment rate, especially in urban centers, along with alleviating the acute landlessness and land-shortage problems their constituents faced and expected them to fix.

With these objectives in mind, Kenyatta initiated the "Back to the Land" movement and put into motion the KANU government's ambitious project of pragmatic agrarianism. This project was a series of development policies and schemes intended to increase the nation's commercial agricultural output by making full-time farming popular with the *wananchi* (citizens). Government-sponsored agrarianism aimed to produce rapid economic development for poor Kenyans by bringing them into the market economy as either productive smallholder cash crop farmers or skilled agricultural laborers working on the plantation estates owned by foreigners and wealthy political elites.[3]

For the Kenyatta regime and its development partners such as the World Bank and missionary societies like the Friends Africa Mission (FAM), the agrarianism project made sense because Kenya was predominately an agricultural country with no way of growing the economy other than through its export farming.[4] Having the Kenyan citizenry maintain the productivity of commercial farms located mainly in Kenya's former "white highlands," an area located in the present-day Rift Valley and Central Province that held the country's most fertile and arable lands that European settler-farmers dominated until independence, was fundamental to the KANU government's nation-building program. The program essentially treated large-scale commercial agriculture as the means to increasing the nation's GDP—the indicator for progress (i.e. development) for economists and policy makers at the time—and thus enabling Kenya's economy to "take off."[5] Kenyatta's clarion call was therefore to convince the majority of *wanachi*, especially unemployed urbanities and poor rural Kenyans, to accept that their prosperity was tied to working (though not necessarily owning) the land rather than receiving government handouts and competing for limited white-collar jobs.

Most Kenyans, however, due to land scarcity did not share the Kenyan government's unyielding faith in agriculture as the key to economic prosperity. Moreover, during the euphoria of *uhuru* (independence), they did not accept that their upward mobility rested solely on getting their hands dirty in the soil. Rather, recipients of the rural "betterment" programs had their own notions of what constituted a "developed" life in the *uhuru* era and thus what it meant to be a Kenyan citizen. Their views often conflicted with the elite ruling class and development agents' agendas for the rural citizenry. Recognizing that the pro-agricultural development projects of the decolonization and independence era were out of touch with their reality and expectations, rural Kenyans either walked away from or modified rural betterment schemes to fit their circumstances.

Landless and land-poor rural Kenyans, in particular, were pragmatists who wanted their nationalist leaders and Kenya's development partners to offer schemes and policies that either provided them with sufficient land to become "rich" farmers or that would altogether alleviate them from the toil of rural life. For instance, Kesyia Mwasiagi, a longtime resident of the densely populated region of Maragoliland, was anything but galvanized by Kenyatta's call to action. From her modest two-and-a-half-acre farm she recalled the betrayal she felt upon learning about the *uhuru* government's development program. "I did not receive that message well," Mwasiagi remembered; "in the first place, they were telling us that the white men were leaving and things would be good and that Africans would pull themselves [up] and that we would get everything that we needed. Now, he [Kenyatta] was telling us to go back to the fields and work . . . I didn't like that."[6] Her neighbor, Melice Onyango, who was subsisting on less than an acre plot of land, was equally displeased with Kenyatta's recommendations for people like herself. "He [Kenyatta] was sitting in an office somewhere getting money and telling you to put your fingers in the soil. I didn't receive it well," she recounted.[7]

Relying on the land as their sole means of survival was neither appealing nor realistic for many Maragoliland residents. Predominately agriculturalists, the people who identified themselves as Maragoli Luhya in rural western Kenya were keenly aware that tilling the soil was an arduous job (irrespective of who they did it for) and that farming provided little financial security. High crop yields were never guaranteed due to unreliable weather patterns and depletion of soil nutrients. In fact, most Maragoliland residents did not consider commercial farming a viable career option because there were hardly any substantial pieces of arable land available. By the mid-1950s, for example, colonial government officials reported that the Maragoli Luhya population had grown at "2% per annum or an increase of 50% per generation" and that some areas in this region had 1,930 persons per square mile.[8]

Hence, even if Maragoli Luhyas wanted to practice cash-crop farming, it would have been on a few acres at most and often much less. Remaining on the land to cultivate small yields on a full-time basis was unappealing for subsistence plot holders in Maragoliland, especially if one was fortunate enough to have opportunities off the land as the result of educational training. This was the position held by Jethro Luseno, who left his two-acre Maragoliland plot for Nairobi in 1967 to pursue a career in dentistry. "After my fourth form when I got the chance to join college, I thought [to myself] OK let me pursue college first," Luseno explained; "I would go to farming if I still wanted, but when I got to college I found it was even easier to make some little money out of that education. So, I thought why go back to farming . . . let others do it."[9]

As Luseno's comments reveal, the Kenyan government's "Back to the Land" appeals, and by extension the agrarianism project, were largely dismissed by educated rural Kenyans, particularly those in Maragoliland, who expected the immediate post-independence years to be the time when they would depend less on the land as "the mother of wealth, development, and general prosperity." [10] For such individuals, a career in small-scale farming did not provide the type of return on investment that they, along with their family members and neighbors, anticipated when they were sacrificing their hard-earned cash to pay for school fees. Tilling the soil was therefore more of a security measure than a necessary occupation for many educated and landed Maragolis.

On the other hand, not all rural Kenyans had the education (nor the desire) to compete with their peers for limited white-collar jobs in overcrowded townships that were far away from their families and the comforts of home. In spite of the KANU politicians' promise to carry out a "crash-program of Africanisation," most of the desirable professional jobs in urban centers were still out of reach for the majority of everyday Kenyans at independence because they lacked the necessary experience and skills.[11] The scarcity of white-collar jobs meant that there were individuals in places like Maragoliland who welcomed the Kenyan government's agrarian schemes and projects throughout the late 1950s and 1960s. However, like their urban-bound Maragoliland peers, they understood the inherent contradiction of the agrarianism project—it required access to more fertile land than was available at home. Thus, they too did not want to practice subsistence farming. Rather, they wanted the developmentalists' schemes and projects to give them access to fertile land in places like the highlands and to less labor-intensive jobs that included posts in the Ministry of Agriculture.

The agrarianism project therefore sorely disappointed many rural Kenyans who expected their nationalist leaders to usher in measurable changes. It presumed that ordinary farmers lacked the knowledge to efficiently use their limited resources, notably land. And, at its worst, the agriculture-as-development philosophy upheld by nationalist leaders and development practitioners sought to acquire the assets of the colonial regime and foreign aid agencies at the cost of addressing local rural Kenyans' structural problems and their expectations. Developing agriculture "on the ground" never got off the ground, because of the absence of alignment of local interests with the agendas of nation builders and foreign developers.

Many scholars and practitioners of development generally consider the ineffectiveness of the late colonial and early independence African agricultural development to be the result of "failed states," "'ineffective' markets," "African ignorance," and either too much or not enough aid.[12] These conventional narratives allege that sub-Saharan Africa's failure to replicate Asia's Green Revolution, and thus its inability to harness agriculture for sustained GDP growth, stems from the corruption, volatile markets, and "tribalism" that were theoretically unique to the continent following decolonization. Such analyses, however, remain largely ahistorical and imply that development programs were largely a one-way undertaking. This rationale not only removes thoughtful local actors from the process of development but eclipses the basic fact that there existed structural constraints that limited possibilities for small-holder farmers while also influencing the way the state and various international agencies organized their development initiatives.

Indeed, the outcomes of nationalist projects and development efforts in sub-Saharan Africa hinged on the various interactions taking place among different groups of historical actors, each of whose own experiences, expectations, and structural constraints influenced decisions and shaped the transfer of power. Present-day philanthropists and policy makers who are focused on locating causes in order to solve Africa's underdevelopment would benefit from closer attention to the host of actors who at the dawn of independence had very different understandings of the potential of that moment, as well as their own notions of development and of what constituted a better life in the postcolonial era. Any discussion of the shortcomings of Africa's development era and critiques of failed nationalist projects must consider the competing interests, conflicting agendas, and structural problems inherent in the process of development at the international, national, and local level.

"Development" in Africa

Development was (and continues to be) a complicated concept that suffers from problems of definition.[13] In its basic meaning, it can denote an improvement in living standards and better opportunities. Similarly, it could be a strategy used by colonial states in the mid-twentieth century to legitimize power, as well as a political project that allowed colonial subjects to demand entitlements from imperial regimes.[14] Development may also refer to an ideological project and normative concept that (Western) nation-builders and scholars of the Cold War era treated as a synonym for improvement and capital growth, which sought to raise per capita income of poorer agrarian-based countries in sub-Saharan Africa to the level of capitalist Western nation-states.[15] In spite of its diverse and complicated meanings, the development project in Africa remains a popular task undertaken by national governments, international aid agencies, non-government organizations (secular and religious), and so-called "experts." It often excludes local people's ideas and conceptions of development.

The attempt to improve the social welfare of "underdeveloped" communities, especially within post-World-War-II British colonial Africa, has its roots in the late eighteenth and nineteenth centuries and with the social betterment activities of religious institutions and their missions.[16] Missionaries were vital allies for empire builders. Great Britain in particular benefited from the efforts of Christian missionaries like the Friends Africa Mission, which was largely responsible for improving the social conditions of Britain's colonial subjects prior to 1929. It was not until the implementation of the Colonial Development Bill of 1929 that the Colonial Office received some funds to carry out its development policy, although the focus was on dealing with the metropole's unemployment crisis rather than colonial development.[17]

The Colonial Development and Welfare (CD&W) Act of 1945 solidified the British government's prewar effort to help finance the economic and social development of its colonial territories and subjects. This legislation extended the initial 1940 CD&W Act, which the British government put on hold during the war. As a consequence, colonial development did not take off until January 31, 1945, a few months before the end of the Second World War in Europe, when the Secretary of State for the Colonies, Oliver Stanley, introduced amendments to the 1940 CD&W Act. Like the first Act, the 1945 CD&W Act sought to make Britain's colonies into self-supporting communities that were prepared to advance along the political framework of the British. Both CD&W Acts were also a marked departure from the initial 1929 Colonial Development Bill.[18] However, all three Parliamentary proposals allowed the British government to abandon completely its *laissez-faire* attitude that it previously held with respect to developing its colonial territories and subjects.

Backed by the Fabian-influenced Labour party, the updated CD&W Act that was finalized in December 1945 increased Britain's investment in its colonies from £50 million to £120 million. The government allocated the funds to development schemes and research work for a period of ten years. This enlarged financial aid package was to equip the colonial governments in the post-World War II era with the means to increase social services such as education and health throughout the Empire. Increasing the government's expenditures for social services in the colonies, according to Arthur Creech-Jones, then the Under-Secretary of State for the Colonies, was well justified. Creech-Jones, who also served as the Chairman for the Fabian Colonial Bureau from 1940 to 1948, had been pushing the Colonial Office to do more to ensure that the colonies be prepared with the research and social welfare programs necessary to bring about equality of opportunity within their local societies—a basic principle of the Fabian Society.[19] "The policy pursued by Britain is not altogether a gesture of altruism; it undoubtedly has this aspect," Creech-Jones wrote, "but at the same time Britain is in turn indebted to the colonies and her expenditure on their social and economic development is largely offset by the important advantages her relationship to the territories brings."[20] The 1945 CD&W Act committed the British Treasury to carrying out Britain's "trusteeship" responsibilities. The Colonial Office was to use the financial aid to build the social and economic conditions necessary for colonized people in places like British Africa to attain self-government within the empire. Realistically, the development funds and technical officers arriving in African colonies as part of the "second colonial occupation" were to help with Britain's postwar economic recovery and to forestall anti-colonial nationalism sentiments that had been brewing since the 1930s in other territories such as Jamaica in the Caribbean.[21]

In order to garner CD&W funds, colonial governments throughout the Empire had to "think in terms of large-scale planning" by preparing ten-year development plans.[22] Centralized planning on behalf of state governments had been popular since the 1920s when Stalin's regime originated the drafting of comprehensive five-year economic plans to accelerate industrialization in the Soviet Union.[23] Western scholars and superpowers in the interwar period and throughout the post-World War II era eventually adopted the Stalinist model for planning economic development. They practiced large-scale planning in their efforts to expedite the modernization process in the less-developed world, because of its apparent success in rapidly industrializing the USSR. In fact, the conditions under which colonial governments were to carry out centralized economic planning was included in the original 1940 Act, but throughout the war years planning rarely occurred in some territories, and the Colonial Office often delayed approving the plans that the colonial governments submitted. British officials hoped that such a stipulation would allow the local people (at least the governments of the territories) some responsibility in building their own higher standard of living. Moreover, the requirement allowed politicians in Whitehall to justify to the global UN community, which was becoming increasingly critical of imperialism in the post-1945 era, Britain's commitment to helping its territories become politically "developed."

The Colonial Office, consequently, required local governments to adopt the top-down statist approach to development by crafting detailed economic plans as a precondition for financial support. In so doing, Britain was able both to intervene in the development process of its sub-Saharan African territories and to impose on the local African political leaders a practice that eventually became popular with modernization theorists working for aid institutions like the World Bank and the United States

Agency for International Development (USAID) throughout the 1950s and 1960s.[24] Modernization theory—and Rostow in particular—favored economic metrics for success such as growth in GDP, and it emphasized centralized planning coupled with purposeful state intervention. The goal was to effect a transition of nascent "traditional" agrarian nation-states like Kenya into industrialized powerhouses that would embrace capitalism and democracy.[25]

Hence, within the context of the decolonization and independence eras, development was primarily a state-directed Cold War project to promote modernization in which "modern" meant adopting the values and culture of either Western or Eastern-bloc countries. It also referred to an organized and centralized intervention on the part of state governments and their development allies to bring about beneficial change in the economic and social condition of individuals and communities. This beneficial change was highly subjective, and often it was international policy makers and practitioners who defined what and who benefited. Yet, as the following chapters demonstrate, this hardly meant that the targets of development lacked the agency to shape the top-down comprehensive economic plans that were in vogue with African statesmen, out-going colonial officials, and development practitioners during the decolonization and independence era.

The act of development planning in particular helped Kenyan political leaders like Tom Mboya and Jomo Kenyatta maintain good relations with their Western benefactors and investors. United States diplomats praised the two Kenyan politicians for establishing a planning and development commission and thus making economic planning a top concern for the 1962 coalition government composed of both KANU and KADU. As a Republic, the KANU government created the Ministry of Economic Planning and Development in 1964 under the guidance of Mboya, who served as Minister in 1966. Under Mboya's influence the Ministry of Economic Planning and Development crafted and issued comprehensive economic development plans that largely favored the West. The 1965 *Session Paper Number 10: African Socialism and Its Application to Planning in Kenya*, for example, specified that Kenya's particular version of African socialism meant capitalism, a definition that differed significantly from its neighbors in East Africa.[26] Kenyatta and Mboya's actions suggested to the US State Department that Kenya's politicians, at least those they regarded favorably, were capable of taking economic development seriously and thus could lead an independent (Westernized) government that was worthy of future financial support.[27]

More than maintaining foreign relations, the KANU-dominated government elected into office in 1963 wanted a comprehensive economic program to mobilize the citizenry to contribute to the economic growth of the Kenyan nation-state.[28] Specifically, the political leaders needed to show the *wananchi* that they had a clear strategy for resolving major socioeconomic problems facing the country at the dawn of independence. These concerns included grievances about land and unemployment on behalf of millions of poor and landless Kenyans, the sharp decline in the Nairobi stock market as foreign businesses halted or limited their investments, and the huge unemployment crisis resulting from the exodus of the European settler farming community who owned plantations and ranches that produced eighty percent of exports and employed nearly half of the Kenyan workforce.[29] The national development plans of the KANU government, in essence, detailed the economic constraints and wishful thinking of the newly-elected Kenyan leaders. In so doing, the Kenyatta regime appealed to all Kenyans, especially those in the rural sector, to put the interest of the "nation" above their own. The process of development in the immediate post-colonial context of the 1960s was a political act that fundamentally compelled people to alter their lives and expectations.[30] By participating in the agrarian development projects ordinary Kenyans would theoretically help grow the nation's agricultural-based export economy and thus increase the GDP—a marker for development.

Capital accumulation and growth in national GDP, indeed, were the marker for development in the early years of independent Kenya and the wider world in the 1960s.[31] This particular meaning and metric of development did not go uncriticized. Scholars and development economists in the 1960s, particularly those affiliated with think-tanks like the Institute of Development Studies (IDS) that was founded in part by ex-colonial experts, critiqued this interpretation of development as a "value judgment," while those who came afterwards challenged its quantitative-focused definition by maintaining that the aim of development should also involve broadening choice and reducing deprivation.[32] Dudley Seers, for example, observed that using narrow economic indicators was "a preference for avoiding the real problems of development."[33] The qualitative redefinition of development by economists and policy-makers resulted in the notion that development meant an improvement in overall well-being rather than an increase in national economic growth. Accordingly, throughout the 1970s, aid agencies such as the World Bank and USAID, along with the United Nations' International Labour Organization (ILO), promoted policies and provided funding aimed at reducing poverty, unemployment, and inequality instead of strictly growing the GDP of "underdeveloped" countries like Kenya.[34]

However, the statist dimension of development in the 1960s and 1970s, which was supported by modernization theorists, was harshly criticized by neo-liberal economists like Peter Bauer, and Deepak Lal, among others. Neo-liberal proponents of deregulation and unrestricted markets maintained that government spending and state protectionism did little to improve (or develop) the conditions of the poor, and were likely contributing to rising interest rates and the slowing of economic growth in the so-called "Third World."[35] By the start of the 1980s, with the abandonment of both the Bretton Woods system of fixed exchange rates and Keynesian economic policy by superpowers like the United States, the World Bank and International Monetary Fund (IMF) acceded to neo-liberal orthodoxy by curtailing the powers of national governments that were seeking aid through structural adjustment programs (SAPs). Specifically, SAPs were economic reforms that limited the role of the state in the economy and reduced government expenditure on social services like health and education that were vital for the type of development projects championed by the ILO and IDS. Yet SAPs were promoted by neo-liberal policy makers and development specialists during the 1980s as the proper way to develop the African continent.[36] By the mid-1990s, however, World Bank and IMF officials reevaluated and eventually abandoned market-oriented interventions. Policy makers did so when it became clear that the free market approach to initiating development seemed to be exacerbating the economic, political, and social problems facing African governments and citizens. Consequently, by the twenty-first century, the concept of development evolved into a bottom-up project aimed at reducing poverty, improving health and education, and increasing productive capacity and per capita income in poorer societies.[37]

Discourses on Development

While the scholarship on development in sub-Saharan Africa during the late colonial era has grown substantially in recent decades, it has historically emphasized the role of foreign development practitioners in shaping projects and consequently the conditions on the ground.[38] James Ferguson, for example, called attention to the ways in which foreign development agencies located within "developmentalist" states like Lesotho sought to de-politicize rural societies and thus discourage local communities from taking part in development projects.[39] Similarly, James Scott faulted "high-modernists," technocrats who used state powers to make the indigenous populations that they sought to improve and govern more "legible," as the sole culprits responsible for the failures of modern social engineering projects throughout the twentieth century.[40] Bowman, more recently, maintained that the technical "experts" in post-independence Zambia were marginalized dissenting figures with little influence over the development process. While Bowman de-emphasizes the role of development specialists, his focus is largely on the ways in which the development policymakers, including the Zambian independent government, were not united in their plans and objectives for bringing forth an agrarian revolution in the countryside. It is still a story of disagreements between elite politicians and policymakers over nation building.[41]

Such explorations of underdevelopment suggest that the process of development was orchestrated by the international community of "experts" and a handful of elite politicians. Absent are local women and men whose decisions and actions also shaped the business of development. Moreover, this top down perspective supports a simplistic notion that the developmentalist state—a state engaged in institutional central planning to promote growth and change—was omnipotent and thus development was a project done to the people, especially to individuals in the rural sector. However, as residents in Maragoliland demonstrate, the development personnel and policy makers charged with carrying out an agrarian revolution in Kenya during the decolonization and early independence years were limited in their ability to influence the household dynamics and expectations of ordinary Kenyans. While the development practitioners' agricultural schemes and programs were invasive and condescending, this scholarship misses an important point: the developmentalist state could not prevent rural men and women from reinterpreting agrarian schemes to promote their own needs.

The constraints facing non-elites in the agricultural sector, which may better explain the "underdevelopment" taking place in twentieth-century rural Africa, have not been completely ignored by Africanist scholars. Goran Hyden, Sara Berry, and Elias Mandala have investigated the reasons for the lack of development in rural communities throughout sub-Saharan Africa by examining the challenges peasant farmers faced in the colonial era.[42] Focusing on the agency of the peasantry, Hyden maintained that rural communities throughout the continent, particularly in Tanzania, remained underdeveloped because they continued to embrace an "economy of affection" that allowed them to opt out of Western-focused development projects.

At the same time, according to Berry, some African farmers were ultimately precluded from effectively engaging in the development process due to the difficulty of accessing land and manual labor. Mandala's historical survey of farmers in the Mang'anja community in Malawi broadened this list of social, economic, and political challenges by arguing that environmental risks also prevented peasant farmers from experiencing development.

Although these studies have directed more attention to local conditions as well as the experiences of ordinary people, most literature on peasant farmers continues to suggest that in one way or another the agrarian revolution that the late colonial governments and early independence African regimes articulated in their grand national development schemes were largely failures. Yet the development projects in rural western Kenya did not fail so much as they were complicated by ordinary people making their own decisions about what was advantageous for them as they experienced the euphoria of decolonization and independence. In the late colonial and immediate post-independence years, the possibilities for progress and social advancement seemed almost limitless. Rural Kenyans, as a result, often did what was best for them as individuals and not what was best for the nationalists, development "experts," and local leaders.

Recently the history of development in Africa has moved beyond this failure and success binary. Historians of Africa and development are providing a more nuanced understanding of the process of development "on the ground" by revealing that local people usually held their own (often competing) ideas of development that differed from those of the project planners and state-builders. John Aerni-Flessner, for example, argues that Basotho youth utilized community organizations and spurred on self-help initiatives that allowed them to build and therefore reimagine Lesotho on their own terms.[43] Similarly, Molly McCullers shows how Herero leaders sought to determine their own political future in the 1960s by rejecting the development efforts of the apartheid regime that was eager to integrate Southwest Africa into the Union of South Africa.[44] An analysis of how Maragoliland residents' reactions to and experiences with agricultural development builds on this local-centric emphasis.

More importantly, focusing on the local has brought to the fore the experiences of those marginalized rural individuals most impacted by grand nation-building projects. Priya Lal's investigation into the meaning of *Ujamaa* (Tanzania's version of socialism) shows how adaptable ordinary Tanzanians were with the controversial project of villagization, which government leaders like Julius Nyerere anticipated would create a more equitable society.[45]

Allen and Barbara Isaacman's work, in particular, focuses on the narratives of the local populations that were displaced by the Cahora Bassa dam project, which developmentalists and "experts" in the colonial and postcolonial era devised with little regard for the realities and the environmental conditions of local communities.[46]

This book aims to expand upon this local-centric approach by showing how rural people became central to the economic and political development of modern Africa. It further confirms the importance of making ordinary Africans heard amongst the cacophony of developmentalism. This bottom-up analysis particularly pays attention to how Maragoli people in western Kenya responded to and made sense of the fundamentally complicated development policies of the late 1950s and 1960s that privileged a pro-agriculture strategy. By placing rural Kenyans at the center of their own history, the shortcomings and unintended consequences of the seemingly never-ending task by outsiders to develop sub-Saharan Africa's farming communities might start to become a bit more rational.

Focusing on rural people in Maragoliland also expands on the African nationalist historiography to include a host of actors that were neither elite males nor urbanites. Such elite characters had been the main focus of political scientists writing about Africa's national movements in the years immediately following political independence.[47] Challenges to this political elite and male-dominated narrative of nationalism emerged soon afterward as scholars like Tabitha Kanogo, Frank Furedi, Terence Ranger, and Susan Geiger, among others included in their political histories Kenyan Squatters, Zimbabwean peasants, and TANU women.[48] Both Angelique Haugerud and Timothy Parsons have widened this scholarship in the twenty-first century, particularly in the Kenyan context, by showing in their works how everyday Kenyans involved themselves in the political process as either African Girl Guide members or vocal *baraza* participants.[49] More recently, Lynn Schler and Joanna Tague have diversified the conversation by examining how peoples beyond the body politic such as seamen and refugees involved themselves in the making of the new nations of Nigeria and Tanzania respectively.[50]

Thus, integrating the experiences of ordinary western Kenyans into the discussions of nation-building widens this literature that has prioritized the role of women and commoners in shaping the new nation. Like landless squatters, disgruntled youth, and jobless city dwellers, men and women in Maragoliland expected better opportunities in the postcolonial state. They wanted more skilled and better-paying jobs, land, and better access to education, among other material improvements. *Uhuru* was supposed to eliminate the class structure created by colonialism. By either engaging in or refraining from the agricultural development program of nation builders and Western "experts," Maragoliland residents demanded the right to a role in imagining and shaping their future in an independent country.[51] The independence movement was not just an urban event carried out by elite politicians. It mobilized and impacted all sectors of Kenyan society.

Missionaries were especially galvanized by Africa's decolonization and the ensuing nation-building project. Mission churches played a central role in promoting and implementing projects to "improve" the material lives of the people in sub-Saharan Africa, especially at the end of empire. As another branch of the colonial enterprise, missions must also be included in any of the critiques of development in both the colonial and national eras. Certainly, the Friends African Mission in western Kenya shared the goals of the late colonial and independent state, along with international development agencies like the World Bank and USAID, by championing programs aiming to meld national development objectives to local needs. The new generation of Quaker evangelists of the late 1950s, in particular, embraced the state's project of agrarianism in order to convert the local Maragoli community and, more importantly, to generate funds for the mission. In so doing, they not only supported the goals of the secular government but were indeed active development agents.

This religious aspect of development was not fully reflected in the literature until recently. Scholars interested in Africa and religion had previously concentrated their attention largely on whether missionaries were effective or ineffective agents of cultural imperialism in colonial Africa. Adrian Hastings's edited volume on Christianity in Africa shifted this trend by exploring the challenges mission churches faced during the African independence era, and more recent works by Brian Stanley and John Stuart have made the links between Christianity, African nationalism, and nation-building more pronounced.[52]

The recent scholarship on missionaries and the end of empire has shown that the evangelists in places like Kenya were willing to assume auxiliary roles at independence. Implicit in this literature is the idea that missionaries were either dormant or uninterested in implementing programs that would allow them to maintain their privileged positions in local church affairs and amongst the communities in which they served. Scholars like Insa Nolte and Julie Hearn have argued that missionary bodies remained inactive developmentalists until the late twentieth century when the new millennium intensified their interests in places like Kenya. This suggests that religious groups *re-emerged* rather than *remained* as development agents in Africa. But the focus on the last decades of the twentieth-century as the period when missionaries became active practitioners of development is inaccurate and reads history backwards. Missionaries have had a long engagement with the development of African enterprise, which extends further than the 1980s and 1990s. Historians of Africa such as Michael Jennings have shown that religious personnel did not abandon their posts in the 1960s when the majority of the African colonies became independent nation states. However, while Jennings argued that the Christian churches, specifically in 1960s Tanzania, redefined their roles and reworked their development programs in order to remain useful and "trusted" partners to nationalist postcolonial governments, this was hardly the end goal for many missionaries. Missions had their own objectives with the arrival of independence. Specifically, they sought to make the mission community into a functioning church that would enable foreign missionaries to continue to play a role in the daily lives of its parishioners at little or no cost to the home church. In short, missions remained key development agents in western Kenya on a par with secular "developers" who supported the government's agricultural development plans.

Maragoli, Kenya: A Case Study

In Maragoliland, the process of development was complicated by conflicting agendas. The Kenyan government and its development partners' comprehensive economic program for the rural sector was often compromised by the personal agendas and goals of the very people it aimed to improve. Maragoliland is a ninety-five square mile region in western Kenya located northwest of Lake Victoria in what is today Vihiga County. Traveling to this area from the present-day port city of Kisumu requires making a sharp climb of 4,800 feet, as well as crossing the equator.[53] These days, the trip by automobile can take anywhere from an hour to two hours depending on the weather, the road conditions and the driver's own agenda. Notwithstanding the usual traffic nuisances and occasional mechanical issues, the drive north away from the bustling Lake Victoria basin town into rural western Kenya is quite picturesque and, for some commuters, can be very serene. The deep red volcanic soils, terraced hill slopes dotted with large boulders, and numerous small farms in which maize and tea bushes grow alongside tall avocado and passion fruit trees, which travelers immediately encounter on the road, are indicators that western Kenya is one of the country's richest farming areas. Accordingly, it is not difficult to understand why Maragoliland was an important arena for state and mission development practitioners interested in improving and utilizing Kenya's agricultural sector.

As previously noted, Maragoliland by the 1950s carried the highest population density in Kenya. A 1951 census report showed that North and South Maragoli, which constituted "Maragoliland," had 606,798 people living within the region's ninety-five square miles. Officials at the time predicted that this number would grow due to advances in health care.[54] The region's high population density meant that residents had little access to land and thus were pragmatic about their options in the decolonization and late colonial period. Rural western Kenyans could not have realistically taken advantage of the agricultural betterment projects in order to become prosperous smallholder cash crop farmers at home. Rather than become "big farmers" in their home villages, a majority of Maragoliland residents were migrant laborers working either on plantations or in urban centers far away from home.

Maragoli residents, who are the focus of this research, fall into four categories: landless, subsistence, smallholder, and large-holder. This classification describes Maragoli residents according to their access to land. Subsistence holders had access to a quarter to two acres of land on which they primary grew domestic food crops like maize, beans, millet, cassava, and other crops. Smallholders held between two and seven acres of land, which allowed them to meet household needs and to produce cash crops like hybrid maize for the market. And large-holders had access to more than seven acres of land, which enabled them to comfortably grow lucrative commercial crops like tea and coffee. Landless people had to work on their neighbors' farms or relocate to the urban centers of Kisumu, Nairobi, or Mombasa.

The Maragoli people in this book were in the great majority of cases landed, educated, and in age cohorts that made them physically able to engage in hard manual labor in the independence era. Specifically, forty-one of the forty-two people interviewed (broken down evenly in terms of gender) who resided in or originated from Maragoliland in the 1950s and 1960s had access to some measure of land either through their fathers or husbands. Following the above categories, eight informants (five males and three females) were large-scale holders from prominent families. From the remaining thirty-three landed Maragolis, twenty people had subsistence units. Only one individual from this group noted that in the 1960s he was landless and thus spent time working and traveling on behalf of the FAM station.[55]

The data explains why the agrarianism project in late colonial and early independence Kenya would seem irrational to a significant number of Maragoliland residents. The way they defined their farm status simply did not align with the categories outlined by development planners. While a Maragoli resident living on eight-acres of land would likely consider themselves a large-scale cash farmer, the reality was that Kenyan agricultural officials, such as Leslie Brown, recognized this individual as a subsistence farmer in their betterment schemes. This difference in definition certainly had huge implications for landed-Maragolis who risked the chance of being passed over on projects and resources meant to develop large-scale farms. The lack of understanding on the part of agricultural experts about local conditions was understandably of concern for some Maragoliland residents. It made them cautious about any type of development agenda and program, either from the Kenyan nationalist government or from foreign development experts, who emphasized the importance of farming as a viable career option.

This skepticism was evident to the Friends Africa Mission agriculturalists who found it increasingly difficult in the 1950s to provide their services to the local Quaker population in Maragoliland because of the region's land scarcity problem. In a 1955 report to the Friends Mission Board, the Mission's agriculturalist Rodney Morris described how the lack of arable land in Maragoliland made it difficult for him to carry out his job to teach better farming practices to the local community. "I am not clear at all what we will say to the Maragoli people, but I know we must help them see the need for learning improved methods even though that in itself my not solve their whole problem," he wrote; "at the present most of them take a negative attitude toward learning improved methods for that very reason."[56]

Maragoliland's population crisis thus provides important insights into why some land-poor people decided to take part in the agricultural development projects while others ignored the project of agrarianism all together, deciding instead to pursue "white collar" jobs in the urban centers. Many in Maragoliland realized that the nation-builders and foreign development personnel in the 1950s and 1960s were promoting unrealistic projects and schemes because land was limited. Nevertheless, they did not completely ignore the government officials and Friends missionaries who were responsible for carrying out "development" in their region. Because they had their own definition of development, they simply engaged with the development practitioners on their own terms when it suited their personal agendas.

Accordingly, for many rural Kenyans, especially in Maragoliland, the project of agrarianism was yet another opportunity they could exploit as *wananchi*.

On Methods and Sources

The data for this study was collected through archival research and open-ended oral interviews. I examined documents housed in state, provincial, and private archives located in the United States, United Kingdom, and Kenya. Reports and memoranda written by senior European and Kenyan government officials and extension field officers working in Kenya's Department of Agriculture and, subsequently, the Ministry of Agriculture during the late colonial and early independence era, contextualized the story of agricultural development in Maragoliland. Furthermore, source material from institutions such as the USAID and the World Bank provided the institutional perspective on the experiences ordinary farmers had with agricultural development policies and projects.

Although the archives held a wealth of information concerning the origins and rationale for Kenya's agricultural development program of the late colonial and early independence years, there were limitations with respect to how revealing the documents were. The institutional records typically dealt with only a thin range of issues, and rarely did the records address the realities of the individuals and communities who were most impacted by the development schemes and policies created in places like Washington DC, Richmond, London, and Nairobi. The contentious nature of the land resettlement program of the early 1960s, for example, factored very little into the official reports that reveal the minutia of the settlement program down to details including soil types and plot sizes. Often missing from the archival records were the rural Kenyan's ambivalence toward relocating to the government-sanctioned land settlement sites because they were far away from their kin and lacked established markets and health clinics.

While the written and printed source material I used came mostly from well-organized and preserved official depositories, I was also fortunate enough to have access to the personal papers of Rodney Morris who was the Friends Africa Mission's inaugural agricultural missionary at Kaimosi in western Kenya. Morris worked in western Kenya from 1955 to 1968 although his tenure with FAM included furloughs that ranged between six months to a year. I discovered Morris's writings at the Friends Collection and Earlham College Archives in Richmond, Indiana, which has an extensive collection of source material pertaining to the activities of the American Friends (Quaker) organization, especially regarding its initiatives in East Africa.

Through some detective work (and luck), I located and subsequently visited Morris in Cortland, New York, in the fall of 2009. He was, unfortunately, unable to verbally communicate with me because of a cognitive condition, so an interview was not conducted. Nevertheless, I left Cortland with a trove of information pertaining to the Friends' Africa Mission's agrarian program in western Kenya during the country's transition from colony to independent nation. The Morris family graciously provided me full access to hundreds of private letters and photographs documenting their time in western Kenya. During his service with FAM, Morris wrote weekly to his family and sent monthly progress reports to the Mission Board in Richmond. Morris's correspondence provided ample details of his efforts to teach local Quaker community members "better" farming practices, as well as his attempts to convince the youth attending the Quaker mission schools in and around Maragoliland the merits of an agricultural education.

For a researcher, especially an historian, gaining access to primary source evidence such as those provided by the Morris family was a windfall. This original material provided an intimate portrait of the missionary enterprise in late colonial and early independence Kenya and, more importantly, emphasized the connection between secular and religious developmentalists that is often overlooked in the development literature. Nevertheless, this source material must be critically read, analyzed, and evaluated in light of the author's background. Morris was an American who had very little practical farming experience prior to his missionary service. Much of his field training, in fact, was from his time as an agricultural science major at Cornell University, where he mostly worked on large-scale industrial farms. As a formally trained agriculturalist, Morris was partial to modern (Western) farm practices and technologies. He often encouraged the local Quaker Kenyan community to use hybrid maize seedlings and to rent FAM's tractor for plowing. His assumptions about the inferiority of African farming methods and his naiveté about the local agrarian culture in western Kenya, particularly regarding subsistence and smallholder farming, were apparent throughout his correspondence. Such biases show that Morris was a product of his time, and his papers offer a glimpse of agricultural development from the vantage point of an outside "expert" agriculturalist.

To get an insider's perspective, I make use of over fifty in-depth oral histories conducted with western Kenyan residents during the period between fall 2010 and spring 2011, with follow-up interviews conducted in the summer of 2016. The bulk of interviews were with individuals from the Chavakali sub-location in Vihiga county, which is located in what is now the Western Region of Kenya and is one of four counties in the former Western Province of Kenya. Vihiga county is predominately home to people who identify as the Maragoli, a sub-group of the Luhya ethnic community. Accordingly, this study focuses on the lived experiences of those individuals who reside in the region colloquially known as Maragoliland, which is described in more detail in chapter 2 below. Rounding out the Maragoliland voices are interviews with former agricultural officers, personnel associated with the Friends Africa Mission agricultural program, and former residents of the region who relocated to the Lugari settlement scheme in the early 1960s.

I connected with my Maragoliland informants largely through my research assistant who is from the Chavakali sub-location. In 2010, he was a field extension officer for the Friends United Meeting's Rural Service Program where he worked with local subsistence and small-holder farmers to increase their yields. The fact that he was from Maragoliland, coupled with his position, made locating informants familiar with agricultural development projects less of a challenge. Several informants were also long-time members of the Quaker church belonging to the local Yearly Meeting, and thus were able to recollect the Friends Africa Mission missionaries' initiatives aimed at improving the farming practices of the local population.

Though the details I gathered from my informants helped to balance the archival material, it is important to recognize that oral interviews are problematic sources. Individuals' memory and experiences undoubtedly shape the details they ultimately discloses to the interviewer. Moreover, informants may answer questions depending on the way they wish to be perceived by others. Present circumstances and the political climate might also color the ways in which individuals perceive their past. Historians therefore are skeptical of oral testimony and question whether the past can be gleaned from listening to personal testimonies. Given that several of my informants were asked about events and affairs that had occurred more than forty or fifty years ago, it is reasonable to assume that some individuals recalled incorrect details because of the limitations of memory, omitted information that did not pertain to their specific circumstance, and revealed perspectives on agricultural development projects that had changed over time.

The methodological challenges associated with the practice of oral history also extends to researchers like myself, who are usually not from the communities and locations that they study. Being an outsider can make capturing the experiences of interviewees challenging. This status, for example, can influence how informants perceive an interviewer's questions and topics of conversation. Discussions about land in particular were difficult due to the historical legacies of Kenya's land-consolidation and adjudication program. My questions regarding land ownership and tenure were often unanswered, because my informants were likely skeptical of my motives and interest in the subject matter.

My outsider status was more pronounced since I did not speak the local dialect, Logoli, and I did not have a command of Kiswahili. Consequently, I relied on my research assistant to translate and to act as the "cultural broker," particularly in situations where my informants indicated they preferred to communicate in Logoli. Employing a translator no doubt influenced the outcome of the interviews and the data collected. Though he was from the community, my research assistant's gender (male) and his occupation (rural extension officer), for example, may have kept elder Maragoli women from revealing their feelings about the male agricultural extension workers who came to teach them "better" farming skills during the late 1950s and early 1960s.

However, despite methodological difficulties, scholars acknowledge that oral histories are valuable because they make clearer the intentions and insights of historical actors that are not visible in written records.[57] The information I captured from my oral interviews certainly made apparent the ways in which rural Kenyans came to terms with the big development projects of the late colonial and early independence period. Such insights help to better contextualize development at the local level.

What's Ahead

Four significant and markedly different types of projects implemented in the late 1950s and early 1960s in Maragoliland—the Chavakali high school project, the Lord's Acre and Stewardship program, the 4-K young farmers' clubs, and the Lugari settlement scheme—reveal the fundamental tensions of development at the international, national, and local level. The four schemes emerged during Kenya's decolonization period, specifically targeting rural people with access to subsistence and smallholding plots—in this case, Maragoliland residents with holdings between two and seven acres of land. Together, the case studies show how the outcomes of nationalist projects and development efforts in sub-Saharan Africa hinged on the various interactions taking place among different groups of historical actors, each of whose own experiences and motivations shaped the transition from colony to nationhood and influenced development projects. Specifically, they show how the project of agrarianism foundered on differences between the agendas of national politicians and international development agencies, and those of rural Kenyans.

Chapter 1 frames the study with a discussion of the role of agriculture in Kenya's political economy in the late 1950s and throughout the 1960s. Specifically, it examines how agrarian projects were embedded in Kenya's decolonization, transition, and early independence years by political elites and development "experts." The chapter also provides an overview of agricultural development programs such as the Swynnerton Plan and the Land Settlement Programs that aimed to improve rural Kenyans' lives as colonial subjects and, eventually, citizens of a nation-state.

Chapter 2 details Maragoliland's physical history and traces the emergence of the Maragoli sub-ethnic community. It situates the region and its people in the larger political, social, and economic context of the mid-twentieth century. The physical boundaries of western Kenya, for example, have not remained constant but shifted over the past century due to the whims of politicians and the ambitions of "ethnic brokers." Administrative changes, both at the local and national levels, also shaped how residents in both Maragoli locations—North Maragoli and South Maragoli—redefined rural betterment schemes in general and interpreted the agrarian projects in particular. Moreover, the chapter shows that the region's population problem had its roots in the colonial era and underscores the point that outsiders, like Friends Africa Mission personnel, have historically viewed the region and people as agricultural.

Chavakali secondary school, the subject of chapter 3, was a place of hope and frustration for the Maragoliland community. The high school emphasized a vocational-agricultural curriculum and was the site where the colonial regime, the nationalist government, and international "developmentalists" attempted to dictate the nature of education, and by extension the place of the rural citizenry, during the late 1950s and throughout the 1960s. This goal, however, was not achieved because ordinary Kenyans challenged the narrative that rural people should only strive to have careers in agriculture and thus remain in the countryside. Chavakali students from Maragoliland in particular used their educational training to enter the wage labor sector on better terms than as simple agriculturalists. Their actions were encouraged by Maragoliland residents who believed that the school ought to serve the interest of the community, especially after having contributed to the initial costs associated with the school's construction through a compulsory special tax imposed by local authorities. The community-funded school was therefore an arena in which local expectations conflicted with national and international development objectives.

Chapter 4 argues that the 4-K Youth Farmers' Club movement did little to convince western Kenyan youths, who were keenly familiar with Maragoli land problems, that agriculture was both a respectable and viable career option in the post-colonial era. Based on the American 4-H clubs, the 4-K club—*Kuungana* (to unite), *Kufanya* (to do), *Kusaidia* (to help), and *Kenya*—was an agricultural youth program that resulted from the 1962 National Conference on Youth. The coalition Kenyan government of 1961 to 1963, along with international government sponsors and non-government development agencies, anticipated that the clubs would cultivate an interest in farming among rural youth. The 4-K clubs were to assist the Kenyan government's agricultural revolution by encouraging young Kenyans to remain in the countryside as productive junior *mwananchi* (citizen) farmers and farmers' wives. While a number of youths from the Maragoli region became involved with their local 4-K clubs, most had no illusions that they would become wealthy cash farmers. This would require access to land—a limited resource. Rather, young Maragolis joined because 4-K clubs provided them with pocket money and a chance to pursue activities with their peers. Maragoliland youths utilized the 4-K movement to gain access to farm-related resources and privileges that they recognized as beneficial to themselves and their families at that particular moment in their lives. Their end goal, in other words, was to address their needs and those of their family members as pragmatically and realistically as they could, without much regard for what their 4-K leaders, elected officials, and development "specialists" expected.

Missionaries were especially galvanized by Africa's decolonization and the ensuing nation-building project. Chapter 5 therefore focuses on the Friends Africa Mission's role as development planners and practitioners in Maragoliland during the late 1950s and throughout the 1960s. Specifically, the chapter focuses on FAM's Lord's Acre Project, which presented opportunities and challenges for the Quaker missionaries in western Kenya who were eager to transform its mission into a strong centralized East Africa Yearly Meeting (or home church). Missionaries implemented the project in the early 1960s as a way to generate revenue for the Yearly Meeting by having participants set aside an acre of crops (usually maize) to donate to their village meetings (churches). Essentially, the project allowed the missionaries to accomplish two important objectives: to turn the mission station at Kaimosi into a financially stable Yearly Meeting and to ensure that local church leaders would still need guidance from foreign Friends missionaries. At the same time, the Lord's Acre Project was encouraging news to Kenyan authorities during the transition period and early independence years because it aimed to convince rural people of the advantages of working on the land. Agricultural officials lauded the project because it placed an emphasis on having farmers in Maragoliland adopt better, "modern" farming practices. In short, the Lord's Acre Project fell in line with the Kenyan government's goals of maintaining a productive rural sector and ensuring that the national agrarian-based economy was stable. Unsurprisingly, FAM personnel experienced similar disappointments and setbacks that their secular counterparts encountered in their efforts to popularize the agrarianism project amongst Kenya's rural communities.

Chapter 6 examines how the planners of Kenya's Million Acre Program's (MAP) high-density land settlement program had difficulty recruiting suitable applicants for the settlement schemes due to their (miss) assumption that rural landless and land-poor Kenyans were desperate. Namely, the chapter argues that MAP planners were incorrect in their belief that all rural Kenyan citizens wanted was land, regardless of the condition and strict provisions associated with the projects. The reactions of Maragoliland residents to the Lugari high-density settlement scheme, in particular, illustrate just how mistaken MAP officials were in their assumptions about rural people and their expectations at independence. The 1962 Lugari Settlement Scheme (LSS) offered participants in the overcrowded Maragoli location at least 10 acres of land, dairy cows, and on-site technical training at the Farmers' Training Center. At first glance, this program should have been popular. However, the coalition Kenyan government and, subsequently, the Kenyatta regime offered such resources to the new settlers under the strict condition that they devote their full-time attention to farming at the new settlement locations, which was located at least fifty miles north of Maragoliland. While land was a socially important and highly coveted resource for young Maragolis, most were unenthusiastic about abandoning their comfortable white-collar jobs in exchange for full-time hard manual work in the fields. Meanwhile, the older generation of Maragoli residents, were skeptical that the government would provide anything, least of all land, without conditions attached. This Scheme consequently did not yield the results that officials anticipated because its targeted audience, specifically sons from small-holder households in Maragoliland, were unmoved by the Kenyan state and development specialists' credo that the rural sector should contribute to Kenya's nation-building process as simple agriculturalists.

The four above-mentioned schemes that the Quaker Africa Mission, the late colonial British government, and the Kenyatta regime had either implemented or were in the process of implementing in the late 1950s and early 1960s epitomize the agrarianism project, making plain the ways in which outsiders attempted to systematize and control Kenya's rural development. More importantly, the case studies reveal how the success of agrarian development initiatives rested on the shoulders of nationalists, "developmentalists," and more importantly, everyday Kenyans. The following chapters provide insight into how the motivations and interests of ordinary Kenyans prevented the expected results that "experts" and nation-builders were anticipating. They explain, in part, why the agrarian revolution of the late 1950s and 1960s was underwhelming in Kenya, especially in Maragoliland.

Chapter One

The Role of Agriculture in Kenya's Political Economy in the Era of Transition and Independence

Mzee kasema turudi mashambani,
Hakuna vya bure,
Rais kasema turudi mashambani tuijenge Kenya,
Mzee kasema, turudi mashambani,
Hakuna vya bure. . .
The old man said let us go back to the countryside
There is nothing for free
The president said let us go back to the countryside to build (develop) Kenya
The old man said let us go back to the countryside
There is nothing for free [1]

The catchy government-sponsored tune, *Turudi Mashambani*, played on radio stations all across Kenya during the early independence years. The song's chorus, as the epigraph illustrates, reiterated Kenyatta's 1964 "Back to Land" speech in which he appealed to the *wanainch* (citizens), especially able-bodied idle Kenyans, to consider the career possibilities tied to the agricultural sector. The chorus's lyrics, in particular, sought to mitigate the high hopes that desperate urban *and* rural Kenyans had placed in their newly elected African leaders. The peoples's expectations included having access to more white collar job opportunities and, for some Kenyans, the provision by the government of free arable plots of land in desirable locations. While ordinary Kenyans assumed that these types of demands were reasonable and well within their rights as *wanainch*, such expectations interfered with the nascent Kenyatta administration's own nation-building plans. Consequently, the *Turudi Mashambani* song was a lighthearted reminder to the public that the *uhuru* (independence) government was intent on pursuing a development program grounded on agriculture, regardless of whether the people themselves had the passion or resources to engage fully in the process. The Kenyatta government's agricultural development agenda therefore was not only disconnected from the realities and expectations of ordinary Kenyans, especially those in Maragoliland, but also made some Kenyans question whether any *real* change had occurred as a result of independence.

As scholars of East Africa have recognized, African farmers living in colonial Kenya were the main targets of agrarian policies that stressed soil conservation practices and population control measures.[2] Having outsiders, whether foreign missionaries or Kenyan agricultural officers, hold village *barazas* (meetings) to demonstrate the latest agricultural practices and to encourage local farmers to meet commercial harvest quotas was indeed a common occurrence experienced by rural men and women in colonial and post-colonial western Kenya where there was a shortage of arable land.[3] Since the mid-1950s, the Kenyan government's aim to improve the conditions of landless and unemployed Kenyans through agricultural development had been a top priority, particularly in places like the Central Province of Kenya, the site of the Mau Mau civil war.

The British coined the term "Mau Mau" to describe the militant landless squatters and disgruntled land-poor individuals who formed the Kenya Land Freedom Army (KLFA). The term had no meaning in any Kenyan language. The Mau Mau conflict was essentially a Kikuyu civil war between the KLFA, a group organized around the bitterness of landlessness, and the land-rich loyalists, many of whom were mission-educated Christians and chiefs.[4] The KLFA demanded the colonial regime return land to Kenyans, especially calling for full access to the European highlands. The Kenyan government eventually ended the insurgency by 1955 with the help of British troops although the emergency did not officially end until 1960. The uprising, nonetheless, unnerved the Colonial Office and compelled the late colonial administration to address the land grievances of ordinary Kenyans. Accordingly, the Kenyan colonial regime attempted to mitigate the land problem responsible for Mau Mau with its 1954 development scheme entitled: *A Plan to*

Intensify the Development of African Agriculture in Kenya. Backed by a £5 million British government loan, the commonly-known Swynnerton Plan was a five-year agricultural development initiative that sought to develop Kenyan African agriculture by reforming customary land tenure practices, eliminating restrictions on cash crops, and instituting a system of land consolidation amongst the local population.

By promoting commercial agriculture in African communities across Kenya, the plan aimed to "raise the productivity of African lands, its human and stock carrying capacity, the income and standards of the people while at the same time effecting a substantial increase in the resources and economy of the Colony."[5] Revitalizing the soil fertility of "native" reserve lands was of utmost importance to colonial administrators who reckoned that doing so would placate the demands of Kenyans for more land elsewhere. In other words, the Swynnerton Plan was to divert attention away from the highlands as well as to ensure that opportunities would be available for rehabilitated ex-Mau Mau insurgents.

Land under the Swynnerton Plan

More importantly, the Swynnerton Plan brought forth a program of land consolidation and the issuing of title-deeds to individual Kenyan farmers who had historically been denied security of tenure by the colonial state. "Tribalistic" District Commissioners and District Officers, for example, were against land consolidation and registration of individual landholdings in the 1930s even though Kenya's Department of Agriculture had suggested at the time that the measures would help alleviate land pressure rampant in the African reserves.[6] The denial of individual title-deeds to local farmers was due largely to the assumptions and biases on the part of European settlers and colonial authorities who presumed that African Kenyans only practiced a communal land tenure system. Of course, this was an erroneous and self-serving understanding of local land tenure practices that local colonial government officials abandoned as a result of the Mau Mau uprising. Subsequently, the Swynnerton Plan was adopted in 1954.

Following the Swynnerton Plan's implementation, the colonial regime required rural Kenyans with dispersed land to engage in a process of exchanging fragments with their family members and neighbors in order to obtain consolidated landholdings. Participants who had consolidated land were then eligible to apply for individual title deeds that they could use as collateral for loans. The colonial regime therefore sought to remove the communal control of land tenure as well as to limit small parcels of land that local colonial agricultural officers had deemed economically inefficient as standalone fragments.

Though allowing for individual land tenure was a dramatic break from earlier colonial policies that treated all African land as the collective property of the "tribe," it seemed a necessary concession in order for the Kenyan government and Colonial Office to deal with the Mau Mau. Specifically, colonial authorities expected the land and agricultural reforms to provide an outlet for large numbers of landless and unemployed Kikuyu, Embu, and Meru ex-Mau Mau detainees being repatriated back into rural society in the mid-1950s.[7] Basically, the security in tenure was to result in a class of loyal landed freehold African smallholder commercial farmers who would absorb the surplus landless population and thus reduce the pressure of unemployment in the rural sector.

The practice of consolidating and registering land was not without controversy and problems. Throughout the Mau Mau Emergency, British officials detained thousands of suspected insurgents in Kikuyuland and restricted over a million people in fortified villages. In this manner, colonial officials easily were able to remake the Kikuyu land system without much opposition.[8] A number of ex-detainees returning home to the Central Province following the Swynnerton Plan's implementation, for example, found themselves landless because their holdings were consolidated and titled under new loyalist owners, many of whom were their own relatives who had the opportunity to take advantage of the colonial state's land reform program. The potential social upheaval unfolding in Kikuyuland because of the land consolidation program was not overlooked by Kenyan officials responsible for implementing the program. Writing to his superiors about the consequences of rapid consolidation in Kikuyuland, A. O. Ongoli warned of the social dangers ahead. "Thousands of rightful owners of land now being consolidated are decaying in prisons," he wrote; "it will not be surprising when these people finally gain freedom to have a spat of cases contesting the rights of occupancy of present consolidators."[9]

In areas like western Kenya where Mau Mau activities were less of a concern, the colonial regime neither strictly enforced the policy of land consolidation and registration, nor did the local community adhere rigorously to the practice. Land consolidation, for example, was extremely unpopular with landed Maragolis because the procedure was costly. Many smallholder farmers refused to spend their limited earnings to merge their fragmented pieces in order to obtain a title that may or may not benefit them.[10] More importantly, since only one person could have their name listed on the title, registering the family's property was unpopular with Maragoli men who had large households with multiple sons. The process essentially called for fathers to stop helping their sons set up their own household because land was no longer supposed to be subdivided once it was registered.[11]

The people's objection to land consolidation was well known to North Nyanza District intelligence officers, who noted that the local leaders were still opposed to the practice after visiting Nyeri District "to study land consolidation methods at the invitation of the Administration." From the confidential intelligence report, it would seem that the visit to Nyeri District only confirmed the suspicions of the North Nyanza leaders that the Kikuyu were "consolidating unwillingly, and only as a result of pressure applied under the Emergency conditions."[12] Land consolidation therefore remained unpopular with local western Kenyans who found no real use for the practice. Nevertheless, at both the international and national levels, the land reforms were strongly backed by the MacMillan government, which supported the idea of individual land tenure among the indigenous population, and were further ratified by the Kenyan government's implementation of the Swynnerton Plan.[13]

The reforms of the Swynnerton Plan revolutionized African land tenure policies and agrarian practices in the years to come. However, the land consolidation requirements, which by 1965 were official government policy, did little to inspire everyday Kenyans to accept smallholder commercial farming as a viable career option in the decolonization and early independence eras because it did not offer land to ordinary people. The Plan was primarily concerned with improving the productivity of land in the "native reserves." It provided no real relief to the major challenge of land shortage that rural Kenyans faced, especially in Maragoliland. The Swynnerton Plan neither divided nor redistributed the large farms and plantations owned by the European settler community to the majority of land-poor and landless Kenyans restricted to overcrowded "native reserves." Instead, the land tenure reforms exacerbated the land problem by allowing wealthier and influential Kenyans to gain larger tracts of land as they were able to convince neighbors and family members of the need for consolidation and could pay the expenses for registering title deeds.[14]

Politics and Land

Landlessness and land hunger therefore remained unresolved as Kenya entered the decolonization period. Though the hostile Kenyan settler community was reluctant to accept the nationalist "wind of change" moving through sub-Saharan Africa by the start of 1960, the events of Mau Mau had convinced the Kenyan government of the vulnerability of white majority rule. Thus, along with the Swynnerton Plan and an active military campaign to combat the insurgency, the late colonial regime in the 1950s embarked on a program to reform Kenya's political institutions that had historically excluded the African majority from representation.

The Kenyan administration, for example, lifted its ban on African political activism that was enacted in 1953 following the declaration of the Mau Mau Emergency with the ratification of the 1954 Lyttleton Constitution. This political reform was limited in that it only permitted regional politics and aimed to retain large elements of the status quo by introducing measures that sought to create a multiracial polity of Europeans and non-Europeans. Eight African leaders were elected into the Legislative Council under a modified 1957 Lyttleton Constitution, with the number increasing to fourteen representatives under the 1958 Lennox-Boyd Constitution. These political reforms essentially allowed the colonial regime to transfer political power to trusted local politicians in the hope they would be able to contribute to Kenya's economic and social development without undermining the settler economy and its social milieu. More importantly, the local politicians were to respect Western investments.[15] The integration of non-European politicians into the central government was, therefore, closely controlled through an electoral system whereby the electorate itself had to qualify for enfranchisement based on income, education, and government service.[16] The ideology of "multiracialism" rested on gradually allowing certain qualified middle-class Africans the chance to participate in the central government, but it never granted majority rule.

Understandably, "multiracialism" did not sit well with the more nationalist Kenyan political elites, such as Tom Mboya, Oginga Odinga, Ronald Ngala, Julius Kiano, and Daniel arap Moi, who emerged to challenge the colonial authorities between 1953 and 1960. These men greatly enlarged Kenya's nationalist movement by establishing the Kenya African National Union (KANU) and the Kenya African Democratic Union (KADU), the political parties that led Kenya into the post-colonial era. Jomo Kenyatta, meanwhile, remained largely absent from the nationalist movement during this period because of his imprisonment. The colonial administration arrested Kenyatta in 1952 on false charges that he was the leader of Mau Mau, and therefore kept him away from the political scene for almost a decade. Kenyatta's detention paradoxically placed him above politics and helped to make him into the undoubted father-figure of the nationalist movement and thus the leader of the independent KANU government in 1963.

The KANU and KADU movements emerged following the first Lancaster House talks in January 1960 when the Colonial Office made it known that independence and thus the principle of African majority rule was its declared goal. The two political factions represented ethnic divisions within the nationalist movement in 1960. Particularly, KANU was composed of the larger, agrarian, and more politically conscious Kenyan communities—the Kikuyu and Luo—who had called for a swift end to colonial rule. The Luo and Kikuyu had historically taken advantage of the opportunities of colonialism because they had better access to good mission schools, enabling them to become the more educated and wealthier communities by independence.

KADU, on the other hand, was the conservative party made up of several different, mostly pastoral, ethnic groups such as the Kalenjin, Maasai, Mijikenda, and Abaluhya who banded together for fear that their interests would be lost under a Kikuyu-Luo dominated government. Although the Abaluhya people largely supported KADU, there were KANU backers amongst the group. Abaluhya communities in the Bunyore, Nyangori, and Tiriki locations of western Kenya, for example, voted predominately KADU in the 1961 Kenyan general elections and thus sent two local KADU members, M. S. Amalemba and E. E. Khasakhala to represent them in the Legislative Council. The Abaluhya constituents in Maragoliland, on the other hand, favored KANU politicians like Joseph Daniel Otiende who was from this particular location and community, showing that at the local level ordinary Kenyans likely became KADU or KANU supporters according to the affiliation of the local candidates rather than by party considerations.[17]

While both groups were united in their call for an end to colonialism, KANU and KADU politicians disagreed over how the country would be governed as well as who would control Kenya's resources.[18] Both KADU and KANU nationalist leaders were particularly divided over how best to resolve Kenya's land problem—a long-term issue that was made urgent in 1959 when the coveted European highlands became open to select African farmers. The opening of the highlands was the direct result of a revised Native Lands Registration Ordinance, which removed racial barriers from land ownership. The law stemmed from the 1955 East African Royal

Commission's conclusions that the racial and "tribal" land barriers inhibited Kenya's rural economy from growing and blocked the creation of African allies.[19] Consequently, the 1959 ordinance permitted interethnic land sales in the once exclusive European enclave. Land, in short, was not to be given to Kenya's indigenous population for free. Settler leaders like Michael Blundell hoped this new policy would safeguard the European community's future interests, especially as it was becoming evident to them that the British government was moving to divest itself from imperial rule in Kenya.

The opening of the white highlands under "multiracialism" hardly resolved the land grievances of ordinary Kenyans. While the ordinance eliminated any further racial restrictions on land sales, real access to the highland farms was strictly limited to prosperous African farmers. These individuals were mostly colonial allies such as the Chiefs and loyalists who had consolidated landholdings. Moreover, and more importantly, they had the resources to practice commercial agriculture. The multiracial land policies, in short, did little to address the grotesque landlessness and land-hunger issues plaguing ordinary Kenyans, especially the majority of land-poor Maragoliland residents, who neither had the capital nor the influence to acquire the land made available under the 1959 ordinance.

The newly-formed KADU and KANU nationalist parties, unsurprisingly, denounced the land ordinance as not adequately addressing Kenya's land problem—notably the demands of poor voters for the reapportion of European lands. Politicians in both parties then proceeded to claim to understand the grievances of land-poor and landless Kenyans as they competed for votes during the independence elections throughout the early 1960s.[20] For instance, as the self-proclaimed vanguard party for *all* Kenyans, KANU politicians made the issue of resettlement a central element of their campaign platform. The party leaders specifically appealed to the squatter population in the highlands in its 1960 political manifesto. "The position of the squatter in the highlands is deplorable and resembles that of the exploited serf in feudal Europe," it read; "if the eradication of this evil system will mean a complete revolution of land tenure in the highlands . . . KANU dedicates itself to face the challenge."[21] Similarly, KADU leaders like Masinde Muliro, then the party's Deputy leader, affirmed in campaign speeches to his western Kenyan constituents that unoccupied Crown lands should be availed to Africans.[22] KADU's position on the land issue, however, differed from KANU's inclusive approach, because it was foremost committed to protecting the interests of the minority ethnic communities who did not want Kikuyu settlers in their home reserves.

Despite their denouncements, the nationalist politicians from either faction could not realistically tackle Kenya's land problem until after the 1961 national elections whereby the first African majority was elected to serve on the Legislative Council. Even then, some of the more radical and populist KANU members, like Odinga and Bildad Kaggia, preferred to wait until after Kenya achieved its complete independence to resolve the land issue. They believed that doing so would ward off the costly demands of European settlers, and would also allow them to make good on their grandiose campaign promise that Kenyans would not have to pay for land.[23] However, the bid to delay addressing the land issue failed to gain traction from within the ranks of KANU, especially with the moderate members who were willing to work with the European politicians in establishing a land settlement and transfer program that would avoid a complete collapse in the Kenyan economy. It was also a nonstarter for both the metropolitan British government and the late colonial regime that were still very much responsible for safe-guarding the interests of Kenya's settler population on the eve of colonial independence.

Settler farmers anxious about their future in a majority, African-ruled Kenya had put considerable pressure on the late colonial regime to address the contentious land issue. The European settlers, in particular, expected their leaders like Blundell, serving as the Minister of Agriculture in 1960, to devise a solution that either protected their farming interests after independence or that would compensate them for their land if they had to return it to the local Kenyans. To this end, in 1961 the late colonial government initiated the first two land-transfer and settlement programs known as the Peasant and Yeoman (assisted-owner) projects with financial assistance from the Colonial Development Corporation (CDC) and World Bank.

The Yeoman Scheme permitted rich progressive farmers the chance to purchase undeveloped yet productive farms of about fifty acres in the European areas, while the Peasant Scheme allowed participants access to fifteen-acre plots in areas that had previously been barred to Africans but that were still outside of the coveted highlands. The colonial regime expected the schemes to help solve the land-hunger problem, and more importantly to maintain the production level of the large-scale farms in the white highlands.[24] The goal was to encourage wealthy and prominent African farmers to participate in the Yeoman Scheme so that they would become the landed gentry who would employ their poor and landless neighbors. In contrast, the development planners expected the Peasant Scheme to relocate 4,500 landless

Kenyan families onto 60,000 less productive acres adjacent to the European regions in the hopes of racially integrating the area.

The likely beneficiaries of the Yeoman and Peasant Schemes, however, were not the majority of landless and land-poor Kenyans. Rather, the Schemes favored employees of the departing European settler farmers, progressive farmers who already benefited from the Swynnerton Plan, and the elite Kenyans (often politicians) who could afford to participate in the Schemes. In other words, the initial land transfer and settlement programs did little to address the needs of the majority of poor Kenyans who could not meet the strict financial and "modern" agricultural experience requirements of the Schemes. It was not until the start of the Million Acre Scheme (MAS) program in the middle of 1962 that the majority of land-poor and landless (male) Kenyans had the chance to acquire farms through the land settlement and transfer programs.

The MAS program emerged during Kenya's transition phase and thus was under the direction of the interim KADU and KANU coalition government. This government resulted from the second Lancaster House Conference held in February and March 1962 and operated under a semi-federalist constitution similar to the United States. Known as the "*majimbo* (regional) constitution," it divided the country into six regional assemblies and allowed for a weak central government in Nairobi. This particular arrangement of government was an expedient compromise made between KADU and KANU leaders and was intended to get the British out. The former group had petitioned for a decentralized system of government while the latter group was intent on upholding the authority of the central government prior to the conference proceedings.[25] The coalition government was responsible for taking Kenya into the final phases of independence, which therefore entailed having to tackle both the land problem and the unemployment crisis.

Accordingly, the coalition government turned its attention to creating a land settlement and transfer program that mandated participants be landless and unemployed. The result was the MAS program, which designated 1.5 million acres of European mixed farmland primarily to high-density (low-income) schemes in order to relieve the over-crowded reserves as well as to provide some land to poor Kenyans who were priced out of the previous schemes. The ambitious settlement program was estimated to cost £25 million and to involve some 35,000 families. Due to its ambitious nature, the World Bank declined to finance the MAS program. The project was therefore largely funded by a British government development loan of £21 million with the remaining financial support coming from West

Germany. Much of the financial support was to be repaid by the newly independent Kenyan government. This condition, consequently, became a major source of contention amongst the nationalist leaders who were divided over whether the land they deemed was taken from Kenyans ought to be purchased back.

The high-density schemes, nevertheless, assisted the Kenyan government and nationalist leaders in their efforts to avert a land grab, as well as to deal with the land problem without much disruption to Kenya's large-scale agricultural economy. For example, the MAS high-density schemes, such as the Lugari Settlement Scheme discussed in chapter 6, offered participants at least ten-acres of land, dairy cows, and technical assistance from Farmers' Training Center instructors. Since the high-density settlement plots were of lower quality and in regions outside of the European areas, the fees participants had to pay were lower than the previous land settlement projects. Similarly, the requirement that applicants be so-called progressive farmers were relaxed though the condition that participants become full-time farmers was upheld by MAS program planners like Blundell and his successor, Bruce McKenzie, who served as Minister of Agriculture into the early independence years.[26]

Even though the MAS program was largely composed of the high-density schemes, the name eventually became associated with the various land transfer and settlement programs unfolding in Kenya during the decolonization and early independence era. These schemes included the 1961 Peasant and Yeoman programs, along with the 1964 Z-plot scheme that provided its recipients with a one-hundred-acre settlement plot inclusive of the former European settler's house.[27] Consequently, the land settlement and transfer programs, continued into the *uhuru* era, even as the government structures and institutions established in the transition period did not.

Majimboism (regionalism), in particular, did not continue into the postcolonial era because KANU won the 1963 general election decisively. The KANU government, with Kenyatta as its leader, passed amendments once it was in power to dissolve the *majimbo* constitution and abolish the regional governments created in 1962. By the end of 1964, the KADU political party had disbanded, with its members joining the party of the government to share the spoils of power. Kenya became a republic in December 1964, thereby making Kenyatta the president and head of a *de facto* one-party state. The ruling party, however, was not centralized and unified and, as Cherry Gertzel has argued, it suffered from more personal rivalries than KADU once it obtained power. While party members banded together to make independence a reality, KANU leaders soon fought over the division of patronage and assets among themselves, and also disagreed about policy issues pertaining especially to Kenya's economic development and land question in the post-colonial era. Consequently, by April 1966, Kenya had reverted back to a multiparty state when KANU members, headed by Kaggia and Odinga, then KANU and Kenya's Vice-President, resigned and established the opposition political party, the Kenya People's Union (KPU).

The KPU was a left-wing party that favored the nationalization of foreign businesses and promised land to poor Kenyans.[28] These populist radical views threatened the Kenyatta regime and, more importantly, challenged the economic policies and ideological sensibilities of its Western supporters. Accordingly, in 1967 the government began its campaign to dismantle the KPU by arresting and levying harsh fines against the party's leadership for minor infringements such as holding rallies without permits. Kenyatta and his supports succeeded in shutting down the opposition in December 1968 as the KPU failed to have the minimum number of members to be recognized as an official party, and thus Kenya reverted to a one-party state by the start of 1969.[29] This reversion to a single-party system allowed Kenyatta to be in control of the gatekeeper state and to carry on with KANU's development program for the rural sector without much regard for the realities of everyday Kenyans.

The Place of Agriculture in Early Independence Kenya

The Kenyatta regime and its Western backers in particular, resumed their efforts to foster a group of politically moderate, educated progressive yeoman farmers—cash-crop agriculturalists versed in Western technologies and cultural practices. It was this group of progressive farmers whom the independent Kenyan leadership hoped would become its privileged rural development partners in the early independence years. The progressive Kenyan farmers were to contribute to the country's economic, industrial, and social growth and thereby improve the lives of everyday Kenyans through a trickle-down effect. Accordingly, similar to its colonial predecessor, the KANU-led government promoted unrealistic (and hypocritical) agricultural development plans that disregarded the land shortage and economic concerns faced by the majority of post-colonial Kenyans.

The KANU nationalists who had won a decisive victory over their Kenya African Democratic Union (KADU) political rivals in 1963, largely relied on the agrarian sector and thereby the project of agrarianism to grow the state's coffers because they had no real alternatives. The Kenyan colonial government, and by extension the Colonial Office, had upheld a neo-mercantilist economy in Kenya since the turn of the twentieth-century. Consequently, by the decolonization era and throughout the early independence years, there were few established non-agrarian industries that nationalists could rely on to help spur Kenya's economic development. The importance of agriculture in general and of large-scale commercial farms and plantations in particular to the economy of Kenya was underscored in a 1961 economic survey conducted by the International Bank: "78% of the total farm output of £46 million," it reported, "came from farms and plantations."[30] Building the newly-independent Kenyan state, in short, required the continued reliance on the countryside and, more importantly, a dependence on large-scale commercial agriculturists who needed access to a skilled labor force.

However, the Kenyan leaders recognized the political necessity of addressing their constituents' immediate concerns regarding unemployment and access to land. Moreover, the KANU leaders who came to power on a populist platform, people like Oginga Odinga and Bildad Kigia, understood that they needed to make good on promises made to their rural supporters who expected not only political independence but real improvements of their socio-economic condition once Africans came to power. In theory, this meant that the Kenyan nationalists were keen to control the large-scale commercial agriculture sector that was historically dominated by rich and privileged (usually European) farmers. Ordinary *wananchi* in particular, expected the Kenyatta government to dismantle the large-scale plantation farms and thus to redistribute the plots of land to them. Kenyan *wananchi* therefore called on their leaders to make available the necessary resources—namely land—for them to improve their particular economic position and social standing.

Their constituents' demands for real change, however, posed a grave threat to the newly-independent KANU-led government, who had no real plans to disrupt the country's agrarian-based export economy—at least, perhaps, not during the state's nascent phase. More importantly, the call to break apart the large-farm estates threatened Kenyatta's ability to reward his cronies (and himself) with the spoils of independence that included claims to the estates themselves. The Kenyan nationalist leaders who assumed power in 1963, understandably found themselves having to readjust their grand promises of *uhuru*.

Thus the Kenyatta regime continued, albeit with some modifications, the agricultural-as-development agenda for the countryside that had begun in earnest during the twilight years of the late colonial period. The development of the nation, according to the 1964 KANU government's economic program, rested on the shoulders of educated small-hold commercial farmers. These individuals were the solution to addressing chronic rural poverty and, more important, to generating capital for future investment. If small-hold progressive farmers "planned an extra row of maize, worked an extra hour per day, planted the recommended seed and followed the advice of the agricultural officer," wrote Kenyatta, they had the ability to start an agrarian revolution that was the "principle means for creating employment opportunities and raising incomes in Kenya."[31] Such rhetoric was a measured effort on the part of the leadership to show its constituents some possible (and tangible) changes in a free Kenya while also ensuring that the state's agrarian-based economy remain intact. Moreover, it shows that the state indeed lacked the resources to make good on the grandiose populist promises made by politicians from both KANU and KADU.

Furthermore, this particular agricultural development model acknowledged the basic fact that only a select few individuals would eventually become privileged small-hold commercial farmers in the postcolony. The majority of rural Kenyan women and men, in other words, were to remain subsistence agriculturalists who were supposed to survive off their limited (and often overworked) parcels, and were to become the agricultural laborers on large-scale commercial estates either owned by select rich Kenyans or multinational corporations. This notion that most ordinary Kenyan citizens would continue practicing subsistence farming stemmed not only from the nationalist leaders' decisions leading up to and immediately following *uhuru*, but it was also grounded in the former colonial government's biases concerning African farmers' place within Kenya's political-economy.

Local indigenous agriculture, after all, was deemed primitive by colonial technical "experts" at the start of British rule in the late nineteenth century, which was used to justify colonialism in Kenya.[32] Colonial agricultural officials in particular constructed a racist narrative of rural Kenyans as "backward" farmers who depleted their soils through traditional practices and thus would eventually require outside intervention to halt and prevent future land degradation and erosion in their villages.[33] In depicting ordinary Kenyans as backward farmers, the colonial government appeased vocal European settler farmers who depended on African field laborers to work on their plantation estates and who were threatened by productive Kenyan farmers.[34] Rural Kenyans, in other words, were to help increase the yields of the settler farming community rather than pose a direct threat to the European farmers' position by producing lucrative cash crops. Through the implementation of restrictive agrarian and land policies, which prevented the majority of Kenyan farmers from growing crops like coffee and tea, the Kenyan government kept ordinary Kenyans from becoming fully incorporated into the formal economy as large-scale commercial farmers throughout most of the colonial era. As previously mentioned, it was not until the mid-1950s, under the Swynnerton Plan, that the Kenyan government lifted the restrictions barring most African farmers from growing cash crops. Nevertheless, the agrarian reforms promoted under the Swynnerton Plan largely sought to reinforce the idea that in the late colonial and the subsequent independent Kenyan state, only a select number of progressive rural Kenyans could become anything more than small-hold commercial farmers, with the majority of the rural sector limited to practicing subsistence agriculture and to providing their labor to advance the ambitions of the so-called progressive farmers.

While the Kenyan government and their development partners called for the rural sector to help with nation-building by embracing the project of agrarianism, in practice the developmentalists' agendas meant little to everyday people who had little access or claim to productive land and who expected more from their politicians than to remain on the farm as *wananchi*. Specifically, a number of residents from the over-populated Maragoli locations of western Kenya were not afraid to individualize the grand nation-building projects at the local level. Maragoliland, as chapter 2 will show, was a site where the process of development was complicated by conflicting agendas and where the Kenyan government and its development partners' comprehensive economic programs for the rural sector were often compromised by the personal agendas and goals of the people it aimed to "improve."

Chapter Two

Western Kenya's Region, People, and the Origins of Population Density

Western Kenya's Historical Boundaries

Maragoliland is a ninety-five square mile region northwest of Lake Victoria. The territory is located in western Kenya, which has undergone significant administrative changes and boundary shifts over the past century. The British government initially laid claim to this part of Kenya in 1894 when it established the Uganda Protectorate, because the area was largely part of eastern Uganda. By 1902, however, it had become part of the East African Protectorate, which subsequently became the Kenya colony in 1920. The transfer of this region occurred due to the completion of the Uganda railway, which reached present-day Kisumu in 1902, thereby opening the region's economy to outsiders.

Throughout the colonial era, officials referred to the western Kenya region as Kavirondo or Nyanza Province, dividing it into four districts: Central Nyanza, North Nyanza, South Nyanza, and Kericho. While "nyanza" is the Bantu word for "lake," referring to Lake Victoria, the definition for Kavirondo meant the place of guns. To the colonial state, the western Kenya area remained North Nyanza or North Kavirondo Province until the early 1960s. The Province split into two separate administrative regions during Kenya's decolonization process: Nyanza and Western provinces. Kericho, formally a district in the Nyanza Province, was transferred to the Rift Valley region.[1] These provincial and district alterations occurred as a result of the Regional Boundaries Commission.

Figure 2.1. Western Kenya, circa 1963. Estate of Rodney Morris. Reproduced with permission from the Morris family.

Following the second Lancaster House talks in February 1962, the Secretary of State for the Colonies appointed an independent commission chaired by Stafford Foster-Sutton to reconfigure Kenya's provincial boundaries to accompany the implementation of the complicated *majimbo* (regionalism) constitution, which as shown in chapter 1 above was a semi-federalist constitution that divided the country into six regional assemblies with a central government in Nairobi.[2] The return to the provincial system after independence meant that the Western Region became known as the Western Province by the middle of the 1960s. This province consisted of three districts: Kakamega, Bungoma, and Busia. The former district of North Nyanza was folded into Kakamega, which became the provincial headquarters. Kakamega district in 1964 consisted of four administrative divisions: Vihiga, Central, Lurambi, and Mumias.

Maragoli People and the Land

Since this study is concerned with the Maragoli community throughout the late colonial and independence period, its focus is on the former North

Nyanza district and, subsequently, the Kakamega district, which is an area situated on a plateau north of Lake Victoria. The Vihiga division of Kakamega, consisting of Nyangori, Tiriki, North and South Maragoli locations, was home to the largest number of people in the country during Kenya's decolonization and early independence years. The latter two locations, which constituted "Maragoliland," were the most populated and where the majority of the division's inhabitants identified as being Maragoli and belonging to the Abaluhya ethnic community.[3]

The Abaluhya supra-ethnic identity, like many African communities, came into being during the colonial era. Gideon Were's historical survey of the Abaluhya argues that this group of Bantu-speaking people emerged as a result of migratory movements taking place around Eastern Uganda and parts of western Kenya during the eighteenth and nineteenth centuries.[4] The colonial state had initially labeled the disparate migrants "Bantu of North Kavirondo," to make administering the area less complicated and more understandable to Westerners. But as Julie MacArthur has argued, the region's cultural entrepreneurs—young mission converts and teachers—rejected this derogatory and foreign-imposed epithet in 1935 by forming the North Kavirondo Central Association (NKCA) and renaming its diverse constituents as the "Luhyia" or "Abaluhya."[5]

Ethnic identities, according to Bruce Berman and John Lonsdale, are best understood as complex and contested social constructions always in the process of creation and re-creation. Ethnicity and ethnic groups are alternative terms for "tribalism" and "tribe," which Thomas Spear described as an "exclusive, territorially bounded, self-conscious collectivity of people sharing a common language, history, and culture."[6] In this fashion, the cultural entrepreneurs' attempt to create a new regional polity and thus a greater Luhyia community had taken root by the late 1930s, as British administrators helped clan "leaders" establish organizations such as the Abaluhya Welfare Association and the Luhya Language committee that would formulate and strengthen an orthography. By the middle of the twentieth-century, the Abaluhya "tribe" eventually consisted of seventeen major sub-ethnic groups, all of which theoretically shared a similar background, custom, spoke a common language, though dialects varied according to locality.[7] Accordingly, as both MacArthur and Spear have suggested, being Luhyia meant speaking a version of Luhyia and residing within a particular region of western Kenya.[8]

The people of Maragoli, also known as Logoli, were among the main Abaluhya sub-ethnic groups residing in the former North Nyanza district by the time Kenya began its decolonization process.[9] The Maragoli speak the

Luragoli language, one of the two largest linguistic groups in the region.[10] Historically, the Maragoli were agriculturalists who primarily grew food crops such as maize and millet. By the mid-twentieth century, however, farming had become problematic for a number of Luragoli-speakers living in the former North Nyanza district due to the rapid population growth in the area, which resulted in crowded homesteads and overworked land with soils depleted of nutrients.

Luragoli-speakers were not the only group worried about Maragoliland's population density in the late colonial era. Kenyan Agricultural government officials and Friends (Quaker) Africa Mission missionaries interested in improving the conditions of rural western Kenyans were also concerned about the land problem in Maragoli. Western Kenyan colonial administrators therefore took it upon themselves, for instance, to offer the Nairobi government solutions they thought would help to alleviate North Nyanza district's population crisis. C. H. Williams, the Provincial Commissioner for Nyanza Province in 1952, proposed resettling people from this region in order to address the land pressure. In a memorandum to his Nairobi superiors, Williams wrote "it is essential an area should be found where a considerable proportion of the population can be resettled."[11] Williams's suggestion, nevertheless, was unrealistic in early 1950s Kenya because of the lack of land available elsewhere in the colony and, more importantly, because the Kenyan government's resources were devoted to subduing the Mau Mau civil war involving mostly Kikuyu people and their grievances over land from 1952 to 1960.[12] The overpopulation in Maragoliland no doubt interfered with the colonial Kenyan state's aims, as well as inhibited some residents from achieving full social recognition within the community.

As with many African communities in Kenya and throughout the sub-Saharan continent, land was (and remains) for Maragoliland people a form of social security. Owning land also allowed adult males to establish households and to become family heads. Land tenure amongst the Maragoli Luhya, according to Gunter Wagner's authoritative yet dated ethnographic study, was on a clan basis with each family having exclusive rights to use and occupy their own holdings. Access to land was gendered in that the family's plot was divided amongst the sons with the children of the first wife in a polygamous household receiving priority over the junior sons. Daughters utilized their mother's plots to grow food crops, but had no claim to this land once they married. Family land was usually acquired either by inheritance from one's grandfather or by clearing and cultivating virgin bush land, which was a viable option in the pre-conquest period. This land tenure system remained

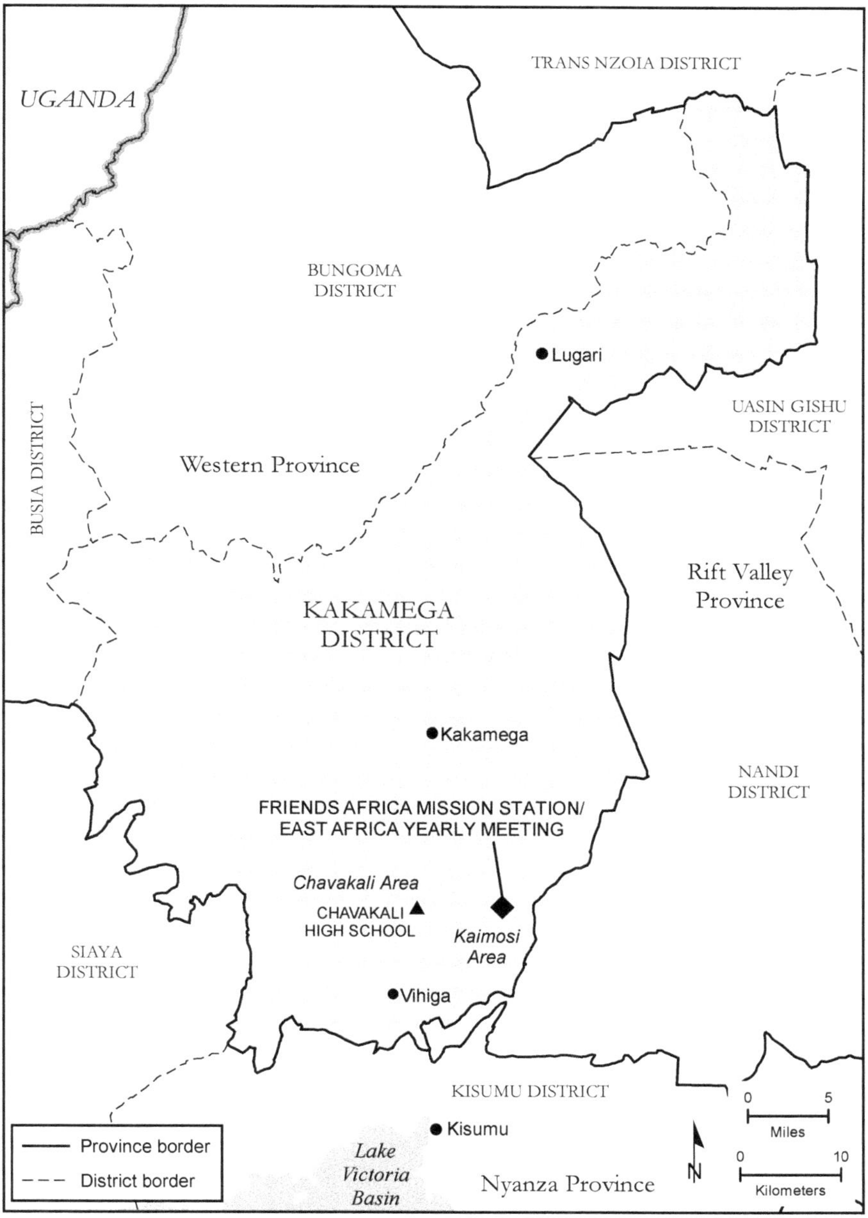

Figure 2.2. Map of Kakamega District. Map by Brian Edward Balsley, GISP

largely in place even after the colonial state, along with missionary societies like the Friends Africa Mission, replaced the *amagutu* clan-heads with the system of paid *milango* (chiefs) in 1926.[13] Land, in other words, had to be in use or the owner risked having to forfeit their property because under the colonial government's "native reserves" system there were no legal titles. Ethnic groups lived on what authorities assumed were communal "homelands" where private property was not recognized. It was not until the 1954 Swynnerton Plan that title deeds and thus individual land ownership became a reality for Kenyans, and even then, it was on a select basis.

The late colonial regime's delayed response to Maragoliland's land crisis meant that the majority of landless and land poor residents in the region continued to experience severe land shortages throughout the decolonization and, subsequent, independence era. For example, reports from agricultural officials like Leslie H. Brown, the Assistant Director of Agriculture for the region at the time, indicated that the average size plot of land for a Maragoli family of eight in 1956 was 5.26 acres. By 1960, this acreage had decreased to 4.7 acres because of a three percent increase in the area's population.[14] Nevertheless, it would seem that Brown and his officers paid little attention to the "Maragoli problem" when they crafted projects to develop the region.

The 1956 "10-year Maragoli Development Plan," for instance, sought to better the conditions of poor Maragoli households by encouraging residents to commit to smallholder cash-crop and subsistence farming, along with work on others' farms as agricultural laborers. The late colonial government essentially aimed to convince the Maragoliland residents of the same message that the Kenyatta regime would champion at independence: working the land would lead to some measure of economic security. Specifically, the architects of the plan, people such as Brown, envisioned having an eight-person household in the region live on a seven-acre holding that the "experts" calculated would provide the family unit with an annual income of £100 in addition to full subsistence.[15] The Maragoli Development Plan's stipulation that households in 1950s Maragoliland live off the ideal seven-acre plot of land, of course, was unrealistic. In fact, as Brown and his agricultural field officers quickly learned, the region's population density made it so that the average land-holding per Maragoli family of eight was about five-aces rather than the seven-acres they deemed appropriate for productive subsistence farming. Moreover, a single nuclear family owning a five-acre homestead in either North or South Maragoli locations also seemed highly unlikely. According to some residents, having this particular size plot of land certainly would not make the family small-hold farmers but rather wealthy "big farmers" in the region.[16]

"Native Reserves" System and the Origins of Maragoliland Land Crisis

The population crisis in the Maragoli locations, which was also present in other parts of Kenya like the Central Province, largely derived from the "native reserves" system and the British government's establishment of a settler colony in East Africa. Since much of the land laying between Uganda and the coast of the Indian Ocean did not seem to have much economic potential, the British government decided to build a railway from Mombasa to Uganda in order to link the economies at the start of the twentieth-century. To finance this project and thus to ease the drain that the new territorial acquisitions placed upon the metropole's treasury, the British government hoped to attract settlers to East Africa. The presence of European settlers would not only help with the economic development of this region, but also served to solidify Britain's sphere of influence and control over its East African territories.

Attracting settlers to this uneconomical part of the African continent required the British government to be very generous in terms of incentives, especially with respect to land acquisitions. The Protectorate administration, which had the authority to lease land that the British Crown deemed "unoccupied" under the 1902 Crown Lands Ordinance, offered potential settlers ninety-nine-year leases to parcels of land between 160 and 640 acres in the fertile East African highlands.[17] The highlands area was hardly vacated or deserted land, however, as the Kikuyu and Maasai communities inhibited this region prior to the British colonizers' inland expansion. But, the population of these local communities had dropped significantly by the time the Crown implemented its initial lands Ordinance in 1902, due to epidemic diseases, droughts, as well as the "pacification campaigns" at the end of the nineteenth century. The 1915 Crown Lands Ordinance extended the leases to 999 years, providing the European proprietors with added security to their land in the highlands. Early administrators like Sir Charles Eliot, the Commissioner of East Africa from 1901 to 1904, hoped that such incentives would attract sophisticated Europeans to the region and thus help to build an elite settler society.

The British government's interest in developing a European settlement in the East African highlands through the Crown Lands legislation of 1902 and 1915 essentially paved the way for the "native reserves" system. Since colonial officials assumed that the communities in East Africa belonged to "tribes," which they understood to be a primitive political organization that could evolve into a modern bureaucratic nation-state with proper guidance, the colonial administration divided the territory of Kenya into reserves and assigned a particular "tribe" to an area. Operating under the erroneous notion that land was collective "tribal" property, Kenyan authorities assumed that the "native reserves" system would prevent the backward "tribesmen" from exploitation and thus losing the "tribal" land to outsiders. The African areas were conveniently located in the periphery of the "scheduled areas," the 7.7 million acres of leasehold and freehold land in the East African highlands, which the Kenyan government demarcated for non-African settlement.[18] By 1920 when the East Africa Protectorate became the Kenya Colony and Protectorate, the establishment of the reserves system and the creation of the "white highlands" was well underway.

In organizing their African subjects into neatly bounded, mutually exclusive, and timeless collectives, each with their own reserve, Kenyan officials were able to cut costs associated with administrating the colony. After all, "tribes" were theoretically under the direction of local "chiefs" and "headmen." Thus, the colonial regime practiced "hegemony on a shoestring" by allying itself with the African leaders whom it designated to administrator the reserves and thus to serve as the local agents of colonialism.[19] This system of indirect rule subsequently began what Mahmood Mamdani asserted as the process by which two categories of people were created: the citizen and the subject in colonial Africa.[20]

In reality, however, most pre-conquest African communities neither belonged to "tribes" nor were they governed by central governing authorities. Rather, the local people lived in changing and dynamic stateless societies, and their ethnicities and boundaries were not fixed but fluid and ambiguous. Governing Kenya indirectly and creating the "native reserves" system, in other words, was convenient for colonial officials as it allowed them to make empire building cost effective as well as to promote the pretense that they were preserving indigenous "traditions."

The colonial rhetoric that indirect rule would preserve local structures of authority and protect "native" customs, nevertheless, did not mask the fact that British authorities created the reserve system as a means to extract revenue, labor and provisions from "uncivilized" individuals. The reserves were essentially situated in relatively non-productive areas that were impractical and inefficient at sustaining the local indigenous population long term. Moreover, confining African communities into specific reserves created soil degradation issues and exacerbated social tensions for the more populous ethnic communities who had outgrown their specific reserves within a decade of its establishment.

For instance, western Kenya's provincial officials were already concerned with the region's growing population and the implications that this growth had on the reserve system in the 1930s. North Nyanza district, which contained the Maragoli community and the Abaluhya reserve, was a particular concern for colonial administrators who realized that the land in the reserve could not adequately sustain the growing population. The Abaluhya "tribe" shared a total area of 7,114 square miles with two other ethnic communities in colonial Kenya's Nyanza Province. According to the 1933 Kenya Land Commission, Nyanza Province's three reserves held an estimated "1,029,422 persons . . . more than one-third of the total population of the Colony."[21] The pressure on the reserves not only led people to relocate (often illegally) to urban centers, but also compelled individuals to migrate into the less populated "native" areas as well as onto the European settler farms in the highlands. The migrants who made their way onto the less crowded reserves were either adopted into their host communities or remained outsiders subjected to regular harassment by local colonial administrators.[22]

At the same time, the individuals who relocated to the highlands, especially the Kikuyu community from the surrounding areas, became laborers on European farms with no secure land rights. The "native reserves" system, in short, had created a squatter system that supported the settler economy by providing cheap laborers whose position in the highland farms were often precarious. It was this insecurity in land tenure coupled with their dissatisfaction as subordinate farm laborers that eventually drove many Kikuyu squatters in the late 1940s to take part in events that would culminate into the Mau Mau uprising.[23] Kenya's native reserves were therefore (purposely) insufficient for the growing local population.

The Colonial Office, under African political pressure, appointed a Land Commission, chaired by William Morris Carter, a Rhodesian Judge, in 1932 to investigate the growing land grievances and population concerns in Kenya that were exacerbated by the "native reserves" system. The Commission eventually ruled that the reserves, with a few minor adjustments, were large enough for African needs. With respect to western Kenya's large and growing population, the Carter Commission estimated that 51,494 people in Nyanza Province's three reserves worked as migrant laborers either on European settler farms or in townships and the Coast throughout 1931.[24] Put another way, an unspoken function of the reserves was to ensure the well-being of the European settlers rather than to protect "tribesmen" from selling communal land to outsiders—a justification British colonialists used in explaining the need for designated African areas. The surplus population in places like North Nyanza district provided the colonial state, the European settler community, and foreign investors with an abundance of cheap African labor.

The Kenyan government, however, could not neglect the overpopulated reserves for too long. Colonial officials, in particular, feared that America's dust bowl disaster would occur in the overpopulated Kenyan reserves. Moreover, following the conclusion of the Second World War, the British Colonial Office realized that in order to maintain a hold on its territories it needed to make Britain's overseas possessions and its subjects economically accountable as well as beneficial to the metropole in the post-1945 era. Imperialism also seemed anachronistic with the creation of the United Nations and the adoption of its Charter. Article 73 of the UN Charter, in particular, mandated that its members who possessed colonies "accept as a scared trust the obligation to promote to the utmost . . . the well-being of the inhabitants of these territories, and to this end . . . to develop self-government."[25] British colonialists, in other words, also had to defend the empire against Soviet, American, and nationalist attacks at the new United Nations. They needed to justify to the global community their continued administration of subject peoples in territories throughout Africa and Asia.

With these objectives in mind, the colonial government in Kenya turned its attention to "developing" indigenous agriculture in the late 1940s, and thus began what John Lonsdale and D. A. Low have termed the "second colonial occupation."[26] This occupation brought in a new wave of metropole and national government interventionism whereby the imperialists attempted to "develop" both the colonial economies and subject populations. Specifically, development planners attempted to increase the production of agriculture because it had the potential to provide sufficient revenue for the colonial state by generating capital through cash crop exports.

More importantly, in the Cold War context, rural development was an area where colonial officials could meddle with the habits of local cultivators and reconstruct social structures by introducing farming practices and polices based on western science and moral principles.[27] Development technocrats from the United States, in particular, arrived in Kenya with their British counterparts in the 1950s ready to recommend solutions and to provide technical assistance that would theoretically lead to positive social and political change for all Kenyans. Through organizations like the International Cooperation Administration (ICA), which became the United States Agency for International Development (USAID) in 1961, the State Department supported the regime's effort to make farming more appealing to rural communities in places like western Kenya. The ICA, as chapter 3 will show, donated farming equipment as well as provided finances to help fund Chavakali Secondary school's teachers' salaries during its early years. The United States government was also a sponsor of the Swynnerton Plan.[28] With the creation of USAID, the State Department seemed only to have increased its involvement in Kenya's rural development process during the decolonization and early national era. Like their secular development counterparts, Friends Africa Mission officials understood that compromises and changes were essential in the post-World War II era.

Friends Africa Mission and Western Kenya

In addition to being one of the most densely populated regions in the country, western Kenya also housed the Friends (Quaker) Africa Mission station. The Quakers, like most religious organizations throughout Kenya and across Africa, had a key role in "improving" the local communities with whom they came in contact during the colonial, transition, and independence era. In particular, by the eve of Kenya's independence, the Friends' Mission Board had initiated programs to develop indigenous agricultural practices. In practice, this translated to the missionaries on the ground telling the local congregation how to be a "modern" and productive farmer citizen. The Friends Africa Mission, in short, operated under the same economic development framework as the late colonial and early independence Kenyan state.

The Friends (Quaker) Africa Industrial Mission was a one-thousand-acre mission station in Kaimosi, a location situated about twenty miles northwest of Kisumu and ten miles north of Maragoliland. In his study of the Friends' early missionary work in western Kenya, Stafford Young noted that the mission's name had become the Friends Africa Mission by 1912 when it came under the supervision of the American Friends Board of Foreign Missions.[29] Three Midwestern American Quakers established this mission in 1902, and because of its location the missionaries primarily interacted with people who eventually identified as the Luhya.

Willis R. Hotchkiss, Arthur Chilson, and Edgar Hole made up the first group of American Friends missionaries to arrive in western Kenya. Hotchkiss was a Midwestern minister who had already participated in a failed African mission in the late nineteenth-century, Chilson was a student at the Cleveland Bible Institute and the mission's first mechanic, and Hole was a businessman from Ohio who acted as the mission's initial business manager.[30] Once their ship landed in the coastal city of Mombasa in July 1902, the men traveled on the newly completed Uganda railway to Kisumu, where they quickly began their search for a suitable site to construct the mission station. They acquired about one-thousand-acres of land located "twenty miles north of the railhead at Kisumu," with assistance from the District Commissioner, C. W. Hobley.[31]

The pioneers selected Kaimosi as the location for the mission's main station because of its proximity to the Goli Goli River and its surrounding forest. They viewed the natural resources as valuable assets that would help them develop a particular type of Christian mission in East Africa: one that was focused on "stressing religious conversion and teaching skills necessary for improved social conditions."[32] Thus, the early Quaker missionaries hoped to create an industrial mission that would essentially transform itself into a "self-supporting, self-propagating native church" for the indigenous people of western Kenya.[33]

The mission station had four departments: evangelical, medical, educational, and industrial. During the initial phase of the mission enterprise, the evangelical department was the most important followed by the industrial division. In a 1903 mission report composed by the original band of missionaries, the reason for this order was explained: "The primary object of Friends Africa Industrial Mission is the evangelization of the heathen. The industrial feature is introduced into the work for the purpose of exerting continues Christian influence over the natives employed."[34] It is evident from the report that the pioneers understood that the local population viewed the church as a place where they could obtain the skills needed to function within a society controlled by foreigners.

Therefore, the promotion of industrial training, which emphasized the teaching of special trades like carpentry and agriculture, became a big focus for the early Friends evangelists, despite some concerns from their American supporters. Their critics expected to learn about the missionaries' success in converting the "heathens," not about their efforts in building mill dams with the Africans. To appease their supports back home, Chilson wrote to the

Mission Board insisting that industrial work and preaching the gospel went hand in hand. "Industrial work is one of the most powerful agencies used of the Lord to bring the Gospel to these people," asserted Chilson.[35] For the missionaries of Friends Africa Mission, the industrial department was central to the mission's overall expansion and spiritual growth.

Industrial work and training, however, did not remain popular among the Luhya men and women for too long. Rather than acquire the specific skills, which would allow them to preform manual and technical tasks around the mission station, the African converts were more interested in learning to read, write, and speak in the colonizer's language.[36] In other words, they were more interested in the practical advantages of Christianity. Many realized that having access to Western education would open doors to better social and economic conditions for themselves and family members. The local population's eagerness for academic education therefore forced the mission to invest its financial resources into developing the educational department at the expense of its industrial program.[37]

Beginning in 1910, the missionaries on the ground devoted much of their attention and the mission's finances to training local teachers and writing textbooks and readers for the Luhya youth and adults who attended classes at the mission station.[38] The Friends' commitment to improve "native" education was neither unique nor specific to the mission, however. The colonial government along with other mission stations throughout Kenya were also promoting a specific brand of African (or "native") education during the second and third decades of the twentieth-century. For example, the British colonial schools modeled their educational program for their African subjects after the segregated American South's rural school system, which stressed vocational skills and manual labor in the curriculum over a scholastic liberal arts program.[39]

Although the local congregation's fervor for education had eclipsed the industrial program's prominence during the first half of the century, by the start of the 1950s there was renewed interest on behalf of the Friends Mission in teaching the practical skills to the local communities again. The mission's return to and its emphasis on vocational training resulted from the fact that in 1946 the American Friends Board of Foreign Missions began the process of transitioning its mission station in Kaimosi into a local church by establishing the East Africa Yearly Meeting.[40] Like their colonial counterparts, mission officials understood that their days were numbered in the post–World War II era. So, they shifted their attention to implementing projects and schemes that would, in theory, help members of the local congregation earn enough revenue to be self-sufficient and thus able to financially support a local Friends Church.

The Friends Mission supported an industrial program centered on agrarian development because they viewed agriculture as a resourceful way for the mission to obtain the funds it required to become self-sufficient and eventually independent of American Friends' support.[41] The focus on developing African agriculture was therefore a pragmatic choice because mission officials recognized the importance of having loyal and productive local converts who were to help the mission transition into a stable home church. The individuals who went to western Kenya to fulfill their missionary services in the late colonial and independence era, as a result, differed from previous missionaries in that they were trained professionals who devoted their time to projects such as "improving" agriculture, which had in the past been overshadowed by educational development. This was a factor behind the Mission Board's decision to appoint Rodney Morris as the mission's first agricultural missionary in 1955. Since Morris was a Quaker with experience working on farms and also had a degree in agronomy from Cornell University, he seemed a suitable candidate to carry out an agricultural mission.[42]

The men and women Quakers who went to Western Kenya to carry out their missionary services in the late 1950s and early 1960s understood that their responsibilities inevitably included preparing the Luhya, especially the Maragoli, for life in independent Kenya. The missionaries' particular idea of the rural Africans' place within the new state was limited to the agricultural sphere, however. Just like the late colonial government and, subsequently, the Kenyatta regime, the Friends Africa Mission's development model rested on encouraging its rural coverts to take agriculture seriously. The Quaker missionaries, in short, intended for their local converts to participate and contribute to the independent church and nation-state as farmers.

Yet Maragoliland's alarmingly high population density meant that residents were often skeptical of the agrarian schemes and farming practices that state officials *and* missionaries introduced to "better" the local community's condition. Maragoliland residents' land holdings, as noted in the introduction, were becoming increasingly smaller due to inheritance practices carried out by the Luhya community and by the population growth in the region. By 1960, for example, a 5.26 acre of land owned by a family of five had dwindled to 4.7 acres because of a three percent increase in the area's population.[43] With these harsh land facts, many in Maragoliland realized that the nation builders and foreign development "specialists" in the 1950s and 1960s were promoting unrealistic agricultural projects and schemes. Nevertheless, as the following chapters highlight, they did not completely ignore the government officials and Friends missionaries who were responsible for carrying out development in their region. The residents of Maragoliland simply engaged with the development practitioners whenever it suited their personal agendas and according to their own terms.

Chapter Three

Chavakali Secondary School: A Place of Learning and Farming

As the seventeenth child of a twenty-one-child household, Joram Clement Chavasuh appreciated that Chavakali secondary school opened in his home village in western Kenya. Chavasuh was a "pioneer student" belonging to the rural high school's inaugural class of thirty-six male students that started on January 12, 1959, in a modest one-room block of four rooms "built of locally fired brick, laid up with mud and pointed up with mortar on the outside, under a sheet iron roof."[1] For Chavasuh, who was twenty years old when he started high school, Chavakali secondary school was the place where he would diversify his skills and explore careers outside of agriculture. Making a living off the land, which was what the late colonial Kenyan government and, subsequently, the Kenyatta regime expected from rural people like himself, was neither appealing nor was it a realistic option for Chavasuh at the time. His status as a junior son, for instance, precluded his making any strong claims to a sizable and productive plot of land on his father's overworked five-acre plot in Chavakali. Moreover, as one of the few in his family to receive an education, Chavasuh's parents expected him to pursue job opportunities in towns, which their national leaders promised would become more available to "learned" Kenyans as the country transitioned from a British colony into an independent nation-state throughout the early 1960s.[2] Chavakali high school, in short, was to help Chavasuh secure a more comfortable future that did not involve having to depend on the land solely for his livelihood in the postcolony.

However, promoting and training young Kenyans for careers in the agrarian sector and thus to appreciate "the significance of agriculture to the future of economic development of Kenya" was a task that Chavakali's administrators, namely the local Nyanza District officials and the American Friends (Quaker) Africa Mission (FAM) missionaries, undertook from the start. They did so largely because of the lack of industries and, to some degree, self-serving local church and government officials who depended on educated young and ambitious people to stay local in order to maintain business affairs.[3] Chavakali administrators and rural "specialists" consequently emphasized practical training in its curriculum, which they hoped would provide students with the skills and mindset to remain in the countryside and to participate in Kenya's agrarian-based economy as skilled farm managers and laborers. By 1961, for example, school officials had adopted an agricultural syllabus entitled "Agricultural Principles and Practice," which included a strong practicum component that required students to take soil samples and learn simple accounting principles, among other activities.[4]

Such contrasting expectations and conflicting visions for Chavakali secondary school provide a window into the chaotic yet euphoric climate of Kenya's transition period and its subsequent independence decade of the 1960s. Certainly, the struggle between local, national, and international "experts" over the proper nature of education and by extension Kenya unfolded at Chavakali. This was the site where both the colonial and the nationalist Kenyan government, along with foreign developmentalists—both secular and religious—tested and contested their theories about the value of vocational educational training in rural secondary schools. It was an ideal place to actualize the state's project of agrarianism. In turn, Chavakali was the arena in which ambitious rural Kenyans adapted top-down development policies to suit their own circumstances, and where they rejected claims by experts that remaining in the agricultural sector was practical and in their best interest as colonial subjects, and eventually as citizens of the postcolony.

The story of Chavakali high school, in short, underscores Frederick Cooper's point that at independence, colonialism was not "turned off like a light switch."[5] Colonial assumptions about development, specifically with regard to rural communities and African education, were indeed carried over into the national era. The Kenyatta regime's program for its secondary schools, particularly its emphasis on vocational agricultural learning, was an extension and continuation of the (limited) colonial educational system and (problematic) neomercantile economy. This continuity, coupled with shortages of arable land in the most densely populated regions, along with the lack of interest in small-hold farming by many ordinary young Kenyans, explains at least in part why the Kenyan state fell short in generating the development it envisioned would take place within the rural sector in the post-independence decade.

Local needs, expectations, and realities trumped those of the Kenyan state and its development partners. The lack of success or the failures of the agrarian revolution of the 1960s in places like Kenya and by extension sub-Saharan Africa was consequently the result of ordinary people challenging the trite narrative that rural women and men should only strive to have careers in agriculture and thus remain in the countryside. The renunciation of this stereotype, which was often championed by urban political elites and rural development practitioners like the Friends Quaker missionaries, underpins the story of Chavakali high school. By neither continuing with advanced studies in agriculture and thus becoming progressive farm managers nor taking up employment as skilled farm laborers upon leaving high school, Chavakali students rejected the school's intended aims and thereby complicated Kenya's nation-building project that was predicated on having its rural citizens embrace the agriculture-as-development model.

The Place of Chavakali

The Chavakali region is predominately home to the Maragoli Luhya, a sub-group of the Abaluhya ethnic community, which is the second largest in Kenya. [6] Thus, it is situated within the North Maragoli sub-location of present-day Vihiga county in what was historically known as the North Nyanza District of Nyanza Province in western Kenya. As outlined in the introduction and second chapter, the District was and continues to be one of the most densely populated regions in the country due to the Kenyan colonial government's "native reserves" system formalized in the early twentieth century.

The average size plot of land for a Maragoli family of eight in 1956 was 5.26 acres, for example. By 1960, this acreage had decreased to 4.7 acres because of a three percent increase in the area's population.[7] This particular statistic reflects a higher average holding size than the "some two acres" revelation made by FAM's agricultural missionary in his report to the American Board in the early 1960s regarding local land-holding size.[8] The difference likely resulted from district officials not accounting that land was often subdivided by family members. Nonetheless, the data suggests that the people in the North Nyanza District, especially young Maragolis, had little or no chance of acquiring sizable arable land from their families because of its limited availability.

Understandably, for many Maragoli people who were all too familiar with the region's land pressure problem and the physical and financial hardships associated with small-hold commercial farming, Chavakali high school embodied possibilities and brighter futures. Though the curriculum seemed limited, the school still offered ambitious young landless and land-poor Maragolis a chance to be "learned" individuals. It was a beacon of hope for North Nyanza people such as the Chavasuh family, who wanted access to a higher standard of living (away from the farm) in the twilight of Kenya's colonial period.

The Founding of Chavakali Secondary School: A Community Affair

The local residents first learned of the Chavakali secondary school project from the North Maragoli sub-location's "chief," Matthew Mwenesis, and FAM missionaries, who proposed the initiative at community *barazas* (meetings) around the North Nyanza District throughout the late 1950s. The project and its objective were straightforward: to establish in North Nyanza District an innovative rural secondary day-school to meet local demands for education. This high school, Mwenesis promised, would provide the region's intermediate school graduates, who were unsuccessful in securing a limited spot in the more prestigious high schools throughout late colonial Kenya, with a type of secondary education required for "useful careers in trade, agriculture, teaching, development of small industries and community leadership."[9] The high school was to recruit only boys, because there were already nearby FAM-administered secondary schools catering to local girls.[10] Thus, for Mwenesis, Chavakali was a solution to the local community's land pressure and unemployment problems even if the school's curriculum fell far short of acknowledging the realities and expectations of his young constituents by privileging vocational subjects like agriculture and carpentry. Focusing on training students for useful careers in places like Maragoliland, in other words, sidestepped the concerns of young rural Kenyans such as Chavasuh, who neither had the resources—land, in particular—nor the desire to remain in the countryside as simple laborers.

Despite his promises that the high school would serve all communities in North Nyanza District, the North Maragoli chief, Mwenesis, only managed to convince the leadership from three sub-locations, his own and those of South Maragoli and Idakho sub-locations, to accept a self-imposed tax known as the Chavakali Special Rate. The Luhya families from the three sub-locations therefore became responsible for an annual tax to jump-start the school's development. Specifically, beginning in 1958 to 1961, the households in both of the Maragoli locations were each responsible for paying Shs.12/- and 50 cents while the Idakho sub-location households were to contribute Shs.5/-. This fee was to be collected by the local African District Council (ADC) in North Nyanza.[11]

Although the local officials believed this tax was reasonable and had initially advertised it at the community *barazas* as a voluntary contribution, paying the Chavakali Special Rate became a burden for a number of residents whose weekly average wage was about Shs.2/-.[12] Rachel Amudava, whose husband was part of the North Nyanza leadership council, made clear that the tax was difficult to collect because it was "a lot of money by then . . . (and) making that contribution was not that easy because there were different levels of understanding in the community."[13] Further, the collection of the Chavakali Special Rate eventually turned into an upsetting event for some Maragoli residents when local authorities made it compulsory in late 1958.[14]

For the women of Maragoliland, the collection of the Chavakali Special Rate tax was especially traumatizing. Since they were primarily in charge of the homesteads while most of their male kin were labor migrants, Maragoli women from subsistence and small-hold homesteads, meaning land units ranging between .25 and seven acres, were the main targets of harassment by local ADC tax collectors. These households were often cash-poor because they lacked the land needed to successfully grow the more profitable cash crops like coffee and tea. Consequently, the female kin of migrant Maragoliland laborers suffered verbal threats and, for some, even physical abuse at the hands of collection agents whenever they failed to contribute the stipulated amount that the ADC mandated. Often, if families had no cash, the tax collectors would leave their homesteads with property that was worth more than the required fee, along with items that did not belong to the family. The confiscation of property in the name of the Chavakali school in the late 1950s created the largest source of agony for several Maragoliland residents, who were left having to explain to their family members and neighbors what happened to their property as a result of collection day.

Keran Magunamu and Epharina Esabu's poignant recollections concerning the collection of the Chavakali Special Rate reveal just how contentious the project was. Like many women in Maragoliland, Esabu and Magunamu both migrated to the Chavakali area after they married their husbands in 1947 and 1957 respectively. Esabu practiced mainly subsistence farming on her family's two-acre land but started dabbling in coffee cultivation in the early 1960s when her husband agreed to have agricultural officials teach the household how to plant the crop. While her husband helped Esabu with coffee planting, he usually worked away from the homestead, so she was often left alone to handle household matters. When describing her former encounters with authorities who were responsible for collecting the unpopular Chavakali Special Rate tax, Esabu was explicit: "It was hell!"[15]

According to Esabu, the collection agents had no respect for people's property and often created tension among neighbors. "A huge animal that you've reared on your farm is maybe about to have milk, [but] someone comes and grabs it and goes away with it to sell for Shs.12/- . . . it was horrible," bemoaned Esabu; "even worse, the animal would be sold in the neighborhood, so you'd look at your animal now in your neighbor's place." Esabu, however, described herself as fortunate given that the intrusive tax collectors did not frequent her homestead outside of their annual visit. She reasoned that it was "because the village elders came from around [here] so I was protected in a way . . . my husband was also good at constructing houses, so he was also a popular man around here." [16] Thus, although Esabu often had to deal with the obnoxious officials on her own, she was often shielded from undue harassment because of her husband's status.

Magunamu, on the other hand, was not fortunate enough to have this type of protection. The fee collectors' visits were more frequent for her, with each episode producing extreme levels of stress. She explained that this was primarily because "whenever they come across and you'd fail to pay them money, they would move away with your chicken, cow, or table." Similar to Esabu, Magunamu mostly cultivated food crops on her husband's 3.25-acre land. The family also dedicated some land for coffee cultivation, which Magunamu attested failed to provide sufficient cash returns. Magunamu was primarily a poultry farmer at the time authorities frequented her home in search of the Chavakali Special Rate in the late 1950s. Her modest poultry business, however, was not lucrative and usually left her with little cash in hand.[17]

Accordingly, it was difficult for Magunamu to continuously pay the local authorities who seemed to have collected the Chavakali Special Rate at their discretion. To underscore her past troubles brought on by the school project, Magunamu remembered the time when collection agents seized chickens from her homestead because she did not have the required payment. "I had no money, but they [administrators] found a lot of chickens around here, so they came into my house and took some maize and throw it on the ground [and] when the chicken came to feed, they got all the birds . . . and they walked away," lamented Magunamu. This particular incident created more financial strain for Magunamu, because the three chickens that the authorities confiscated belonged to her neighbor who demanded that she pay for the missing poultry since the chickens were taken from her property.[18]

The abusive treatment that local residents experienced on behalf of the ADC tax collectors were made known to the North Nyanza District officials through letters by residents and in reports by local administrators who detailed the harassment. James Mage Aluda's letter to the North Maragoli chief in January 1960, for example, captures the frustrations that local residents felt about having to pay for the mandatory Special Rate. Upset that the ADC collectors had confiscated a table from his home to serve as payment, Aluda implored his chief to explain how the Special Rate collection process worked. "I would like to know how many times one pays in a year," he wrote, "does it mean that when I am not at home your people can take my things without any information? Don't you think it is against the civilized principles?"[19]

While the collection of the Chavakali Special Rate was objectionable, some Maragoliland residents were still in favor of the school being built in the region. Even those individuals most scarred by the collection process praised the school. "It was a good thing for this area to have a school," Magunamu maintained.[20] Sharing Magunamu's sentiment, local officials pushed forward with the four-year tax initiative because (in theory) it would generate the initial capital needed for the secondary school's basic construction.

Particularly, the Chavakali Special Rate allowed the community to move forward with the goal of building a secondary school for their children. Rather than wait until 1961, which was when the Government of Kenya indicated to local authorities it would be willing to allocate funding to such a project, the local Maragoliland government used the tax revenue it collected throughout the 1958 cycle to open the school on January 1959.[21] Consequently, as Chavasuh proudly noted, "it [Chavakali secondary school] was sponsored by the community and was purely for the local people."[22] The secondary school, in other words, stands as a testament to Abaluhya efforts, particularly those of the Maragoli Luhya, to provide their sons with a literary education that many hoped would lead to well paying jobs far away from the family's overcrowded homestead.

The Role of Adapted Education

Even though the local community supplied the start-up funds, the majority of ordinary Maragolis neither governed the Chavakali high school nor developed its curriculum because Kenyan law provided the Education Department supervisory control over all independent or community-sponsored schools. Accordingly, FAM missionaries and, by February 1960, faculty from Earlham College (located in Richmond, Indiana) along with staff members from the International Cooperation Administration (ICA), the predecessor to United States Agency for International Development (USAID), were the school's administrators and curriculum planners.[23] For the developmentalists, the Chavakali high school was to offer the local community an adapted education.

Popularly known as the Tuskegee philosophy of education, this type of schooling was what American philanthropic organizations like the Phelps-Stokes Fund and Jeanes Foundations transplanted to British territories in Africa starting in the 1920s. Proponents of adapted education like Thomas Jesse Jones, who served as the Phelps-Stoke Fund's Education Director, argued that it was appropriate for the rural African milieu because it was utilitarian and rooted in a strong agricultural bias.[24] Through adapted education, the Colonial Office hoped to foster compliant African subjects who would serve the interests of Europeans within and outside of its territories for years to come. Technical and agricultural (as opposed to academic) education, in other words, was to prepare Kenyans to be productive individuals who would gradually assume their own (political) affairs in the distant future thereby preserving the political status quo. More importantly, the Colonial Office hoped that a non-conventional education program in the African territories would also avoid creating a class of problematic Western-style nationalists like Gandhi and others who formed the Indian National Congress in British-ruled India.

Given the unpopularity of practical educational programs throughout the colonial period, which manifested in events like the Kikuyu independent-school movement of the 1930s and 1940s whereby local Kikuyus rejected the vocational-agricultural training model by funding independent schools that provided only liberal arts education, it would seem reasonable that

Kenya's Ministry of Education would discontinue this type of schooling.[25] However, the Kenyatta regime in 1964 moved forward with expanding and implementing Chavakali's vocational-agricultural program into its rural secondary school curriculum.[26] It did so because of individuals like David M. Mulinidi. As the Secretary of the Busali Development Committee, Mulinidi reminded his Provincial Education Officers in 1962 that "we have no industries to keep the boys and girls busy . . . in this way crimes will increase in the country."[27]

The Busali location was also in North Nyanza District, and thus its local leaders like Mulinidi were very much aware of Chavakali's aim, and they were also desperate for solutions to the unemployment crisis that was prevalent throughout the colony on the eve of decolonization. Consequently, Busali officials sent a delegation to explain to the Provincial authorities in western Kenya that this particular secondary education would "be an indirect industry to keep them [boys and girls] until they are full grown up ready to hold or do some reasonable service for the community."[28] Chavakali's curriculum therefore seemed to meet the needs of local administrators facing challenges resulting from lack of industries and land.

Moreover, adapted education and thereby the notion that working on the land was key to an individual's social upward mobility and prosperity supported the colonial regime's and, eventually, the Kenyatta administration's economic policy of neomercantilism. This economic system, which stressed large-scale production of agricultural materials for international markets, had prevented industrialization and economic diversification throughout the colonial era. The agriculture sector, particularly large-scale commercial farming, unsurprisingly was the backbone of Kenya's economy when the British government in 1960 announced plans to divest itself of the colony within a three-year period.[29]

The quick onset of decolonization and political independence meant that the 1961 Kenya African Democratic Union (KADU)-led government, the 1962 coalition administration of KADU and Kenya African National Union (KANU), as well as the KANU-led nationalist regime that assumed power on December 12, 1963 continued to support the idea of export-oriented agriculture. In so doing, it maintained the colonial economic development model of neomercantilism—a system that consequently benefited elite, land-rich Kenyans at the expense of ordinary land-poor Kenyans in the postcolony. Neomercantilism also meant that the Kenyan government needed a productive and cooperative agricultural labor force. The fact that in 1964 the Kenyatta regime requested additional funding from USAID, the successor of the ICA, to expand agricultural teaching, especially Chavakali's agrarian-focused curriculum, within the country's rural secondary schools was in many ways a realistic acknowledgement that Western colonial rule had failed to produce a viable and diversified capitalist economy.[30]

As the introduction shows, the Kenyan state's reliance on the rural sector and the continuation of the neomercantile economic system into the post-colony was due in large part to its Western allies espousing the virtues of modernization theory throughout the independence decade. KANU's economic program in 1964, for example, reveals how Kenyan leaders adapted modernization theory into its nation-building program by underscoring the importance of the agrarian sector within the process. The development of the nation, according to the ruling party, rested on the shoulders of progressive small-hold commercial farmers, who were seen as the solution to chronic rural poverty and to growing Kenya's agricultural-based economy in the postcolony. If small-hold farmers "planned an extra row of maize, worked an extra hour per day, planted the recommended seed and followed the advice of the agricultural officer," wrote Kenyatta, they had the ability to start an agrarian revolution that was the "principal means for creating employment opportunities and raising incomes in Kenya."[31]

More importantly, the agriculture-as-development paradigm allowed the transitional government and, subsequently the Kenyatta regime, to confront a direct threat to the political establishment: young, semi-educated, land-poor, and unemployed Kenyans to whom Mulinidi's comments referred. The 1960 Dalglesh survey of unemployment estimated that only 435,000 of the 1.5 million Kenyan males between the ages of sixteen and forty-five seeking employment outside of the rural areas had wage-employment. Locally, the survey indicated that 600,000 residents were either jobless or underemployed in the North Nyanza District, making it the largest area of unemployment in Kenya at the time.[32] Such statistics were understandably threatening to nationalist leaders and foreign investors who were concerned with young people migrating into urban centers in search of employment in both the formal and informal sectors.[33]

By Kenya's complete independence from Great Britain in 1963, the unemployment issue was exacerbated by the fact that rural *harambee* (community-funded) or independent high schools had mushroomed.[34] The growth of *harambee* schools essentially resulted in an increasing number of educated yet idle Kenyans in the countryside. These schools were often inadequately staffed and lacked appropriate resources to carry out a high-quality academic program. As a result, the graduates of the *harambee* schools usually were limited in their educational experiences compared to their peers who graduated from the more elite and mission-administered schools like Alliance High School.

Nevertheless, like their ambitious and better trained peers, the *harambee* school graduates expected to acquire employment off the land and to live comfortably in urban centers. Such expectations from this particular demographic, especially in light of the Mau Mau uprising, concerned foreign development agents, late colonial administrators, as well as politicians from the transitional government and then the Kenyatta administration. Town officials particularly feared that this group would become hostile and cause unrest by aligning themselves with communist rabble rousers if the government failed to meet its expectations for employment, which seemed possible given that there was not a significant private sector in Kenya and the reality that Kenyatta had to retain a number of colonial officials at independence.[35]

Such circumstances essentially meant that the desirable non-agricultural jobs were scarce and out of reach for the majority of *harambee* school graduates, who were unable to compete for the coveted jobs because they lacked the necessary training and education. The Kenyan government in the late 1950s and the 1960s was therefore enthusiastic about the Chavakali secondary school project because of its aim to motivate rural Kenyans to remain on the land as skilled farm managers and laborers. The school's commitment to offer its students a vocational-agricultural education grounded in practical rather than theoretical training, in particular, supported the newly-independent Kenyan state's nation-building program that prioritized export-oriented agriculture as the driver of economic development and the solution to keeping young and able-bodied rural citizens occupied in the countryside.[36]

Along with the Kenyan and British government, the FAM missionaries throughout the first half of the twentieth century promoted technical training over academic instruction in its educational program. The Quakers, like most religious organizations in Kenya and across Africa, had a key role in "improving" the local communities with whom they came in contact such as the Maragoli. Consequently, upon receiving from the British Crown a title lease to the impressive one-thousand-acre property at Kaimosi, western Kenya in 1902, the founding Midwestern American evangelists aimed to establish and operate schools with a vocational-industrial focus.[37]

FAM missionaries intended for these schools to attract loyal converts whom they anticipated would become leaders responsible for developing the mission into a self-sufficient local church.[38] In practice, however, the pioneering FAM missionaries offered an adapted education program to the local communities in North Nyanza, which included training in brick making and "modern" farming practices, because they were limited in terms of supplies and personnel to start their desired local chrch. Moreover, the Midwestern American Friends evangelists were farmers more than theologians: they favored an agricultural curriculum because it supported their practical orientation for the mission, which hoped to foster a group of literate Christian farmers and farm workers who would use the land to financially sustain the local church and its activities.[39]

Consequently, supporting the Chavakali secondary project in the mid-1950s fit in with the Quaker church's mission. The emphasis on practical over traditional academic training was necessary for young ordinary Kenyans, FAM and Earlham College representatives argued, because it prepared them to garner jobs in the rural sector that would enable them to become good Christians and citizens. Particularly, FAM personnel anticipated that graduates of Chavakali would remain in the countryside and assume leadership positions in the home church since they would acquire the practical training necessary to manage the mission's religious work and its one-thousand-acre property at Kaimosi. Put another way, Chavakali secondary school was a means by which missionaries could directly influence and foster the younger generation of Luhya Quakers into becoming "proper" church leaders in the late colonial and postcolonial era. Its establishment and, more importantly, Chavakali's vocational-agricultural education program, catered more to outside interests and expectations than to the people in the Maragoli area whom the school was supposed to serve.

From Community Project to International Scheme

That rural Kenyans' place within the newly independent state was limited to the agricultural sphere was one of the main reasons why FAM leaders like Fred Reeve, the mission's Executive Secretary at the time, strongly backed the campaign by the North Maragoli sub-location chief, Matthew Mwenesis, to build a rural high school in Chavakali. Reeve's enthusiasm for the school project led him to solicit support from officials at Earlham College in the late 1950s. The Executive Secretary's efforts resulted in the two religious (Quaker) Friends institutions working jointly in 1957 on grant proposals to the United States' ICA and to the British government. Reeve and Landrum Bolling, who was Earlham College's president at the time, appealed to officials in Nairobi, London, and Washington DC for funding and resources to assist the Maragoli community's effort to establish the first day secondary school in Kenya. Bolling and Reeve proposed that Chavakali secondary school would borrow elements from American rural high schools that included adopting a day rather than a boarding (over-night) structure, as well as privileging agriculture and industrial arts over conventional academic subjects in the school's curricula.[40]

On February 16, 1960, over a year after Chavakali secondary school's grand opening on January 12, 1959, Reeve and Bolling secured a grant for $310,685 from ICA. This financial support was for four years, meaning it carried over into the independence era and effected the transition of the high school from a local community-financed initiative into an ICA (and eventually USAID) pilot project with Earlham College in charge of overseeing the contract.[41] Consequently, the college was responsible for providing staff and leadership while the British Colonial Office and Kenyan government were to offer these same services (on a limited basis) and to furnish the classrooms with equipment and tools.

In its role as an ICA-AID pilot project, Chavakali intensified its vocational curriculum by having faculty and administrators implement agriculture and industrial arts courses. The ICA-AID contract brought Robert Maxwell, the assigned agricultural instructor, to western Kenya in 1961. Maxwell, an American farmer from Iowa, arrived at Chavakali tasked with creating an agricultural program that was to appeal to students and their families.[42] This assignment was certain to be a challenge for Maxwell given that in 1960, prior to his arrival, some parents had threatened to pull their children out of Chavakali after they witnessed an instructor working on his demonstration farm plot at the school's facilities. The parents demanded that Morris Kirck, then the Headmaster, compel this particular teacher to refrain from working in the field and to dress more professionally.[43] It is unclear if Kirck formally addressed the parents' concerns, but Chavakali's student rosters for this time period do not reflect a significant drop in enrollment numbers but rather the opposite, suggesting that the angry parents likely did not carry out their threat to withdraw their sons from the high school.

In spite of the community's reluctance to have Chavakali students learn farming skills from their instructors, Maxwell implemented an agricultural syllabus in the early 1960s that Kenya's Ministries of Agriculture and Education supported and, more importantly, was Cambridge Syndicate approved. The syndicate's endorsement was vital because it organized and regulated the curriculum and examinations for Kenya's secondary school programs, and thus it was the organization that issued the coveted Cambridge

School Certificates that were often required for admission to a university and white-collar jobs.[44] Maxwell, in other words, provided Chavakali students and parents with a reason to take the subject of farming seriously because agriculture was now part of the Cambridge School Certificate exam, an examination that most (if not all) Kenyan students in the late colonial and independence decade worked diligently to be eligible to take and to pass.

Nevertheless, even if rural Maragoli students were interested in learning "better" agriculture skills, the lack of land available prevented many pupils from practicing at home what they were learning on the school's demonstration plots. Colonial education and farm policies, in effect, were inherently irrational and nonsensical in western Kenya. The reality was there was no free land and the practice of fragmenting holdings through inheritance was forcing future generations to make due on smaller and less fertile plots.

The Practicality of "Practical Education"

Whereas the Kenyan government and FAM missionaries throughout the independence decade sought to create a specific type of rural citizen using the Chavakali secondary school, students and their parents had their own objectives for the high school. For a number of Maragoli residents, the school offered them a way to provide their children with a conventional literary education, which they understood was essential for socio-economic upward mobility within any Kenyan state. The school, in other words, represented more than a place to receive vocational-agricultural training: it was to enable western Kenyans to acquire an education that would lead to a well paying job ideally far away from the family's overcrowded homestead. The school's emphasis on vocational-agricultural training, understandably, frustrated parents and community members who likely viewed the agrarian training a waste of their sons' time and was perhaps even offensive since the instructors anticipated that students would demonstrate their scientific techniques to their parents on the family's farm.[45]

That Chavakali students and their parents were unenthusiastic about the school's emphasis on application and demonstration was reasonable, especially in light of significant political events taking place nationally and across the sub-Saharan African continent in the late 1950s and early 1960s that expedited the end of colonial rule in Kenya.[46] Chavakali high school officials' aim to make vocational-agricultural education a priority started during the twilight years of colonization and subsequently continued during the country's decolonization and transfer of power, when expectations for better working and living conditions were high among all Kenyans. Accordingly, like most ordinary Kenyans at this time, Chavakali parents expected material improvement in their family circumstances.

Community expectations seemed warranted given that they contributed to the school's development by way of the Chavakali Special Rate Tax. Indeed, as tax payers, many parents who sent their children to Chavakali felt that they were entitled to have some influence over the school's affairs and curriculum. Administrative control, however, belonged to Friends missionaries, Kenyan officials, and US development representatives who ideally had the local community's best interest in mind. Keran Magunamu, for instance, provided insight as to why the local population had little sway over Chavakali's academic program: "most of the villagers were uneducated, so that did not allow us the opportunity to dictate what was supposed to be taught at the school."[47]

The lack of education, nonetheless, did not keep parents from feeling that they ought to have some control over their children's schooling. This feeling of entitlement, in fact, ultimately engendered complications for FAM missionaries and authorities during Kenya's transition period. For instance, the school's acting-superintendent, Rodney Morris, wrote to the Mission Board in 1960 about the challenges missionaries faced in carrying out the mission's agenda for the school under these circumstances. "The outcry was tremendous with many rumors being circulated about the school being second-rate," Morris explained; "the people really have a feeling that the school belongs to them, a feeling that we don't want to discourage, but one that makes any proposed changes all the more difficult."[48]

Along with being problematic for the missionaries, the local community's attitude about the school's main purpose essentially undercut the efforts of the Kenyan government and its developmental partners who were eager to have young rural people investing in their communities and, more importantly, participating in the national economy as either skilled agricultural workers or productive small-hold commercial farmers. For example, as Robert Maxwell discovered during his return trip to Kenya in 1969, a number of former students from the first five classes, meaning those who entered between 1959 and 1963, neither remained in western Kenya nor became successful small-hold commercial farmers once they left Chavakali secondary school.

Of the 266 former Chavakali school students with whom he interviewed for his doctoral research, Maxwell learned that only twenty-three students (eleven percent) indicated they worked in the agricultural sector, but they did not specify if they were either commercial farmers or officials working for the Ministry of Agriculture, with the latter being more likely. Compared to the 108 respondents who reported that they were clerical workers residing in places like Nairobi, the twenty-three people working in the agriculture sector signaled to Maxwell that the school's vocational-agricultural program that he implemented fell short in its goal to influence students' career choices.[49] More importantly, these statistics highlight that ordinary western Kenyans hardly shared the same vision as the political elites and development practitioners about what it meant to be a "developed" Kenyan citizen.

Similar to their parents, the former Chavakali students protested that school administrators wanted them to remain on the land and involved in agriculture after completing their education. Student concern particularly stemmed from first-hand knowledge that their high school agricultural training program had limitations. Jethro Luseno, whom we met in the introduction, questioned the agricultural education he received at Chavakali high school from 1964 to 1967: he recalled that the training, at best, prepared students to become simple laborers on large farms outside of Maragoliland. Specifically, Luseno remembers how the lack of arable land in the Maragoli region prevented some classmates from practicing what they learned at home, and thus they had to use their skills elsewhere upon graduation: "I know some of my friends actually joined big farms . . . when they joined big farms like Kericho [tea plantation] farms it was easier for the managers to teach them and bring them into line on how to manage the place."[50] Luseno's comments essentially underscore that the local Abaluhya community recognized the main contradiction with agrarian education in Kenya: the lack of access to land.

More specifically, they did not have access to sufficient land at home to make practicing commercial farming worthwhile. Nicholas Ben Ganira, for example, enjoyed working outside and had considered attending Egerton upon graduating from Chavakali in 1962. Opened in 1939 as a farm school for Europeans interested in pursuing agricultural careers, by 1955 Egerton had become a premiere agricultural college offering diplomas and training certificates to all Kenyans.[51] Post-secondary education opportunities, in other words, were available to students such as Ganira, who were passionate about farming. "I didn't want to be sitting in the office," Ganira explained, "I wanted to work as somebody dealing with crops, cows, cattle, whatever."[52]

Despite his ambition to utilize his vocational-agricultural training, however, Ganira continued his post-secondary education at Siriba College, where he focused on earning a teaching credential rather than building on his high school agricultural training at Chavakali. His decision to become a primary school teacher was likely due in large part to the fact that Ganira was born in the Kaimosi area of the North Nyanza District where his father had neither the land nor the finances to support his son's ambitions. While Ganira did not reveal how much land his father held, based on the land statistics described previously, the family's property in North Nyanza was likely less than five acres and was thus insufficient to sustain Ganira's big farm dreams. Land shortages in places like western Kenya that were due to the commercialization of agriculture and land consolidation policies, understandably discouraged Chavakali students and their families from engaging in agricultural ventures.

"I Do Not Want to See You Here in Khakis": Career Farmers and the Community

Although land scarcity in western Kenya may have been enough reason to make some parents and students skeptical of Chavakali's vocational-agricultural curriculum, the sentiment that subsistence and small-hold farming was a "dirty job" reserved for illiterates kept many local people determined to have the school administrators continue providing their children with a conventional liberal arts education. Someone who had the privilege to obtain an education, in other words, was expected by family and community members to aspire to be more than cash-crop farmers in an independent Kenyan state.

Magunamu, for example, was a parent with educated children who shared this sentiment. Particularly, she did not want her two sons whom the family was struggling to put through secondary school in the early 1960s "to learn how to write, to speak English, and [then] come back [home] and start doing all kinds of rubbish with soils." However, when questioned further, Magunamu conceded that had her sons wanted to work in jobs dealing with the "rubbish soils," she probably would have supported their career choice on condition that they "teach agriculture instead of coming to do farming."[53]

The negative stereotypes associated with farming unquestionably also discouraged some Chavakali students from taking their agricultural training seriously. Sammy Akifuma recalled how his family and neighbors had an unfavorable opinion about vocational-agricultural training because they could not fathom the students doing more with this kind of education than "ploughing the home." Akifuma started at Chavakali high school in 1963 at the age of seventeen and was very much cognizant of the unflattering attitude that some individuals in his local village harbored about farming as a career option in general and about the school's agricultural program in particular. "Teachers like Dan Beane were expecting us to be farmers," he remembered, "but, those days, not today, farming was considered [by locals] to be a field for the illiterates . . . they would say, I do not want to see you here in Khakis . . . people were not impressed with that kind of clothes."[54] His community's position about agricultural training and farm workers, along with his modest upbringing, likely motivated Akifuma to concentrate his attention on subjects like math, and subsequently, to become an employee at a bank in Nairobi after finishing high school.

North Nyanza residents' judgments and skepticism concerning farming as a viable full-time career were not the only reasons why some Chavakali high school students may have opted to pursue post-secondary education at conventional colleges instead of at agricultural training centers like Bukura Farming Institute in western Kenya. Farming, indeed, is labor-intensive and often can be unpredictable because of changing weather patterns and soil conditions. Put simply, being a farmer is physically and emotionally taxing. This difficult task was something that the Maragoli Abaluhya community, as agriculturalists, knew first-hand; therefore, they sought to avoid such difficulties if other opportunities were available. Although tilling the soil may have been part of many young western Kenyans' daily activity, farming was a secondary commitment for a number of Chavakali students fortunate enough to have an education and thereby options off the land.

Luseno, as a matter of fact, had no intentions of making agriculture his chosen profession because of his status as a "learned" person. Despite having access to at least two acres of his father's six-acre holding in Maragoliland, he did not share the developmental goals that his school administrators and the Kenyan government imagined for young educated rural people. Rather, he practiced the farming techniques that he learned from his teachers in order to receive a passing grade and only did farm work on the school's demonstration plots.[55] Similarly, having passed his Cambridge School Certificate exam in 1962, Chavasuh applied to and attended Kaimosi Teacher's Training College. His decision to teach rather than farm, Chavasuh explained, was because his village elders expected him to contribute to the community's needs. "I received a delegation from the community requesting me to take up teaching because there was no teacher in the community," he said; "not even a single teacher."

While there may have been a teacher shortage in the North Nyanza region, Chavasuh's career choice was due to the fact that teaching, unlike agriculture, was not physically demanding, offered a relatively stable income, and gave him respect as a "learned" person in the local community. Chavasuh also understood that becoming a teacher did not mean that he could no longer practice what he learned from Chavakali school's agricultural instructors. Like many educated rural Kenyans, Chavasuh simply became a part-time "telephone" farmer relying on family members' time and labor to maintain the land. Agriculture, namely cash-crop farming he revealed, "helped to generate funds . . . (which) was my interest."[56] Chavaush's white-collar teaching profession allowed him a higher chance of securing a comfortable future during a time of transition and change in 1960s Kenya.

Conclusion

The controversy surrounding Chavakali high school's vocational-agricultural curriculum specifically underscores the disjuncture between rural Kenyans' ambitions and urban elite politicians, as well as foreign developmentalists' goals in the independence decade. More importantly, it highlights the unintended consequences of colonial policies that continued into the postcolony. Chavakali students and their family members in the late 1950s and the 1960s disagreed with using their education to pursue only agriculture-oriented careers, and moreover they lacked the main resource—land—to fulfill the nation-builders' expectations that the rural sector would develop and continue the export-oriented agricultural economy of the colonial era. Unsurprisingly, Chavakali students looked beyond their fathers' overcrowded homesteads for opportunities and ways to improve their condition. In so doing, they frustrated the secular and religious developmentalists' plans to turn young, semi-educated, rural Kenyans into productive rural citizens.

Specifically, the land issue in Maragoliland and their own career ambitious kept a number of students off the land and uninterested in pursing agricultural training at the post-secondary level. The community's attitudes about practical education being second-rate training, for instance, encouraged Chavakali students like Akifuma, Luseno, and Chavasuh to continue appropriating the schools' resources to suit their own agendas rather than to carry out the expectations of their school officials and nationalist leaders in the postcolony. Put simply, the local community's actions and reactions toward Chavakali high school's vocational-agricultural program shows that the nation-building project was in large part unsuccessful because the everyday realities and expectations of Kenyans in the countryside differed significantly from their nationalist leaders in Nairobi and from foreign developmentalists. As such, the experiences of rural Kenyans in general and Chavakali students in particular illustrate how vocational-agricultural education in rural high schools hardly produced the cadre of "modern" small-hold commercial farmers whom the Kenyan state hoped would socially and economically stabilize the countryside. They also make clear how rural communities that were far removed from Nairobi were both objects and agents of developmental change, especially through education, during the late 1950s and 1960s.

Indeed, not all rural people aspired to become small-hold farmers who would sustain themselves and their families on a small piece of land that was often depleted of nutrients and lacking in productivity. Owning large farm estates and becoming commercial farmers were indeed desirable goals for Maragoliland residents, but Maragoliland's alarmingly high population density meant that residents were pragmatists. Moreover, Chavakali provided its students with less ambitious goals. Chavakali students and their parents recognized the school for what it was—a stepping stone—and utilized this resource to their own advantage to the exclusion of outside goals. Similar to the Chavakali Secondary School, the motivation behind the national 4-K farmers' clubs, which is the topic of chapter 4, was to encourage young rural Kenyans to embrace farming and to remain in the countryside. Not surprisingly, the 4-K officials faced similar challenges as the Chavakali school administrators in their goal to promote agrarianism.

Chapter Four

"Doing Their Part": 4-K Farmers' Clubs

> "I couldn't become a farmer . . . farming was dirty . . . I didn't even want my own children to think of it . . . even my own father, I remember my own father, there were times when we joined together as young men and we would go and dig land and plant . . . if he [my father] found me, he would've told me 'I took you to school, I didn't take you to go dig for people,' so, we were forced not to think [about farming] . . . so long as they [my parents] saw me reading my books that was enough."[1]

As a high school student in early 1960s rural western Kenya, Pierson Zavani understood very well what his privileged position meant for himself and his household. He knew, for instance, that his parents expected him to take schooling seriously by refraining from extracurricular activities that were distracting. Among other things, this translated to Zavani devoting his free time to his studies rather than to helping his parents (and neighbors) prepare their farms for the seasonal harvest while not in classes. He made his parents' expectations clear in the above comments when he explained his choice to "stay off the land" upon completing high school. In short, Zavani was discouraged from "digging land" for anyone, including for his own parents who had a five-acre farmstead in Maragoliland, because he was a "learned" person.[2]

Despite his father's objections, however, Zavani was an active 4-K club participant (4-K refers to *Kuungana* (to unite), *Kufanya* (to do), *Kusaidia* (to help), and *Kenya*) during a period when the Kenyan government and its development partners hoped to capture the imagination of rural people by way of its agrarian project, which championed the notion that prosperity was tied to working on the land. 4-K clubs specifically aimed to cultivate an interest in small-hold cash farming amongst the rural youth between the ages of ten and twenty-two years in regions like the Maragoli heartland in the North Nyanza district of western Kenya.[3] This agricultural youth organization was popular in the early 1960s, especially with nationalist Kenyan leaders and their British counterparts and American advisers who recognized the importance of encouraging the younger generation residing in the countryside "to play their part in building the new African economy and society" by taking farming seriously.[4]

Nevertheless, even though Nairobi officials hoped that the 4-K program would "help these young people develop their (farming) talents to the fullest extent," it was indeed a pastime activity for Zavani.[5] He particularly associated the 4-K clubs as a way to earn pocket money and an opportunity to visit different parts of the countryside because the organization often sponsored excursions to large (European-owned) plantations. Put simply, the 4-K organization offered real incentives to young people who were hoping to acquire some measure of economic independence from their parents, as well as to those individuals who were eager to network with "rich" farmers whom they otherwise would not have met in their remote villages.

Such incentives were no doubt appealing, but they were by no means strong enough to convince the organization's targeted club members like Zavani to change their minds (and their parents' positions) about pursuing small-hold cash-crop farming as a viable full-time career in an independent Kenya. Zavani accordingly did not consider his 4-K club membership to be defying his father's wishes. Like many 4-K club members in and around the Maragoliland region, he rightly understood this organization's practical appeal and, more importantly, its limitations.

The 4-K movement and, by extension, the project of agrarianism of the late colonial and early independence era was thus paradoxical. It promoted a lifestyle that was incompatible with the realities and motivations of most members, particularly in areas like the densely-populated North Nyanza region of western Kenya. Poor 4-K members with little or no formal education—namely, the majority of Maragoliland residents from this region—had neither sufficient arable land nor the family support to realistically pursue small-hold commercial farming on a full-time basis. In turn, those individuals whom club officials hoped would take the 4-K mission seriously—landed and educated youths such as Zavani—did not and would not allow themselves to entertain the idea of depending on the land for a living as Kenyan citizens. These members, along with their parents, assumed that *uhuru* (independence) would result in more jobs and opportunities that were less labor intensive, more prestigious, and away from the overcrowded homestead. The 4-K agenda, in effect, contradicted the targeted members' expectations for independence.

Yet *uhuru* certainly meant different things to different people, especially in the countryside and within places like Maragoliland. Not all rural Kenyans aspired to go to town and to work in offices far away from their families and the comforts of home. Some *wananchi* (citizens) no doubt expected their nationalist leaders to provide prospects that would allow them to have a better standard of living in the countryside.[6] The 4-K clubs, in other words, benefited some Maragoli men and women who either had no desire to leave the countryside or who had returned home from townships throughout the 1960s after an unsuccessful pursuit of a better life away from the land. For such individuals the 4-K project was anything but a nefarious government-sponsored rural development scheme aimed at controlling their place within an independent Kenya. Rather, it was a useful organization that provided them with "professional" agricultural training, a community of like-minded peers, and a sense of national pride and purpose *at home*. Put another way, the 4-K movement was a resource easily appropriated by ambitious rural Kenyans who willingly sought to make the most of the independence era on their own terms.

Development of 4-K Clubs

The 4-K agricultural youth program was a collaborative effort between the United States Agency for International Development (USAID) and the 1962 coalition government, which as outlined in chapter 2 was composed of the Kenya African Democratic Union (KADU) and Kenya African National Union (KANU) political parties.[7] In the context of the Cold War, America's State Department became increasingly interested in Kenya's decolonization process because it wanted to prevent any future Kenyan government from falling under the influence of the Soviet Union and thus from embracing communism as a political and economic framework. Kenyan politicians such as Oginga Odinga who were vocal about their dealings with eastern bloc countries in the late 1950s and throughout the 1960s unquestionably threatened American sensibilities.[8] Accordingly, the United States' foreign policy in sub-Saharan Africa included financial support for programs and projects that both American diplomats and Kenyan politicians deemed would be in the best interest of the rural *wananchi*.[9]

In practice, however, the foreign aid and development personnel that American government organizations such as USAID (and its predecessor, the International Cooperation Administration) sent into the African territories throughout the decolonization era and early independence years were meant to transition the former colonial possessions into "modern" nation-states that would not stray from a Western-oriented free-market and democratic system.[10] By the start of the 1960s, for example, there were already government aides and agricultural technocrats from the State Department's African Bureau office advising Nairobi officials on how to craft policies meant to "help the African farmers greatly expand their participation in the cash economy."[11] Tasked with the difficult responsibility of having to formulate policies and programs to address the country's mounting poverty and land problems, Kenya's Coalition Cabinet, especially KANU right-wing Ministers like Kenyatta, Mboya and James Gichuru, welcomed this assistance from the industrialized West.[12] At the local level, this translated into the Kenyan transition government's using finances and personnel provided by USAID to develop social clubs that aimed to make farming appealing to young rural people.

Accordingly, in late 1962 Kenya's 4-K organization was instituted as a result of a national conference on rural youth clubs organized by Kenya's Deputy Director of Agriculture at the time, J. C. Templer, along with advisers from USAID.[13] Between the 7th and 9th of November 1962, Kenyan leaders and American officials examined several possible strategies to promote rural development and economic growth. One such solution became the 4-K farm youth club program. The American foreign aides likely embraced and championed the rural farm youth clubs because they were modeled after the 4-H organization of the United States. The iconic 4-H American organization, referring to head, heart, health, and hands, began at the end of the nineteenth-century as "an effort by the federal government to modernize rural America and, in the process, to make American agriculture more rational, profitable, and efficient."[14] The USAID Extension team, consequently, transplanted the 4-H model to Kenya in the early 1960s intending to "Westernize" rural African communities.

4-H clubs also promoted capital-intensive farming that fit right into the late colonial government and the subsequent Kenyatta regime's aim to maintain Kenya's mercantilist economy grounded on intensifying cash-crop farming among the African Kenyan population. The pro-capitalist development planners heading the conference therefore agreed to implement this particular youth program throughout rural Kenya and, more importantly, to name it the 4-K because it connected the organization with similar groups in other countries and Kenyanized the program. The 4-Ks referred to the Swahili words: *Kuungana* (to unite); *Kufanya* (to do); *Kusaidia* (to aid); and Kenya.[15]

Nation-Building through 4-K

The 4-K organization was a tremendous asset for Kenyan politicians. The clubs helped political elites spread the government's message about Kenya's future economic success: that prosperity still depended heavily on land and export cash-farming even with the advent of *uhuru*. The 4-K model and its objective essentially provided Kenya's nationalist leaders with a way to hold their rural constituents accountable, rather than themselves, for improving living standards in the postcolony. Put another way, Kenyan political leaders from both KANU and KADU arguably embraced the 4-K movement because they could not realistically fulfill the grandiose promises they made during the decolonization era to the large number of rural men and women supporters desperate for upward mobility as Kenyan citizens.

Particularly, the clubs were a practical and cheap stop-gap solution for concerned nationalist leaders and their (international) development partners who were anxious to address Kenya's significant unemployed rural population. In the North Nyanza region, for instance, some 600,000 residents were either jobless or underemployed.[16] National and local authorities, were understandably worried about the large number of idle rural Kenyans who seemed to grow increasingly impatient with their poor economic status throughout the decolonization process. Large numbers of frustrated ordinary Kenyans, for example, made their way to the overcrowded towns in search of more lucrative white-collar jobs that they assumed would be theirs in a Kenya governed by Africans. This increasing urbanization heightened the anxieties of Kenyan government officials, because urban employment opportunities for Africans with little or no formal education were minimal and largely nonexistent in the more populous urban regions like Nairobi.

Kenyan leaders and British authorities were particularly concerned with young people moving into urban centers in search of employment in both the formal and "informal sectors." Many young people who made their way to places like Kisumu, Nairobi, and Mombasa did not have the qualifications for the white-collar jobs that were being vacated by Europeans following the 1962 government's effort to Kenyanize the formal sectors. These rural migrants often found themselves living in poverty and engaging in petty crime, prostitution, and politics.

For these reasons, desperate young Kenyans crowding into urban spaces disturbed late colonial British officials, European settlers, and eventually, Kenyan nationalist leaders. The administrators worried that such transplants would result in the expansion of an uncontrollable "informal sector" and thus lead to political and social chaos similar to the Mau Mau civil war. Furthermore, Mboya, who eventually served as Kenya's first Minister for Economic Planning and Development, had feared that this type of instability would hinder the country's economic growth, especially since foreign investors already had doubts and questions about the future of Kenya as it transitioned from a colonial entity into a Republic.[17]

Accordingly, 4-K clubs were to assist with the country's nation-building process by providing young rural Kenyans with some measure of purpose *at home* and far away from the urban centers. 4-K club members were to hone their farming abilities, which club administrators assumed most rural Kenyans had, and to learn how to appreciate their agrarian setting. Moreover, the Kenyan government hoped that 4-K participants would eventually apply their technical agricultural training (albeit limited) toward becoming productive small-hold junior *mwananchi* farmers and farmers' wives who would produce enough food and cash crop yields to sustain themselves and their families.

Indeed, the 4-K mission was to "teach young [African] people the dignity of labour and the respect for agriculture as a profession" in an independent Kenya.[18] It sought to motivate and train a future generation of progressive small-holder farmers who were supposed to practice cash-crop farming successful enough to employ some of their land-poor and semi-educated neighbors who could not secure employment elsewhere. Kenyan government officials and rural development experts assumed that this class of farmers would eventually ameliorate some of the socioeconomic tensions that seemed to be mounting at the dawn of colonial independence.[19]

The 4-K agricultural program, in short, offered the nationalist leaders and their foreign aid advisors a means to cultivate political content and stable rural communities in a transitioning Kenya. The aim to have 4-K club members embrace small-hold cash-crop farming and thus their "proper" role as *wananchi* was made clear during a meeting among the organization's leadership in 1965. "The future of Kenya will depend upon the future of agriculture and the future of agriculture will depend upon the people engaged in farming . . . the farm youth of Kenya have a most important role to play in the future of Kenya," the meeting's minutes reported.[20]

In theory, this meant that 4-K participants were to learn "improved" farming practices and domestic science skills through hands-on projects completed on their family's homestead and within their own homes. "Girls," according to Grace Wagema, "should be taught cooking . . . personal hygiene, like the care of nails, teeth and hair . . . (and) simple sewing." Wagema, who was the Home Economics Extension Supervisor in 1965, worked closely with the 4-K program to ensure that female 4-K club members were involved in projects that taught them to "be useful in the home."[21] At the same time, 4-K program officials anticipated that some of the more ambitious male club members who came from land-owning households would "assume their place in agribusiness and government . . . to become the future leaders in their farming community as well as in their country."[22]

Kenya's Other Farm Youth Clubs

Even though the 4-K organization took off in the decolonization and independence era, the concept of developing a youth program that would convince rural children that there was value in manual farm labor was nothing new to Kenyan officials. (What was novel at the time, however, was that the international community had a more vested interest in nurturing a cooperative young Kenyan rural sector.) Colonial education programs and youth clubs for ordinary Kenyans like Britain's Young Farmers' Clubs promoted agriculture, aligning closely with the racist sensibilities of late colonial authorities, who maintained that it was the proper type of training for their "backward" African subjects. The notion that rural Kenyans ought to pursue anything other than farming was therefore a sentiment shared by colonial officials and Kenyan nationalist leaders.

In 1956, for example, the Kenyan Assistant Commissioner of Community Development, J. L. Porter, had suggested that a special educational program focusing on "new methods of agriculture" with extramural activities in the form of youth clubs be created in rural areas throughout the colony.[23] Porter's recommendation came at a time when Kenyan officials were searching for effective measures to rehabilitate and reinstate Mau Mau detainees, many of whom were young, landless, and unmarried males and females back into rural society and, presumably, under the gaze of local elders and colonial authorities. In 1960, the District Commissioner of Vihiga in western Kenya echoed Porter's suggestion in his response to a national unemployment survey when he recommended that the local administration tackle the Maragoli unemployment crises, along with the younger generation's aversion to manual farm labor, by placing "a greater emphasis on the government-sponsored schools' curriculum on "rural science" or agricultural activity."[24]

Along with the Kenyan government and its secular international development partners, religious organizations like the Friends Africa Mission (FAM) also had a strong interest in preventing rural Kenyans, particularly the youth, from migrating to urban centers at the dawn of colonial independence. In September 1958, for example, FAM board members in Richard, Indiana, along with their counterparts at the Kaimosi mission station headquarters in western Kenya, had agreed to a "meaningful agricultural program (to be established) in Friends Intermediate Schools (grades 5–8)."[25] Similar to their government counterparts, FAM's agricultural youth clubs were also molded after American 4-H clubs and the British Commonwealth's Young Farmers' Clubs. This replication was not surprising. FAM American and British missionaries who were familiar with these agrarian-focused organizations in their respective home countries were the same individuals responsible for implementing and administering the church youth clubs throughout western Kenya.[26]

FAM board members, however, intended for its agricultural youth clubs to do more than help the Kenyan government address its unemployment crises while maintaining the state's agrarian-based economy. Specifically, the mission-backed farm youth clubs were a way to create loyal converts who were to use their agricultural labor to financially sustain FAM's local activities once Kenya achieved its political independence. By the late 1950s, Quaker officials in Kaimosi and Richard understood very well that they would have to transfer control of the local (and main) church in western Kenya, the East Africa Yearly Meeting, and thereby relinquish control over FAM's affairs to local church leaders due to the impending political changes.[27]

Hence, the Friends' agricultural youth clubs were to attract the growing number of poor young Quakers from places like Maragoliland to remain in the countryside so that they would become the dutiful and responsible future Christian leaders in the postcolony. By late 1959, for example, FAM leaders recruited and sent a married couple, Rodney and Joan Morris, to western Kenya to implement agricultural youth programs into the Friends' secondary school curriculum.[28] Maragoli Kenyans, particularly those individuals attending Quaker schools such as Chavakali secondary school, were familiar with and, perhaps, even active members in FAM's agricultural youth program by 1963 when the 4-K organization arrived in their villages. The 4-K clubs, consequently, complimented both FAM and the Kenyan government's development strategy for the rural sector, which was predicated on the success of the project of agrarianism producing compliant agriculturalists and farm laborers.

Capturing the Local 4-K Community

With this development objective in mind, the Department of Agriculture, under the direction of the 1962 coalition government, created material symbols, slogans, and 4-K pamphlets that largely targeted rural Kenyans who hardly anticipated to remain on their family's homestead upon the advent of *uhuru*. The organization's propaganda particularly focused on convincing privileged young educated people that farming was a viable and respectable job for them to hold as Kenyan citizens. These 4-K prospects usually came from land-owning households, so it was likely that they had access to some portion of their family's homestead and so could theoretically commit to advancing the program's mission. However, it was these same individuals who often sought opportunities off the farm and away from the countryside once they completed their educational training. The rhetoric and message in the government-sponsored booklets, consequently, reinforced the notion that young Kenyans with access to land had a patriotic duty to take up farming as a full-time career. Through its 4-K paraphernalia, club authorities aimed to convince its land-rich members that by learning better farm and home practices they were carrying out their civic responsibilities and would "contribute towards better nutrition, health, and higher standards of living (nationally)."[29]

The 4-K emblem became a distinguishable material representation of the 4-K members' participation in Kenya's nation-building project. It was also the most recognized symbol of the movement. This badge was cut into the shape of the map of Kenya with a four-leaf clover laid upon it. The letter "K" was inscribed on each of the clover leaves, and at its center was a Boran cow's head, which was meant to symbolize the importance of cattle within "traditional" Kenyan society. The color of the emblem was green in order to express youthfulness, life, and growth. Although the emblem was not mandatory for membership, local 4-K leaders strongly encouraged their club members to purchase and, more importantly, to wear the badge as it demonstrated to one's family and community that the wearers wanted to improve themselves through agriculture.[30]

The 4-K organization badges were priced at about Shs. 3/- each, making them an affordable alternative to expensive uniforms usually associated with popular and elitist school-based organizations like the Kenyan Boy Scout Association and Girl Guides. Accordingly, for a small fee, the majority of poor 4-K members could be like their peers who wore the coveted Scout and Girl Guide uniforms that most Kenyans accepted as representing a Western version of adolescence and prestige.[31] Thus, 4-K club members, too, could publicly display their association with an important government-sponsored movement. More importantly, by purchasing and wearing the emblem, 4-K members were assisting the nationalist leaders in promoting a specific agenda for the younger generation of rural Kenyans in the newly independent state.

Along with the 4-K emblem, club officials also encouraged its members to put into practice the 4-K movement's motto: "to learn by doing." This motto served to remind 4-K members that they were to become proactive agriculturalists who were responsible for their own (economic) development.[32] The organization's motto indicated that 4-K members were to learn to appreciate the value of manual labor and farm culture by independently planting crops, rearing animals, and keeping detailed records of their progress. These club activities all supported the government's larger goal of trying to convince rural youth, especially from land-holding and educated backgrounds, both to love farming and to accept it as a full-time job prospect.

4-K officials and the Kenyan authorities also hoped that by practicing the "to learn by doing" motto the wealthier 4-K members would aid them in their efforts to convince poor Kenyans to embrace the notion that working on the land was important for building the household and, by extension, the entire nation. 4-K club leaders therefore encouraged landed 4-K members to carry out food cultivation and animal rearing projects alongside their parents and extended kin. The 4-K club members' progress and achievements, whether in the form of higher crop yields or healthier animals, were often displayed for family, neighbors, and friends to inspect and thus to admire. It was exactly these types of 4-K activities that Kenyan government officials hoped would allay the skepticism expressed by club participants like Zavani, whom we met at the start of the chapter, and Mary Ganira. Both 4-K members were from land-holding families, but neither one envisioned becoming a full-time farmer on the eve of colonial independence. Rather, Ganira wanted to become "a working-class person" while Zavani focused on becoming a secondary school teacher.[33]

Moreover, having young people from land-holding households actively engaged with the 4-K movement allowed the Kenyan government to show itself to be innovative in its handling of the glaring land problem in regions like Maragoliland. Proponents of the 4-K movement, for example, aimed to address the land issue by encouraging the more impoverished and land-poor club members to carry out 4-K projects with their privileged landed peers. This type of collaboration, officials argued, would allow *all* club participants the chance to practice the "learning by doing" motto.[34] Advocates stressed that the collaboration between the landed and land-poor 4-K members would provide the latter group with certain skills, along with some confidence, to locate (farm) employment once they completed the program.[35] Convincing privileged young people that they had a future in the agricultural sector was a main goal of the Kenyan government, especially because it desired greater control over the rural population's manual labor and movement in the postcolonial era.

However, even if the 4-K club propaganda material succeeded in persuading young Kenyans from landholding families that there was dignity to working on the land, the program's supporters understood it was not enough: the entire rural community *needed* to also buy into the program for any type of agrarian revolution to be successful. "Everyone must consider it [4-K] as part of the local society," officials concluded.[36] As a result, 4-K officials diligently outlined in the propaganda materials the types of services the organization could offer *all* Kenyans, trying especially hard to capture the attention of the impoverished and uneducated person who either had limited or no landholdings whatsoever.

The 4-K booklets and posters, for example, emphasized the organization's utility to land-poor households by arguing that the youth clubs provided valuable agricultural training and farm knowledge to their children. Poor 4-K club members, the materials suggested, would be able to increase their family's modest yields, as well as improve their own chances of gaining employment in the agricultural sector, if they were active and engaged. 4-K booklets, for instance, conveyed the message that 4-K members who attended regular club meetings were highly successful because they listened to agricultural "experts" lecture on subjects like how to make compost and the benefits of using hybrid seeds. Indeed, the 4-K propaganda was aimed at convincing those poor Kenyans who might have been the biggest skeptics of these kinds of rural "betterment" programs.

4-K organizers also made their informational materials overly simplistic in order to reach every rural Kenyan. The brochures were primarily pictorial in content, appealing to those individuals with little or no formal education and would have found it difficult to read and comprehend literature about the 4-K program. For example, the "4-K Clubs: What They Do" booklet had several pages of illustrations depicting club members leading meetings, planting vegetables, and caring for farm animals.[37] Through these simple informational pamphlets, the semi-literate subsistence farmer was to learn the functions, goals, and benefits that 4-K clubs supposedly offered his household and the community in which he resided.

A Club for the Community

Because officials and the Kenyan government needed the entire rural household to change their attitudes about agriculture, 4-K clubs were eventually "built into the local community rather than the local school."[38] In so doing, the program officials were also tackling a major issue faced by their counterparts: namely, the waning of student interest in farming while they were away from the oversight and encouragement of their teachers. In other words, officials did not want to risk the chance that young participants would discontinue farming when they were on holiday from school, especially when 4-K members were supposed to be model junior *mwananchi* farmers in their communities and households.

The concern that student members might allow their 4-K activities to fall by the wayside upon returning to their homesteads was not unfounded. Several students from land-owning households in Maragoliland in particular found it difficult to continue with their agricultural projects while on holiday from school. It would seem that a number of parents, who sacrificed their hard-earned income to pay for their children to become "learned" individuals, had stigmatized farming as a career option for illiterates.

Rachel Zavani, who was a young student in 1962, explained that her parents would not have supported a decision to pursue agriculture as a profession even if she wanted to practice large-scale commercial farming, because she was educated. Further, as stated in this chapter's opening comments, Rachel's husband, Pierson, also encountered similar push-back from his parents, who wanted him to do more with his education than "dig" land for a living.[39] Similarly, Keran Magunamu, another long-term resident of Maragoliland, admitted that she did not want her two sons, whom the family was struggling to put through school in the early 1960s, to "learn how to write, to speak English, and come back [home] and start doing all kinds of rubbish with the soils." Instead, Magunamu expected her children to "teach agriculture instead of coming to do farming," if they wanted to seriously take up any career having to do with soils.[40]

Although some Maragoliland parents disapproved of their educated children embracing small-scale commercial farming as a full-time career option, which they rightly believed was a risky venture because of insufficient land and the difficulties in accessing markets due to unreliable infrastructure in western Kenya, the 4-K movement still attracted a large number of households throughout rural Kenya. By 1965, for example, there were over three hundred active clubs with a membership of almost eleven thousand across the Kenyan countryside. This statistic included 532 members belonging to seven 4-K clubs in western Kenya.[41] The large membership number was likely the result of the 4-K club organization being an out-of-school and home-centered program. The fact that it was not a school-sponsored activity, for example, opened the 4-K club membership to any community member between the ages of eight and twenty-two years old. Moreover, the organization did not levy membership fees, which were costs associated with popular youth organizations such as the Boy Scouts and Girl Guides, because of accounting difficulties. In so doing, the organization managed to attract an even greater number of (poor) young rural Kenyans to become 4-K members.[42]

The popularity of 4-K clubs at the ground level could also be attributed to an unofficial and silent compromise between the local administrators who were intent on getting the rural young people to appreciate the value of agriculture and those Kenyan parents who expected their children to work on the family land, but who were first and foremost determined that their children focus on academic subjects while at school. Having their children (usually sons) versed in the latest "modern" farm techniques was important for some of the landed Maragoli Kenyans who wanted their family farms to be well maintained (and productive) for future generations. More importantly, parents like Trofosa Kaneri expected her two educated sons to understand and to learn that taking care of the family's ten-acre plot "meant food security."[43] Similar to Magunamu, however, Kaneri did not want to spend the money she earned as a tailor to support her children's extracurricular agricultural school activities. She was adamant that the expensive school fees she paid went toward providing her sons with a conventional academic training that would prepare them for white-collar career opportunities.

Kaneri's expectations were common and shared by many African parents across rural Kenya. In fact, Kenyan parents' reluctance to allow their children to engage with agriculture made it difficult for school administrators and state authorities in the late colonial and early independence period to promote and thus sustain in-school activities that dealt with farm education. In a 1962 annual report, for example, the coalition government's Department of Agriculture alluded to the failure of school-based agricultural youth clubs when it noted that the 4-K club movement was replacing the Young Farmers Clubs that "were started at schools (but) never made a great deal of headway in African schools."[44]

Consequently, 4-K clubs became popular with parents like Kaneri who allowed her sons to participate because it was independent of the academic system. Put another way, the 4-K program neither interfered with her children's learning at school nor did it diminish her lesson that "farming meant food," which she wanted to impart to her sons. Interestingly, her sons' participation in the local 4-K club seemed to have reinforced Kaneri's message about the importance of food crops as her children mostly planted vegetables for their club projects.[45] 4-K clubs were therefore a middle ground for parents like Kaneri who recognized the importance of providing both a conventional liberal arts education and technical agricultural training to their children.

The Benefits of Membership

While local parents' support may have influenced the 4-K club membership levels in Maragoliland, the practical (and material) benefits of the program were often just as effective in attracting young rural participants. The chance to earn money from their club projects, which members were free to use whatever way they wanted, became a major incentive for Maragoli adolescents who had no intention of remaining on the land full-time. This opportunity was due largely to the fact that the Ministry of Agriculture oversaw the 4-K program. Farm cooperatives and foreign canning factories operating in Kenya, for instance, were encouraged by the Ministry of Agriculture to purchase some of its produce from 4-K members in their respective areas.[46] 4-K members were also allowed to sell their goods at their local village markets and at the annual District and National agriculture shows. As a result, they often profited from their horticultural and poultry farming projects, which 4-K organizers expected the participants to continue year-round and, more importantly, to do so on the club members' own family plots.

Zavani, for example, happily participated in his local 4-K club during school holidays where he earned extra spending money by selling cabbage grown on his father's land. "I got about Shs. 30/- for them (cabbages) . . . during those days (that) was a lot of money for a student," exclaimed Zavani.[47] Horticulture was not the only means by which young 4-K members could earn cash. The *Kenya Weekly News*, for instance, chronicled members who went beyond planting vegetables and collecting chicken eggs in its "Keeping Posted in Agriculture" section. This section profiled some of the more profitable projects that 4-K members across Kenya conducted such as what Ezekiel Masambu carried out in Maragoliland. In 1968 the periodical featured an article about Masambu's success as a 4-K participant who decided to collect honey in addition to carrying out the standard farm projects advertised by the organization. Masambu explained that he pursued this unconventional project after discovering a beehive on his father's farm. His business acumen seemed to have paid off as Masambu was able to sell a barrel of honey for Shs. 25/-, allowing him to contribute significantly to the household economy during that year.[48]

Earning money by way of 4-K club projects was not restricted to land-rich members. In fact, a number of Maragoliland 4-K participants whose families had little or no land to devote to the program's activities usually found creative ways to carry out their club activities and thus to participate in the local cash economy. Their landless-status, in other words, did little to dissuade ambitious members from becoming active (and profitable) 4-K members. Joram Clement Chavasuh, for example, was a resourceful young 4-K member who profited from his horticulture projects even though he had no access to family property in the mid-1960s. As chapter 3 revealed, Chavasuh was the seventeenth child from a twenty-one children household and had no legitimate claim to his father's five-acre farm located in the Chavakali location of Maragoliland. Not allowing his status to exclude him from Club activities and its advantages, Chavasuh sought assistance from his 4-K leader who was a "big farmer" in the region. This particular individual provided seedlings and a small area on his farm for Chavasuh to plant tomatoes and cabbages.[49]

It is unclear whether or not this arrangement between member and leader eventually turned into a quasi-tenant-farmer relationship. The change in the status of their relationship, however, likely did not matter for Chavasuh, who reasoned that having access to seeds and land was of utmost importance for him because he wanted to make money through agriculture. "My interest was to carry out projects because the way I look at them (farm projects), they helped to generate funds . . . my interest was mainly that . . . I saw agriculture as a way to make money."[50] Though the 4-K projects hardly generated enough cash income for young Kenyans to establish their own households, it still allowed poor members like Chavasuh a sense of pride and purchasing power among their peers. This did not go unrecognized by the more affluent members of the community such as Rachel Zavani, who revealed that with some 4-K members "you knew there was some pocket money."[51]

Figure 4.1. 4-K participants. Estate of Rodney Morris. Reproduced with permission from the Morris family

Along with having extra cash in their pockets, 4-K club members regularly traveled outside of their home villages to network with peers and influential "big" farmers. This particular perk thrilled young members like Pierson Zavani who enjoyed the fact that the excursions were frequent and free. "4-K clubs used to make so many trips . . . you would be taken to agricultural shows in Nairobi [and] wherever they were . . . you would go to the shows for free . . . you did not pay," he explained.[52] The excursions undoubtedly allowed 4-K members the chance to network with farm men and women from across Kenya. This socializing often happened at District and National agricultural shows where admission was free for the members because of 4-K's partnership with the Ministry of Agriculture and the Agricultural Society of Kenya.[53] The agricultural shows attracted a number of specialists from diverse backgrounds and various regions because it was held across Kenya. 4-K club members were therefore able to witness first-hand the latest "modern" agricultural practices and techniques used by the so-called progressive farmers who usually had demonstration plots at the shows.

4-K participants also learned from their own peers at the organization's annual shows. The yearly 4-K club event followed a similar blueprint as the government's official agricultural shows, except that 4-K offered its members the opportunity to exhibit their club projects. Members visiting the 4-K annual meetings, in other words, were not simple bystanders like they were at the District and National agricultural shows. In fact, competitions were held for club members, which encouraged the participants to display their best produce, farm animals, and even bookkeeping skills. Masambu, for example, competed in the 1967 annual 4-K show by entering a pair of doves and some cabbages for the best produce and animal competitions respectively. While he did not bring home any prizes for his entries, Masambu still "enjoyed the contact with other members" at the show.[54]

His comment underscores an important purpose of the 4-K agriculture show: networking with other 4-K members. Officials specifically rotated the annual shows throughout the Kenyan countryside, hosting them in central locations so that "all people can come without inconvenience."[55] Consequently, 4-K club members from various regions were expected to exchange ideas as well as copy projects from one another. It is difficult to know if members actually discussed club work or if they simply related the current local gossip. The 4-K annual club show, nonetheless, provided its participants with something to look forward to during the year. The 4-K annual meeting was especially pivotal for young Maragoli residents who were interested in agriculture, because it allowed them the chance to show off their hard work to their neighbors as well as to the "big" farmers whom they admired and hoped to become in the future.[56]

Aside from social-networking at the annual shows, 4-K members were able to cultivate closer bonds with family members and neighbors by engaging them in conversations about club projects. Such ties were important for 4-K members in the Maragoliland region who wanted to remain at home as *uhuru* became a reality. Members like Jescar Lumire Chanyisa, who was seventeen years-old when Kenya gained its independence, appreciated her 4-K membership. She was especially grateful that her 4-K leaders encouraged her to practice the "learning by doing" motto with family members. This type of encouragement, according to Chanyisa, motivated her to be more proactive in helping her subsistence-farmer parents improve their yields. Despite facing initial resistance because "it was very difficult to change the mentality of parents," Chanyisa succeed in teaching her parents "the importance of planting in lines."[57] Likewise, Julia Awinjah convinced her father to use fertilizer on his maize crops after she had learned about it at her 4-K club meetings. "He used to buy and we would explain to him and we would plant," Awinjah recalled; "he'd see the harvest was good and then continue (using it)."[58] In helping their parents increase crop yields, both Awinjah and Chanyisa usefully applied their 4-K training. This involvement was unquestionably satisfying for both women, who enjoyed farming and wanted to contribute to their households.

Appealing to Adults

Younger Maragoliland 4-K participants were not the only residents who embraced the program. Older residents throughout western Kenya also welcomed the organization into their communities and used 4-K resources to advance their own personal agendas. Maragoli Luhyas, like most of the marginalized ethnic groups throughout the nation, expected for their western Kenyan leaders, whom they elected to represent them in Nairobi, to make good on their grandiose political promises made throughout the late 1950s and 1960s.[59] Thus, for these individuals, the 4-K program was not a top-down state project that arrested the development of rural men and women eager to make the most of an independent Kenya. Rather, it symbolized the coalition government and subsequently the *uhuru* administration's attempt to provide for all *wananchi*.[60] In other words, a number of mature Maragoli Kenyans who *wanted* to make a living by cultivating the land, rationalized that the 4-K organization's resources and club activities denoted their political leaders' efforts to provide them with the tools to improve their quality of life in the village. Participating in the 4-K organization was thus a sensible choice for ordinary Maragoliland adults who had little interest in taking part in the "rat race" prevalent in 1960s urban Kenya.

Individuals like Nicholas Ben Ganira, for example, benefited from having a local 4-K chapter established in his home location of Kaimosi, western Kenya. Since he was already beyond the age limit to participate as a regular club member, Ganira ultimately joined his local chapter in 1963 as a volunteer community leader. Ganira was explicit when he explained his decision to take part in the 4-K movement: "I didn't want to be sitting in the office . . . I wanted to work as somebody dealing with crops, cows, cattle, whatever."[61] Put simply, Ganira sought membership in the 4-K club because he considered it to be a practical step toward obtaining his idealized progressive farmer lifestyle that he envisioned having in an independent Kenya. However, such a lifestyle in the postcolony was never a realistic option for Ganira, who came from a modest family that lacked sufficient land to support his large-scale commercial farming ambitions. Therefore, Ganira sought to please both his family and himself by enrolling in a teacher's training college housed at the Friends' Africa Mission station and by engaging with his local 4-K chapter in Maragoliland as an active club leader. In so doing, Ganira successfully laid the groundwork for his future, eventually becoming a local secondary school teacher and "modern" agriculturalist who readily adopted the latest farming practices on his homestead.

A major perk that the 4-K offered its members and that proved to be valuable to mature 4-K participants like Ganira, was access to the Farmers' Training Center (FTC) or Farm Institutes. Although the 4-K farm courses for its adult volunteers were mainly to familiarize them with the fundamentals of club administration, the participants often attended courses at the FTCs in order to "brush up their knowledge on the particular projects on which they will be dealing."[62] The popular FTCs initially began as Agricultural Stations created by the colonial regime during the 1930s as a way to train government (mostly European) officers. By 1959 the late colonial government had transitioned thirteen Agricultural Stations into FTCs tasked with training African farmers and their wives in the latest farming methods and theories. The shift in the government's agenda was likely due to its efforts to carry out the recommendations outlined in the Swynnerton Plan, which in chapter 2 was shown to be aimed at addressing the landless and unemployment crises of the late colonial period by investing to increase the African agriculture sector.[63]

The late colonial regime and subsequently the coalition government, which assumed responsibility for the FTCs in 1962, expected the farm institutes to train successful progressive farmers in places like western Kenya who would presumably hire their family members and landless neighbors to work as field laborers. The main focus of the training centers was to teach a select number of landed Kenyan farmers "intensified farming methods . . . (through) intensive farming courses and lectures on veterinary and forest matters and on a general civics."[64] The institutes were molded along the lines of the Jeanes School's agricultural program, which provided practical training to its local students, particularly married men, by giving them small holdings to use at the institutions.[65]

Unlike the Jeanes School program, the FTCs did not seem to offer its students access to demonstration plots at their training facilities because its courses were much shorter in duration—often lasting no more than a week.[66] This meant that participants were supposed to apply what they learned on their own farm plots. FTCs were therefore conveniently located throughout the nation's agricultural regions, situated in locations throughout rural western Kenya that were easily accessible by either public transportation or, for some, within a day's travel by foot. This convenience became an important factor for the 4-K organization as it was intent on having its members abreast of the latest farming practices and, more importantly, concerned with having 4-K members conduct their club activities at home where they could showcase their prowess as farmers to their kin and neighbors. Accordingly, any person who joined their respective 4-K chapter had the chance to take courses and to interact with agricultural instructors at the FTCs located near their home villages.[67]

For 4-K participants in the Maragoli region this meant traveling a short distance to the Bukura Farm Institute, which held specific classes and activities for them at no cost as a result of an agreement with the Ministry of Agriculture.[68] The 4-K courses, however, were not as extensive as other courses offered at Burkura. Yet the free access was certainly a valuable fringe benefit, especially for the majority of Maragoliland 4-K members who neither had nor wanted to pay the Shs.10/- fee to attend a regular Bukura agricultural program. Ganira, who was already financially committed to his teacher's training certificate program, thoroughly enjoyed this particular 4-K perk. His enthusiasm was evident when he explained how attending courses at the training center refined his understanding of animal husbandry. "We had cows, we had pigs, we had poultry, all sorts of things at the agricultural institute," stated Ganira, "so, we used to learn more." Studying at Bukura, even if limited, seemed to have satisfied Ganira's penchant for farm life. His Bukura experiences in the early 1960s prepared him for his 4-K responsibilities and provided him with first-hand experience that he would not have acquired at his own expense because of his modest upbringing.[69] Indeed, complimentary access to the FTCs was important for determined 4-K members who were eager to enhance their understanding of both the practical and theoretical underpinnings of farming during the colonial and postcolonial periods.

While practicing the skills learned from their Farmers' Training Centre sessions would have been a challenge for the majority of 4-K members who lacked land and farm animals, it was still a coveted benefit. The opportunity to take courses at places like the Bukura Farm Institute at little or no cost, for example, ensured that Maragoliland 4-K members would be able to receive training that made them stand out to nation-builders expecting to grow Kenya's agrarian economy. Specifically, rural Kenyans who had taken courses at FTCs were noticed by the selection committees responsible for finding "qualified" participants to take part in development schemes such as the land settlement, financial loans, and resource allocation programs of the late colonial and early independence era,[70] which were intended by the Kenyan government and its development partners to attract and retain progressive African farmers. FTC graduates, in effect, had the potential to obtain resources to improve their conditions within an environment that was comfortable for them.

Moreover, the Kenyan government's support of FTCs seemed to have emboldened some ambitious western Kenyans bent on doing more with their agricultural training than develop their modest farms in the decolonization and early independence years. The notion that participants could use their training for other purposes was not unfounded because this had been a popular unintended consequence of the FTCs throughout the late colonial period. Specifically, trainees in the late 1950s had attempted to use the certificates they received from completing their courses at the farm institutes as evidence that they were qualified to work as government agricultural instructors.[71] A 1956 memo from the District Agricultural Officer of North Nyanza to Bukura Farm Institute students suggests that the misappropriation of FTC certificates was rather a common practice amongst western Kenyans. In the memo, the Officer alluded to the problem by reminding students that "the idea of your [FTC] training is not to go and find jobs, but to go back to your farm and work on it."[72] By using their certificates to make a claim to an occupation that the colonial state had reserved for advanced (usually

European) personnel, the FTC graduates threatened the late colonial and, eventually, the *uhuru* government's development agenda. Put simply, this action flew in the face of the late colonial regime's efforts to use the FTCs as a means to promote a rigid lifestyle for ordinary rural Kenyans.

In order to combat the problem, Bukura officials stopped issuing certificates in 1956. Officials apparently resumed awarding certificates by 1963, however. Ganira, for example, received training certificates from Bukura upon completing his courses throughout the early 1960s.[73] While it may have been a stretch for 4-K members to use their completion certificates as official credentials that would allow them to work as bona fide agricultural instructors, 4-K authorities in western Kenya reported in 1965 that they had difficulty retaining local leaders who wanted to be paid for their services after they trained at Bukura.[74] It is therefore reasonable to assume that some of these individuals discontinued their volunteer work with the organization after finishing their training at Bukura Farm Institute in order to seek paid employment elsewhere. Accordingly, the 4-K program was useful for everyday farm people who sought to improve their material conditions and wanted to expand their understanding of the agrarian society in which they lived.

Conclusion

The 4-K club program was started in the summer of 1962 by the coalition Kenyan government and its foreign (American) development allies, in the hopes of creating a productive agrarian sector that would continue to grow Kenya's economy in the postcolony. The 4-K movement sought to convince young people, especially from land-owning households, that they ought to contribute to the nation-building project by remaining on the land as productive *wananchi* small-hold cash farmers. Moreover, Kenyan government officials, working under the same development framework as their colonial predecessors, hoped that rich and successful 4-K members would help them to alleviate the unemployment crisis by hiring their peers. 4-K programs, in short, were to help the *uhuru* regime in its efforts to advance agrarianism.

4-K clubs, however, rarely worked the way development "experts" and government personnel had envisioned. For instance, 4-K members whom the organization hoped to attract, namely educated members with access to land, were unapologetic about their decisions to pursue opportunities away from the farm. 4-K officials therefore had difficulty persuading its landed and educated 4-K members that working in the agricultural sector as farm managers and small-hold commercial farmers was an honorable career choice for them to pursue. For these privileged 4-K members, the organization essentially became a pastime activity while they completed their education and prepared for life off the farm. It was never meant to be taken seriously, especially when their family members believed agricultural work to be a "dirty job" meant for uneducated people with little or no options.

At the same time, the lack of enthusiasm for agriculture did not mean that ordinary Kenyans failed to understand the value of 4-K clubs. Indeed, the 4-K movement attracted ambitious youths and adults who had little interest in pursuing life away from their home villages. Several creative Maragoliland 4-K members were able to make the most of their memberships by accessing farm-related resources and tapping into a wider-agrarian community even though they lacked access to land. Use of the FTCs proved valuable for ambitious and daring 4-K members who parlayed their limited training into more prestigious jobs in the agricultural sector that likely paid more.

The Kenyan government's agenda to revolutionize the rural sector via the 4-K program, at the very least, was a complicated task. To the disappointment of the nation builders and their development allies who planned to jump-start Kenya's economy through an agrarian revolution, 4-K members hardly thought of themselves as the next generation of progressive farmers. Rather, as the experiences of Maragoli 4-K members show, rural Kenyans were determined to dictate the course of their own lives as *wananchi* and thereby appropriated the organization's services accordingly. Like the Kenyan government, the Friends Africa Mission was motivated to have rural western Kenyans, especially in Margoliland, take an interest in agricultural development projects. As chapter 5 will show, Friends missionaries who arrived on the scene in the late 1950s implemented programs that they deemed would create "good" Christian stewards able to use their farming skills to contribute to church (and state) coffers in the post-independence era.

Chapter Five

Friends and Acres: The Friends Africa Mission Stewardship Program

In May 1962, Rodney Morris, an agricultural missionary with the Friends Africa Mission (FAM), wrote to the local leadership of the East Africa Yearly Meeting (EAYM) to explain the exact nature of the relationship between EAYM and the World Neighbors Organization, an American non-governmental aid institution. In so doing, Morris hoped that he would be able to attend to some concerns that the local EAYM leaders had about this new partnership that commenced in April of that year. Namely, Morris's memo addressed the Kenyan Quaker leaders' "widespread interest" over what the partnership would mean for themselves and their congregation within the context of decolonization and, more importantly, how it would impact EAYM's final phase of transition.[1]

In his memo, Morris revealed that World Neighbors would provide funding to expand a program that he was heading—the Stewardship Rural Service Program. This program was an agricultural and village development initiative aimed at helping the local Christian community in western Kenya "gain the various skills necessary for them to contribute to and share in the economic and social development of their communities."[2] The partnership with World Neighbors was to enable Morris to bring the Stewardship Program to some 400 village meetings (churches) in western Kenya's Elgon and North Nyanza regions. Both regions were located in Kenya's most densely populated areas with some locations, like Maragoliland, holding over one thousand people per square mile.[3]

Though the goals of the Stewardship Program were clear, Morris assured the Yearly Meeting leaders that the financial assistance from World Neighbors would support initiatives that local church officials, *himself* included, deemed useful. Specifically, he stressed that the funds would help him carry out his agricultural ministry, which was centered on "modernizing" local Quaker farmers. His work was of the utmost importance, Morris maintained, because "modern" (and productive) farmers would be able to contribute to the local meetings and thereby help expedite EAYM's transition into a financially and locally-operated independent church. "East Africa Yearly Meeting will stand or fall according to the strength and dedication of individual village meetings," warned Morris, "in the same way the new free Kenya must rely on the small villages and people who earn their living from the land."[4]

Though seemingly innocuous, Morris's memo was interpreted by some EAYM officials as troublesome. It signaled to them that the Friends missionary body was far from winding down its affairs even if the local church (and the nation) moved closer to becoming independent entities.[5] EAYM, an umbrella organization composed of the Friends Quaker village meetings in western Kenya, had entered the final stages in the spring of 1962 to displace FAM as the highest Religious Society of Friends organization in the country. FAM's "Kenyanization" process began in 1946 when the Friends Board of Foreign Missions, FAM's governing board, established EAYM and allowed the African leadership control over the church's religious matters. By the early 1960s, with the prospect of Kenya's independence a given and the nationalists' political slogan of "Africanization" too hard to mute, the Board of Foreign Missions recommitted and refocused its attention on establishing policies and programs that would result in "leaving the nationals in control."[6]

The complete hand over of the mission's affairs to local church leaders was therefore to coincide with Kenya's impending sovereignty set for some time in 1963. The newly-created alliance with World Neighbors, unsurprisingly, was of great interest to the African Yearly Meeting leaders who were anxiously awaiting to take over FAM's administrative affairs and properties, including the one-thousand-acre mission station in Kaimosi. The fact that World Neighbors' officials were working directly with Morris, rather than the Kenyan EAYM leaders, to grow the Stewardship Program at the eve of independence seemed to undermine the governing board's rhetoric and promise that it would devolve control to EAYM.

Morris's memo, therefore, provides a unique window into the ambivalent nature of the mission enterprise during Kenya's decolonization and development era. In many ways, the missionaries during the late 1950s and the 1960s accepted that the demise of imperialism was a necessary step in the right direction and that they would have to be "prepared to be told what to do."[7] Nevertheless, missionary organizations like FAM continued implementing projects and sending a number of professional missionaries with technical background training into the field to both proselytize and "modernize" the local population in the final days of empire. The arrival of the professional missionaries and the newly-created alliance with World Neighbors, in effect, created tensions between foreign and local church personnel, casting doubt over whether the missionary personnel were ready to embrace their auxiliary status once EAYM leaders assumed control. More importantly, it suggested that EAYM's future would continue to be influenced by outside "experts" who often had their own agendas and projects that were largely out of touch with the realities and expectations of local converts.

This is why the Friends mission agriculturalist struggled to get his Stewardship Rural Service Program off the ground. Specifically, Morris had difficulty sustaining a major component of the Program—the Lord's Acre Project. This voluntary agricultural scheme encouraged the local congregation to set aside land, preferably an acre of their farm, to plant crops that were to be donated to the church. The Lord's Acre Project fit with Morris's mission to improve the farming practices of the local Quaker population so that the parishioners would be able to earn more from the land and "at the same time build a Church more able to stand strong."[8] The Project, however, was hard to carry out in places like North Nyanza's Maragoli location where a number of subsistence and small-hold Quaker farmers rarely had an inch of productive soil to give and where young mission-educated residents rejected Morris's message: that there was value, monetary and moral, in working as either an agricultural instructor or skilled farm laborer in an independent Kenya.

For these reasons, the majority of Maragoliland Quakers were at best part-time participants in EAYM and, by extension, in Kenya's agricultural development. They engaged in the church's farm "betterment" schemes in their own time and on their own terms, often basing their decisions about the use of their talents and their skills upon their needs and those of their families instead of the expectations of Friends' missionaries. In so doing, they defined the extent of their involvement in Kenya's agricultural revolution, and thus their participation in the nation-building process.

The Stewardship Rural Service Program in the Era of Decolonization

The Stewardship Rural Service Program was one of the key ways that FAM missionaries continued to interact with and to influence the local congregation as Kenya transitioned into an independent nation-state in the early 1960s. Stewardship, in the Friends' context, meant that the church members were responsible for providing their tithes by "taking care of God's gifts and getting maximum benefit from them."[9] Accordingly, FAM missionaries hoped to use this program to teach Christian women and men in western Kenya better agricultural methods and, more importantly, to impress upon the local Quaker community that they had a moral duty to financially sustain the Yearly Meeting in the postcolonial era. Morris made these aims clear in the 1962 grant proposal to the World Neighbors Organization by noting that the Program's objectives were increasing the financial support of EAYM from the local Friends and developing "an awareness of man's responsibilities to care for God's gifts of the soil in the best possible way and in so doing increase production."[10]

The church's Stewardship Program initiative officially started in August 1961 with a two-person team, consisting of Morris and a Kenyan field worker. Morris served as the program's advisor though his responsibilities were those of a program director. Having Morris not be the official head of the program (at least on paper) was important for FAM administrators to ensure because it would have stoked the anger of certain EAYM leaders already frustrated by the mission's lengthy transfer of power process. The lack of official title seemed to neither limit Morris' involvement with the program nor to interfere with his ministry. Both he and the Stewardship Program's lone field worker, for example, traveled to Friends village meetings scattered throughout western Kenya to teach the Quaker farm men and women the latest "advanced" agricultural practices.

As FAM's main agriculturalist, Morris had petitioned the Board about establishing a more definite agrarian-focused Stewardship program since his arrival at the mission's headquarters at Kaimosi in 1955. Instituting a program that would improve the conditions of local farmers was indeed what Morris expected to do as soon as he settled at the mission station. Upon his arrival, he began studying the farming patterns and habits of the men and women whom he hoped to assist. He spent time on and off the mission site familiarizing himself with the types of crops the local communities grew on their farms, noting that "the basic food of the African is ground corn or maize."[11] Morris also devoted time to teaching weekly classes to "local fellows" on how to improve their agricultural yields.[12] In his classes, Morris stressed planting in rows and using fertilizers that he made and sold to his students and to local farmers on behalf of the mission. Although the people with whom Morris interacted seemed eager to adopt the "modern" agricultural practices he demonstrated to them on FAM's experimental farm plots, it was impossible to know if the procedures were being followed at home. Mike Simkin, a FAM missionary who worked with Morris, acknowledged that the missionaries often did not know if their efforts were leading to impactful changes off the mission station. "It was difficult for the missionaries to visit the people at their homes so we did not do regular follow-up meetings," Simkin admitted; "we did not really know if they were doing what we taught them to do at home . . . some did not have the money to purchase the fertilizers (while) those who did spent it on school fees and other expenses."[13] This lack of information likely motivated Morris to push for the creation of the Stewardship Program, which would allow him the opportunity (and resources) to witness first-hand whether his ministry was bearing fruit within the community.

Friends' Board members and FAM administrators, however, kept Morris from starting the program in the late 1950s on the claim that there were no finances available.[14] However, gleaning from private correspondences between FAM's Executive Secretary and the Board of Foreign Missions' General Secretary, it is evident that a main reason for the Board's lack of support was due to the officials' concerns over Morris's agricultural background. Morris, who was an American from upstate New York, started his agricultural ministry at FAM with minimal practical farm training. While his resume indicated that he spent time as a general farm laborer, Morris often held this position sporadically during the summer months of his formative years. FAM's agricultural missionary, in other words, never actually operated his own farm prior to accepting his post in rural western Kenya. Instead, most of Morris's agricultural development training was theoretically-based and accumulated while he was an agronomy student at Cornell University.[15]

His limited experience with practical farming ultimately became a main concern for Fred Reeve, then FAM's Executive Secretary, who oversaw all missionary activities on the ground. After observing Morris in the field, Reeve had major reservations about having him return to FAM as an agricultural missionary once Morris concluded his services in late 1958. In a memo written to George Scherer, who was then General Secretary for the Friends Board of Missions, Reeve complained that Morris was "still too young and impractical and lacks experience to understand much of a program." He continued his complaint by stating that "this was shown over and over again during his stay here . . . it is more evident than ever that my judgment concerning the impractical approach which he has had as a young student coming directly from school here, is a true judgment."[16]

Reeve was not alone in his conviction that Morris ought to carry out a different kind of ministry if he was sincere about continuing his work at FAM. The treasurer for the Board of Foreign Missions in the late 1950s, Martha Tubesing, was concerned enough about Morris's inabilities as a farmer that she wrote directly to a financial contributor after receiving his donations to finance Morris's return to Kenya. "In the first place, Rodney has had no experience in actual dirt farming," she confided; "he has not been able to start a project and carry it through to completion but gets off on tangents of one kind or another . . . he also finds it very hard to work under supervision or to take constructive criticism."[17]

Though the Board and FAM administrators seemed to be convinced that Morris was not a suitable farmer, it was likely not the main reason why the mission agriculturalist was unpopular with his superiors. Rather, the more reasonable explanation for Morris's unpopularity was because he was advocating for changes to FAM's land policy and thereby drawing attention to the vast amount of land the missionaries owned in a region where it remained a scarce resource for the majority of Kenyans. Morris, for example, became a major target of criticism at the start of his ministry when he suggested FAM initiate a settlement program that would allow landless and land-poor farmers and their families with whom he worked to have access to four and ten acre plots of land on the one-thousand-acre mission property.[18] While Morris's idea was in accord with the types of agrarian development schemes championed by Kenya's Ministry of Agriculture at the time, such as the Swynnerton Plan discussed in chapter 1, it still shocked Reeve and other Board members who read the idea as foolish and dangerous.[19]

Since land access was a highly contested political issue as well as a main grievance behind the Mau Mau uprising, FAM officials were undoubtedly nervous about sponsoring any projects that highlighted their status as large landholders in the late 1950s. Morris's proposal therefore vexed the mission administrators in both Kaimosi, Kenya and Richmond, Indiana. They would have preferred for FAM missionaries to remain apolitical and to turn a blind eye to Kenya's volatile land problem. Of course, this was delusional. The fact that the Friends Board of Missions since 1902 had held title to a large piece of property located in Kenya's most densely populated region made it difficult for FAM to ignore the local and national tensions surrounding land.

The events of the Mau Mau uprising in particular motivated the missionaries to pay closer attention to how their status as landholders were being perceived by the communities in which FAM facilities resided. Notably, the Quaker missionaries were fearful of being seen by local Friends as a sub-set of "White Highland" European plantation owners.[20] This association, understandably, disturbed the Quaker missionaries who likely imagined themselves to be part of the local communities in which they served rather than as part of the loathed settler community population.

The mission body's concerns eventually led to FAM's Executive Security commissioning a land study in 1958. The purpose of the study was to help the American Friends Board of Missions determine how best to use the land in Kaimosi so that it was "in accord with the future interests of the African people."[21] The Board sent a three-person team to survey the mission's land policy and use. The survey team consulted with FAM missionaries and EAYM leaders about the land situation and discussed the types of agricultural projects underway at Kamosi.

It was probably his interaction (and eventual disappointment) with the land study commission that motivated Morris to put on paper his own solution to FAM's quest for "a new course" concerning the use of the mission's land. The study's final recommendations for FAM, indeed, did not include implementing a radical land redistribution and resettlement program for the local community, which Morris championed. In fact, the notion of redistributing the mission's land deeply perturbed the survey team's soil scientist, James Thorp, who warned FAM officials in a private correspondence about its potential dangers. "I can think of nothing that would be more likely to wreck the Mission, and probably the African community as well, than to attempt to give 'unused' land 'back to the Africans,'" Thorp cautioned.[22] Thorp's warning, coupled with FAM officials' reservations about his training, made it so that Morris would be unable to start and operate a Stewardship program during his first assignment in western Kenya, which concluded in late 1958.

In spite of the confidential protests and major revelations about his shortcomings, Morris resumed his agricultural ministry with FAM in the early 1960s. It is unknown exactly why the Board members and FAM executives agreed to his return, but Morris may have demonstrated that he was serious (and stubborn) about carrying out an agricultural ministry in Africa by completing a seven-month farm agrarian training program at St. Faith's Mission

Farm in what was then Southern Rhodesia during his furlough from FAM. It probably also worked in Morris's favor that he was able to attract financial donors who supported his work in Kenya.[23]

Upon his return to western Kenya, Morris worked diligently to implement projects that he presumed would "strengthen the witness of stewardship and improve farming methods" of local village meeting members.[24] He devoted time in the fall of 1960, for example, traveling to the village meetings throughout North Nyanza District to familiarize himself with the challenges that seemed to have prevented the church from maintaining a system of giving or tithing amongst the congregation. From these visits, Morris concluded that in order for EAYM to survive the "challenging days ahead, economic development must not be encouraged among Friends without a corresponding emphasis on giving for the work of the Lord."[25] Morris, once again, urged the local officials and the mission's governing board that a formal Stewardship program was necessary as it would help the majority of subsistence and small-hold Christian farmers in western Kenya develop their land so that they could better meet their financial responsibility to the Yearly Meeting.

Morris's recommendations seem to have fallen on deaf ears until the summer of 1961. By this time, the British government had accelerated its program to divest itself of Kenya and thus the colonial regime was transferring political power to local representatives who had promised their constituents that they would have opportunities to improve their lives in an independent Kenya. Recognizing the changing political climate, FAM and EAYM officials authorized Morris to employ a field worker to help him implement a major component of the Program—the Lord's Acre Project. The Board's initial rejection of the Stewardship Program, however, seemed to have bruised Morris's pride, leading him to doubt his relationship with his FAM supervisors. For example, in his candid letter to Norman Young, an American Friends representative, the mission agriculturalist blatantly questioned the Board's real motives behind their initial decision to not support his Program. "I am quite frankly unconvinced that lack of finances is the only reason the Board did not accept this program," Morris wrote; "in the past we have had rumors regarding the feelings of some Board members regarding my ability, maturity, etc."[26]

Stewardship Program Growth

The Board's lack of enthusiasm and its meager financial support eventually led Morris to seek out external funding that was, in theory, to hasten

EAYM's financial independence from the American Friends' Board of Missions. The external funding that Morris secured in order to supplement the development of the Stewardship Program, as previously noted, came from a cooperative project alliance between World Neighbors and EAYM that began in April 1962. While this partnership was technically between the local Friends church and the non-governmental aid organization, Morris was actively involved with the process from the very beginning. He drafted the grant proposal himself, for instance. Morris's intimate involvement with the process was made possible due to the fact that EAYM had just assumed complete control of the church's affairs from FAM at the start of the 1960s. Thus, its leadership was still coming to terms with redefining tasks for missionaries who were on the ground. Morris therefore easily took over administrative responsibilities for the Stewardship Program because the Yearly Meeting officials were hardly in the position to assume all aspects of the missionary body's activities when the partnership with World Neighbors and EAYM commenced.

The partnership was especially convenient for Morris and World Neighbors officials. Both institutions—FAM, in the case of Morris—was in the business of "developing" rural people's livelihoods by offering practical (vocational) training. As a private international development organization, World Neighbors collaborated closely with religious groups like the Religious Society of Friends who already had an established presence at the local level in "underdeveloped" regions of the world. Its main objective, "training and educating communities to find lasting solutions to the challenges they face—hunger, poverty, and disease—rather than giving them food, money or constructing buildings," ensured that the types of projects World Neighbors sponsored since its inception in 1951, primarily focused on improving the lives of subsistence farmers.[27] For this reason, the Friends' Stewardship Program was of special interest to the World Neighbors' overseas director at the time, Merlin Bishop.

It was during a February 1962 visit to Kaimosi when Bishop first learned about Morris's ambitious task to make the Yearly Meeting capable of supporting itself financially by developing the agricultural practices of ordinary farmers in the area. According to Morris's memo to the EAYM leadership in late May 1962, Bishop was particularly impressed by the potential that the Lord's Acre Project had in terms of developing the local farm communities in western Kenya. "World Neighbors seeks to apply a very practical way of the scripture," Morris explained to the EAYM executive committee and FAM Board members; "it seemed a natural step to ask the World Neighbors to help us expand the Stewardship Program." To make this new partnership even more appealing to the Kenyan leaders and FAM personnel, Morris wrote, "with this help we can be able to reach more people with the message of better care of the soil for a better life and a Church more able to support itself financially."[28]

Having the Friends' local parishes and therefore the EAYM financially self-sufficient was an important goal that some FAM missionaries in Kaimosi were striving toward in the early 1960s. Missionary personnel like Morris were especially eager to have a financially independent local church since they often found it difficult to work with insensitive Board members who were far removed from the local circumstances yet still in charge of imposing tight budgets and conflicting agendas. Financial independence essentially meant that the missionary body in western Kenya would be less answerable to and dependent on aid from the American Friends Board of Missions. More important, making the village meetings financially self-sufficient was important for some of the professional Friends missionaries who arrived in the late 1950s and the 1960s with the aim of improving the conditions of the local Quaker community. It essentially allowed the missionaries to continue with their services and to maintain their positions of power unchecked during Kenya's transition phase from colony to nation-state.

Accordingly, with a five thousand-dollar grant from World Neighbors, Morris set out to recruit workers to join his Stewardship field team. This financial aid, which was renewable so long as the Program was meeting "this genuine need of helping others help themselves" allowed Morris to expand his one-person staff into a nine-person team by the end of 1962.[29] The mission agriculturalist had hoped to recruit and train bright, mostly young male, Quakers throughout rural western Kenya. However, even though Morris had received "some 85 applications" at the start of his search in May, Morris was extremely disappointed with his applicant pool. It appeared that the majority of the applicants were unqualified for the "more skilled" positions like the film unit operator or clerk translator and were unwilling to consider the main post—agricultural extension field officer.[30]

The absence of skilled male applicants should not have come as a surprise to Morris, who appeared to have been cognizant of western Kenya's historical skilled labor shortage problem. In fact, he had reported to World Neighbors officials in 1962 that the male population in and around the Friends' region of western Kenya, such as Elgon and North Nyanza, often sought employment in the cities due to the region having no real industries and because of the population density that had left most young men in North Nyanza with either insufficient or no land on which to subsist.[31] Presumably, a large number of the western Kenyan males relocating to urban centers like Nairobi and Mombasa in the early 1960s were highly skilled and educated individuals. Morris's disappointment in the "unskilled" applicant pool, however, did not stop him from quickly hiring men to join the Stewardship Program team.

By August 1962, Morris had submitted a report to EAYM officials that contained a list of the names of the eight additional Stewardship field workers, all of whom had already visited their assigned village meetings to discuss the Lord's Acre Project and were wrapping up their second month of special training by the date of Morris's report. [32] This group of individuals were training at the FAM Bible school in Kaimosi, along with taking agricultural courses at the government's Farmers' Training Centers closest to their homesteads. This training program fit with Morris's ministry and, more importantly, aligned with the World Neighbors agenda. Since World Neighbors was highly interested in establishing an outreach program that would develop the whole person and the community, the new staff members were required to possess a broad array of knowledge and practical skills. A prepared Stewardship field officer, for instance, was responsible for increasing crop and livestock production, demonstrating good hygiene practices as well as teaching basic accounting principles among other practical things, which the Friends and World Neighbors' officials considered necessary to improve social and economic conditions of the individual and the church.[33]

Morris's new recruits, therefore, received courses in the general principals of agriculture, agricultural extension methods, health education, and Christian Stewardship. Morris proposed this broad (and quick) training program so that the newly-revitalized Stewardship Program would have extension workers "who know how to help others move forward with new ideas and simple improved methods and how to get expert technical help when it is needed and wanted by the people."[34] In short, the rural development program that Morris implemented throughout western Kenya's Quaker communities was executed by field workers who were only moderately prepared to deal with the multitude of financial and agricultural challenges that their assigned village meetings undoubtedly faced on the eve of colonial independence. In so doing, the FAM mission agriculturalist was able to secure his position as the advisor and thus to continue shaping the program.

The Stewardship Program's training scheme was unique in that it was preparing the extension workers to carry out an ambitious village and farm development program that allied closely with the nation-building projects of the 1960s. This mission-directed village and agricultural reconstruction undertaking correlated specifically with the Kenyan coalition government's development program for the rural sector. The nation-building agenda of the KANU and KADU coalition regime, which came to power in 1962, rested heavily on developing the exhausted agricultural sector and was a continuation of late colonial rural betterment schemes. Like their colonial British predecessors, Kenyan nationalist leaders were keen to address the grievances of poor rural Kenyans by implementing agricultural development schemes that sought to improve cash crop yields and land usage through the introduction of "modern" practices and technology. The colonial government, for example, implemented the Swynnerton Plan and initiated land redistribution schemes in the late 1950s meant to support the development of a commercial African farmer middle class.[35] The coalition regime and subsequent Kenyatta administration continued these same programs and measures in the postcolony.

The Kenyan government therefore embraced and collaborated with nongovernment organizations and religious organizations such as the Friends Religious Society to bring forth an agrarian revolution at the local level. In a progress report sent to EAYM in early 1964, for instance, Morris noted the amicable relationship that the Stewardship Program had with Kenya's Ministry of Agriculture: "I have had many officers express to me warm appreciation for the work that our men are doing in the field and the way in which they are joining hands with Government officials in the common task of building the community," Morris reported.[36] The collaboration between FAM and the Nairobi government was indeed beneficial for both parties. Morris received the validation he needed to justify to his supervisors that his ministry was working and worth its continued sponsorship. The Nairobi government, on the other hand, was able to minimize its expenditures on national development and still have the rural areas that it had previously neglected as a result of the Mau Mau uprising, such as western Kenya, become developed through this collaboration. In other words, the Friends Stewardship Program provided Kenyan politicians with the evidence to show their rural western Kenyan constituents that they were, in fact, committed to raising the standard of living of every *mwnainchi* (citizen) regardless of ethnicity or "tribal" affiliation.[37]

Although the Kenyatta government had validated the importance of the Friends' Stewardship Program to its nation-building program by complementing Morris on his efforts at the village level, the missionary agriculturalist still faced challenges when it came to his relationship with the EAYM executive committee. It appears that the FAM officials and the local Yearly

Figure 5.1. Morris (center) and Rural Service Stewardship Team. Estate of Rodney Morris. Reproduced with permission from the Morris family.

Meeting personnel at Kaimosi were in agreement when it came to their assessment of Morris. Specifically, the EAYM's complaints regarding Morris was that he was unprepared for his post and, more importantly, too eager to spend the church's finite resources on a project that many of the Yearly Meeting leaders understood would prolong the transition period with FAM. In retrospect, it was perhaps the Yearly Meeting's reluctance to accept any more foreign control over the local church affairs that lead to the initial rejection of the Stewardship Program by the Board. In an April 1961 letter to Morris, for instance, Norman Young included minutes from a meeting between EAYM and FAM officials regarding the Stewardship Program that showed how the Kenyan Friends were apprehensive that Morris would continue to dominate the program once it was firmly implemented at the local level. "The Program should be carried out by Africans as quickly as possible," Young quoted.[38]

Put Simply, the Yearly Meeting leadership did not see a real purpose in allowing a *mzungu* (foreigner) to initiate and direct an ambitious rural development program during a time when the missionaries were supposed to be "Kenyanizing" the church. Some leaders firmly believed that the missionaries ought to have been winding down their activities and preparing to hand over all their administrative duties to the local leaders. Morris's proposal for a Stewardship program, not surprisingly, alarmed certain local Quaker leaders who rationalized that this kind of scheme would essentially allow the foreigners to remain in certain positions of authority in the home church. Ben Wegesa was one of the Yearly Meeting officials in western Kenya who recognized that the Stewardship Program contradicted the Board's aim to hand over complete control of the church to the local leadership by independence. Wegesa, accordingly, called for the 1961 meeting with FAM personnel to discuss and outline the specifics of Morris's role.[39]

EAYM's concerns over Morris's motives hardly meant that the local Friends leadership did not understand the need for developing and improving the conditions of their congregation, who were predominantly poor subsistence farmers. For example, they understood and shared in Morris's observations that the village meetings had to be more financially responsible and committed in order for a truly independent home church to evolve from the Friends' mission. It was likely due to this willingness to address the dire financial situation of the church and the economic concerns of its parishioners that convinced the EAYM leaders to permit Morris to execute his proposal in the summer of 1961. Yearly Meeting officials, however, appointed Tom Lung'aho, a prominent Kenyan Quaker member, as the director of the Program while Morris served as the overseas advisor.[40] Keeping Morris as an advisor was a move the EAYM officials wanted because it was supposed to allow for an easier transition at the local level.[41] It was also a concession that the EAYM leaders made because, like their nationalist leaders, they understood the importance of maintaining ties with foreigners even in the postcolonial era as it meant continued access to aid and resources for which the local home church (and country) was in desperate need at independence.

There is little evidence available to infer the kind of working relationship that Morris actually had with Lung'aho. However, based on the few private letters written to his family in which the missionary referred to his supervisor, it was clear that Morris appreciated and respected Lung'aho's authority. A suitable explanation for why there might not have been more sources from which to extrapolate the nature of Morris and Lung'aho's relationship was because the latter did not remain in charge of the Stewardship Program for long. By May 1962, Morris was reporting to family members that Lung'aho had become Fred Reeve's understudy and was preparing to assume the Executive Security position for the Yearly Meeting per the "new devolution plan that the Board recently approved."[42] Morris also revealed to family members that EAYM had yet to decide on a replacement for his supervisor, which presumably meant that for all intents and purposes Morris was in charge of the Stewardship Program when the World Neighbors partnership began.

Thus, even with some hesitation on the part of Yearly Meeting officials, it was Morris whom the Stewardship extension workers were reporting to about their progress in the field. World Neighbors also communicated directly with the FAM agriculturalist regarding their own expectations for the Stewardship Program expansion. Morris, in short, had managed to assume a position that would allow him to continue shaping the affairs of the local church and to impose his own (Western and often impractical) agrarian program on the ordinary Quaker farmers in western Kenya during the decolonization era and throughout the immediate years following *uhuru*. He was the Program's advisor from 1962 to 1966, during which time he strove to improve the conditions of the local people and church primarily through the Lord's Acre Project.

Lord's Acre Project

The Lord's Acre Project was the vehicle by which Morris sought to impress upon the rural Friends congregation the importance of adopting "modern" farming practices and to committing themselves to the development of an independent Yearly Meeting. This agrarian scheme was the largest component of the Stewardship Program. It was what FAM and EAYM personnel hoped would make the individual village meetings throughout western Kenya's North Nyanza district financially accountable for their own affairs in the independence era.

In essence, the Lord's Acre was a voluntary project that required the members of the village meeting to cultivate a portion of their land—a limited resource that was highly exhausted in the Maragoliland region by the 1950s—for the church's development. The entire harvest from the Lord's Acre portion of the land was to be donated to the village meeting as a tithing. "It was the so-called plot of God . . . if it is maize, if it is sorghum, whatever crop it is . . . every harvest you make out of that particular plot, you'd take it to the church," recalled Melice Onyango.[43] Onyango had briefly carried out the project in the 1960s on behalf of her local village meeting in Chavakali. Similarly, Keran Magunamu remembered that the officials at her local meeting would sell the congregation's donated crops in order to support social programs, construct church buildings, or pay for any other religious-based activity and event.[44]

The concept of the Lord's Acre was neither unique to the Friends Religious Society nor was it restricted to western Kenya. Rather, its origins were rooted in the American south. A 1941 *Time* Magazine article, for example, reported that the Lord's Acre project had originated "outside the churches eleven years ago" as a result of James G. K. McClure, then president of the Farmers' Federation of North Carolina, and that "over a thousand churches of 20 denominations" had established a Lord's Acre program.[45] McClure had promoted this systematized form of tithing for churchgoing farmers as a solution for those who often lacked cash yet had extra yields available. The project eventually took root outside of the United States due to informational pamphlets the Federation commissioned and distributed to American missionaries stationed abroad who learned about the Lord's Acre in media outlets like *Time*.[46] McClure also invited inquisitive missionaries to Ashville, North Carolina to witness first-hand the types of activities carried out by local parishioners under the Lord's Acre program, which included raising poultry and pigs for church donations.[47] As the agricultural missionary for FAM, Morris likely received (or was aware of) the Farmers' Federation publications. It was also plausible that he learned of the Lord's Acre program in 1958 during his furlough at home in Cortland, New York since the program was commonly practiced by congregations throughout rural America. Indeed, it was upon his return to Kaimosi in the early 1960s when Morris began his campaign to have local Kenyan Friends support their village meetings through stewardship of the land.

Since it was a voluntary initiative, Morris and his Stewardship field staff visited the village meetings scattered throughout North Nyanza district advertising the Lord's Acre Project. The missionary agriculturalist felt compelled to personally convince the local congregation of the material benefits and moral value associated with the agricultural scheme. His activism was driven in large part because of the church officials and Board Members who were dubious of his Program and his practical farming credentials. Having Lord's Acre participants, in short, meant success for Morris and allowed him some kind of evidence to show his critics that the Stewardship Program's projects, at least the Lord's Acre, were attractive to local rural Kenyans.[48] Furthermore, through the Lord's Acre plots, Morris had the opportunity to demonstrate to the local community and, more importantly, to his superiors, the types of skills and knowledge he possessed as a farmer. It was on the Lord's Acre plots where the mission agriculturalist intended to help the local Quakers practice "modern" farming by introducing them to agricultural inputs like fertilizes, along with synthetic II and hybrid maize seedlings to increase crop yields.[49]

During his visits to the village meetings, Morris spoke to the local church members about the agricultural resources, informing them of the assistance that they would receive from the Stewardship extension field officers if they were Lord's Acre participants. Morris had hinted at the fact that participants would receive this type of special attention from the agricultural workers in his memo to the church leaders in 1962: "the field workers will give guidance and instruction . . . to help them see clearly the objective they want to achieve and then how to go forward . . . it should be the goal of every Christian to care for his land in such a way so that it will yield 15 bags of maize on an acre," wrote Morris.[50] The Stewardship field staff, in other words, were in the villages for the sole benefit of the congregation if the parishioners committed themselves to the Stewardship Program's goal. The field workers were especially dedicated to the Lord's Acre participants given that it was these church members who were taking the steps to develop their farming practices so that they could be in a better position to financially support the village meetings.

Similarly, the Friends' mission agriculturalist hoped that his informational visits would enlighten local Quaker leaders about the benefits of sponsoring Stewardship projects in their respective village meetings. Morris especially wanted to convey to the village meeting leaders that the Stewardship team and the Program's activities had the potential to transform the local church into a responsible institution whereby the congregation would be willing and confident to invest their limited financial resources in the postcolonial era. Morris had previously revealed to EAYM leaders in a 1960 report that a main factor preventing the local village meetings from becoming economically self-sufficient was the "careless and improper handling of what little money and produce is given . . . it is too often looked on as supporting the officers."[51] Thus, that local village meeting leaders often struggled to collect funds to cover the church's basic needs was not lost on Morris, who used the information as an entry point to discuss the benefits of his program.

Morris expected that the Stewardship extension officers with limited backgrounds in financial planning and management would appeal to church leaders interested in keeping pessimistic church members from leaving their village meetings. As a result, he made certain to stress to the village meeting pastors that encouraging their church members to partake in the Lord's Acre Project was advantageous to them. The field workers would "spend their time giving direct help to the Meetings by teaching proper accounting, making budgets or estimates and many other practical things Friends need to know to improve the financial position of our churches," Morris explained.[52] That is to say, working with the Stewardship field team benefited the village meeting pastors since the partnership would demonstrate to the local congregation that the church officials were attempting to become more responsible and transparent about the church's finances, at least with respect to the Lord's Acre donations.

The exact date when Morris initiated the Lord's Acre Project into his agricultural ministry for western Kenya is unclear, although some Christians from other denominations in the Maragoli region of western Kenya were already familiar with the Lord's Acre Project prior to the Stewardship team's campaign in 1962. David Sagala recalled that the project was "introduced in the early 1940s, that's when it was started in Kaimosi."[53] Epharina Esabu also referenced this decade as being the time when she first learned about some neighbors dedicating a portion of their harvest to support their churches.[54] Both Sagala and Esabu's familiarity with the Project suggests that other missionary bodies in the region such as the Salvation Army church may have introduced the Lord's Acre project to their converts. While western Kenyans might have been familiar with the Lord's Acre Project before Morris's initiative, it does not seem to have taken off amongst the Friends Village Meetings until the early 1960s with Morris at the helm.

In February 1962, for example, Morris wrote to family members boasting that "we had our first pledges for Lord's Acre Projects—20 altogether which is most encouraging."[55] Not only does this correspondence provide some insight into when the Lord's Acre may have taken off in western Kenya, but it also suggests that FAM's main agriculturalist may have faced challenges at the local level. The modest number of pledges shows that Morris probably had a difficult time convincing local Quaker farmers that western farming practices and technology would produce results that could dramatically improve their limited holdings and thus better their material conditions enough for them to donate a surplus to the church. They were likely not captivated by the "modern" farming techniques and "advanced" technology, which included a tractor used by the FAM missionary in his farm Stewardship Program.

The inability to win over ordinary Kenyan famers was undoubtedly disheartening for FAM missionaries, but it seemed the norm for agricultural missionaries and secular development "specialists" during the decolonization era. Morris in particular was familiar with the local cynicism surrounding his ministry. In a 1959 letter to his family, he mentioned that his position with FAM was of particular interest to some local Friends; "A group of elders from the local meeting came over Tuesday afternoon, sat down and wanted to know just what we were here for," Morris confided; "an agricultural missionary was rather a new species to them and they didn't understand just quite what we were going to do."[56] The local community's unfamiliarity and skepticism toward his work seemed to have done little to deter Morris from his overall conviction that revolutionizing the agricultural sector was the most effective way to improve the living standards of the local congregation at the eve of Kenya's colonial independence.

Joseph Edalia, a Stewardship field worker under Morris, explained that the FAM mission agriculturalist campaigned vigorously for the Lord's Acre Project because "it was the way he [Morris] wanted to assist the church . . . to assist the church to find means and ways for the church to raise funds." Edalia further elaborated that his former supervisor was convinced that the rural Friends community would greatly benefit if they properly maintained and utilized "god's gift of the soil." [57] It was through the establishment of the Lord's Acre Project that Morris was able to satisfy his ministry to "modernize" the local agricultural farming practices in the hope of transforming the village meetings into financially self-sufficient entities.

The Lord's Acre and Maragoliland Quakers

Morris's activism evidently galvanized some Friends from the Maragoli region to take up the task of making their churches more profitable and thus make EAYM less financially dependent on outside support. Practicing Quakers from the Chavakali location of Maragoliland in particular responded to Morris's call for the local meetings to be more accountable for their own affairs and thereby pledged themselves to the Lord's Acre Project. Residents such as Jones Ndagadwa and David Sagala, for example, were both actively involved with the Project in their respective village meetings following their church leaders' gentle yet not so subtle encouragements in the early 1960s. Both Sagala and Ndagadwa likely participated because they were land owners. Specifically, they each had farmsteads that averaged between two and seven acres. The size of their properties was significant given that the standard holding in the region was less than an acre.[58] Their larger pieces of land therefore allowed them the opportunity to cultivate larger yields to meet household and church needs. "We would be advised to put aside a section, a small piece of land, like this room, and you'd plant the crop of your choice," explained Ndagadwa.[59] Sagala echoed Ndagadwa by indicating that the "Lord's Acre was taught in church . . . we were told to put aside a section of the farm . . . a small plot where crops that were planted in that particular section would be taken to the church."[60]

Upon agreeing to set aside an area of their family land for the Lord's Acre, both participants recalled how careful they were to make sure that everyone in the household, themselves included, remembered to not use the land for other purposes. "We used to demarcate," said Ndagadwa, "we would make a heap of soil and make a boundary, so it was easy to recognize that, that was for the Lord's Acre."[61] Similarly, Sagala revealed that it was morally important for him to disclose to his family members and neighbors that he was starting the project. "I informed them that I'm putting it [land] aside for the lord," he recollected, "it was a vow, and when you vow, and god blesses that particular plot, and you fail to take that harvest to god and church, god does not like that."[62]

The procedures that both Sagala and Ndagadwa undertook in order to keep the Lord's Acre plot and its harvest strictly for church use were strategies that the Stewardship extension workers taught and encouraged participants to observe. These stringent measures were necessary, especially given that the Lord's Acre was a voluntary initiative with little oversight and limited resources. "There was no one that would come and supervise you . . . it was you and your god," explained Sagala.[63] In fact, Edalia remembered that he was responsible for making signs with the Swahili phrase, "Kegero cha Nyasaye" (Lord's Acre), for his assigned village meeting participants to put on their designated plots. This sign not only publicly reminded participants of their commitment to their village meetings, but it assisted the Stewardship team in easily identifying the plots on which they were to demonstrate during their field visits.

More important, the signs directed Morris and his field assistants to the farm households where they were to share the bulk of their finite farm inputs like fertilizers and hybrid maize seedlings. Morris initially purchased such inputs with funding from the American Friends Board of Missions, but his source of revenue changed when EAYM allied itself with the World Neighbor's Association in 1962. Although this alliance unquestionably boosted Morris's confidence when it came to his dealings with the Board members who were critical of his overall development program, the World Neighbor's financial assistance was minimal and restricted to two specific locations in western Kenya—North and Elgon Nyanza.[64] The aid, in short, was hardly sufficient to cover all the Stewardship Program's expenditures, especially those expenses related to the growth of the Lord's Acre. In his 1964 annual progress report, for example, Morris noted that "some 300 villages had Lord's Acre Projects with about 2,400 people participating."[65] With this number of participants, Morris was careful to ration resources and to use the

Figure 5.2. Family with "Kegero cha Nyasaye" sign. Estate of Rodney Morris. Reproduced with permission from the Morris family.

limited aid he received for developing projects that he presumed would generate income to help make the village meetings and subsequently the EAYM more independent. The "Kegero cha Nyasaye" signs were therefore useful for Morris as they helped him be pragmatic and efficient in his dealings with the local Quaker farmers.

Along with helping Morris and his field workers identify Lord's Acre participants, the "Kegero cha Nyasaye" signs and the participants' disclosures to their families and neighbors aided in popularizing the scheme throughout western Kenya. Friends' Lord's Acre Project was common knowledge for many people residing in and around Maragoliland, for example. Individuals like Esabu, who belonged to a different Christian denomination but lived in the Chavakali location, were familiar with the purpose of the Friends project because they had neighbors who participated in the program. "You're supposed to plant and commit that harvest from that particular section to the church," Esabu recalled; "I did not have a piece set aside for such a program, because those who mainly did it were Quakers."[66]

Even if it were strictly carried out by members of the Religious Society of Friends, the well known agricultural project did not necessarily appeal to all local Quakers. Rather, the Lord's Acre Project participants were primarily land-owning elder Quaker members in Maragoliland. In explaining why she refrained from taking part in her village meeting's Lord's Acre program, Keran Magunamu quickly answered: "I did not decide to practice this because I had a small piece of land."[67] Magunamu's statement essentially underscores the impracticality of Morris's agrarian development scheme for the majority of ordinary Quakers in Maragoliland. Even if they wished to take advantage of the Stewardship Program's resources, they were prevented from doing so largely because of their lack of land.

Like other communities in Kenya, the Maragoli people dealt with soil degradation and land shortage since the colonial era. By the 1930s, for instance, a number of Maragoli people residing in what was historically known as North Nyanza District were already confronting soil erosion as a result of the region's population density and the colonial government's effort to commercialize maize cultivation in the region. [68] Accordingly, by the time Morris arrived in the region in the mid-1950s, Maragoliland had poor soils, along with the highest population density of any district in Kenya. Morris, in fact, informed World Neighbor's officials of the severity of North Nyanza District's overpopulation problem in his 1962 grant proposal by noting that the district had a "rapidly increasing population estimated to be as high as 3% increase per annum."[69] Maragoliland's population density no doubt influenced the ways in which the local Quaker community, notably the young land-poor or landless residents, received Morris's agrarianism program that was grounded on participants' planting an acre for the church.

Although Morris may have been well intentioned, he was naïve and unwilling to accept that the Lord's Acre Project may have been impractical and perhaps insensitive toward the very people he sought to help. Morris exhibited this kind of naiveté from time to time in his updates to his family members back in America. In a 1962 letter, for example, Morris expressed his discontent at the young Quakers who had refused his recruiting advances to join the Stewardship field team: "It is rather disturbing to find the number of young men that are qualified but do not have sufficient Christian concern or dedication to even be seriously considered."[70] Morris was unwilling to acknowledge that the lack of enthusiasm for his agricultural mission was likely because most rural western Kenyans did not have an inch of soil to claim as their own, despite his strong commitment to implement the Lord's Acre project in places like Maragoliland. By definition, the project was only open to individuals who had enough arable land to cultivate food crops and, perhaps, some kind of cash crop. It was this group of church members rather than the majority of ordinary Quakers whom the Stewardship Program was helping. Though Morris's naiveté certainly did not help grow the Stewardship team, the actions of some Lord's Acre Project participants also caused the Friends missionaries and village meeting pastors to completely abandon the project after only a few short years.[71]

Morris's Lord's Acre Project was unsustainable because a number of participants failed to donate the harvest, which was often higher in quality and quantity, to their respective village meetings. Many in the community either knew someone or had learned through the rumor mill about the Lord's Acre participants who "had decided to take the harvest from that particular plot" and thus broke their promise to the church.[72] This kind of behavior on the part of certain church members was not only frowned upon, but also kept many local parishioners from either initiating or continuing with the collaborative effort to support their local meeting's activities and their pastors. Magunamu emphasized this point by noting that the "corrupt" participants in her village meeting "began to eat the harvest from the Lord's Acre . . . so, when people saw that, that's what really discouraged people from doing the project."[73]

Both Sagala and Ndagadwa recalled that the success of the Lord's Acre plots created temptations that many Maragoli Quakers simply could not resist, especially in the 1960s when unemployment rates were high and thus a time when poor rural Kenyans found the crops they cultivated on their Lord's Acre plots to be more beneficial to them than to the church. "Things that were planted on the Lord's Acre used to do just wonderful . . . (on) one stock of maize, for example, you would have two or three maize cobs . . . so, someone would just say that no one is watching me so I would not take this to the church . . . that just created problems," explained Sagala.[74] Similarly, Ndagadwa remembered that a few participants in her village meeting did not honor their pledges as they would keep the higher quality crops for themselves and "take some other harvest from elsewhere to the church."[75] The technical advice and farm inputs that Morris and his Stewardship team provided to the Project participants seemed to have inadvertently allowed some local farmers in Maragoliland to become profiteers. The Lord's Acre Project in other words was working too well at meeting the everyday needs of the people rather than at achieving its larger aim—to make EAYM financially independent.

Although Ndagadwa and Sagala both insisted that they upheld their Lord's Acre pledges, given the circumstances it is understandable why some of the participants found it within their right to keep the crops they cultivated on their Lord's Acre plots. It was, after all, their land and labor that was utilized. Thus, they rationalized that they were entitled to reap the plot's harvest and its benefits, especially if it meant being able to feed their families and to meet household expenses such as school fees. Simply put, a number of participants neglected to share their crop yields with their village meetings because the harvest was needed elsewhere.

This unwillingness on the part of some participants to honor their pledges both undermined the project at the local level and jeopardized the Friends' overall rural development strategy for western Kenya. Particularly, this lack of commitment on the part of the Lord's Acre participants threatened Morris's plans to have the village meetings financially solvent. The agricultural missionary was therefore extremely displeased to learn that certain individuals were not fully committed to fulfilling their pledges. "People have had very difficult time adapting themselves to any new idea and we're finding that while many people have pledged projects, there are very few who really understand the significance of what they are doing," bemoaned Morris.[76]

Once he realized that a number of participants were not turning in their crops, Morris and the Stewardship field workers drastically limited their resources and decreased their commitment to the project. The pull-back on the part of the Stewardship team essentially made it difficult for poor Lord's Acre participants to continue producing the higher quality harvest to which they had grown accustomed because they lacked the fertilizer and hybrid seedlings. Unsurprising, most participants stopped working on their plots and consequently by the late 1960s had abandoned the notion of committing an acre of their limited land to sustain their village meetings.

Several Quakers in Maragoliland, however, did not attribute the sudden decrease in the productivity of the Lord's Acre plots to the decisions made by Morris and his team. They also failed to recognize that it may have been caused by soil erosion resulting from the owner's overuse of the land. These devout Maragoli Quakers instead rationalized that the unproductive soil was the sole result of God's punishing the "corrupt" individuals who knowingly used their Lord's Acre crops for other purposes than intended. This particular threat—punishment by God—seemed to have been a legitimate fear amongst the Friends community in and around the Chavakali location. According to former Lord's Acre participants like Ndagadwa, it was a significant cause for the Project's demise in the area: "later on, people did not really continue doing it because in a way people would get curses and punishment from god."[77]

Local gossip about the misfortunes and tragedies of participants who were rumored to have been taking from their Lord's Acre plots seems to have only compounded this unsubstantiated fear, leading some Friends to continue shunning the Project. For instance, even though she did not participate in the Project primarily because of the lack of land, Magunamu became even more cautious of the Lord's Acre scheme after learning about a neighbor's tragic situation. This particular neighbor, according to Magunamu, suffered because he refused to give his bananas that he grew on his Lord's Acre plot to their local village meeting. "What happened was that god punished him . . . he went somewhere and died and the ants fed on him . . . that was a lesson!" she explained, "when you vow that this was the Lord's Acre, don't joke about it . . . God blesses that acre and anyone who goes to eat from that one will bring problems . . . that's why I decided to avoid it."[78] While there were likely more plausible causes for her neighbor's death, Magunamu's tale is a prime example of the ways in which some Quakers in Maragoliland reconciled the community's eventual abandonment of the Lord's Acre Project in the late 1960s.

Specifically, the Lord's Acre Project appeared to have moved down the Stewardship Program's list of priorities by 1967. In its place was the Better Maize scheme, which was a project that Morris had attempted to convince the local farm communities to adopt alongside their Lord's Acre plots. This particular scheme encouraged mostly large-holder western Kenyan farmers to increase their maize yields to an excess of "30 bags per acre" by using fertilizers and hybrid maize seeds.[79] Furthermore, by 1967 Morris was also no longer in charge of the Program. His missionary services with FAM had concluded in the fall of 1966. Rather than continue his work, he and his family decided to return home to the States. Even though EAYM's executive committee, along with Morris, were determined to have a Kenyan Quaker take full charge of the Stewardship Program by 1965, it would appear that the American Friends Board of Missions was unable (or unwilling) to provide the necessary funding for Morris to hire and train his understudy.[80] The Stewardship Program, as a result, moved forward under the direction of Sven Rasmussen, a Dutch missionary with special training in horticulture. Consequently, the Stewardship Program remained in the hands of yet another FAM missionary who arrived with his own specialty and agenda for the local people in western Kenya. The Program was finally transferred to a local Quaker after Rasmussen finished his services in the early 1970s, a decade after it began.[81]

Conclusion

Development projects in general and mission-directed modernizing programs in particular rarely turned out the way their planners envisioned in 1950s and 1960s Kenya. Specifically, the Friends Africa Mission's ambitious Stewardship Rural Service Program did little to convince its western Kenyan parishioners that they ought to contribute to the building of the church in the postcolony, and by extension the independent Kenyan nation, as stewards of the land. This lack of interest on behalf of Kenyan Quakers, especially amongst the Maragoli Friends, was due to the mission's agrarian-based development agenda championed by out-of-touch "professional" missionaries who were too eager to proselytize and "modernize" the local farming communities in and around western Kenya during a time when they were supposed to wind down their affairs. Local western Kenyan Quakers, in other words, recognized the Stewardship Program for what it was: an opportunity for FAM missionaries to continue dominating church matters in the postcolonial period.

FAM's agrarianism project also reflects how the missionary personnel were mainly paying lip service to addressing the expectations of the local congregations at independence. Missionary bodies such as the FAM, in other words, were not yet ready to admit that they were promoting an agrarian lifestyle that was unattainable for some and undesirable for most. Unsurprisingly, the mission's agriculturalist experienced disappointments similar to those of the secular development state and international aid agencies who were committed to showing rural Kenyans that there was economic (and political) value in staying on the land as full-time "modern" farmers. Some of the educated and land-poor young Maragoli Quakers, for example, rejected the agricultural missionary's call to participate in agricultural development schemes. Similarly, a number of community members who took advantage of the Stewardship Program largely put their own interests above those of their local village meeting by keeping the fruits of their labor.

Overall, FAM's rural-development undertaking in western Kenya rarely motivated local Quakers to become efficient stewards of the land and thus "good" Christians. Instead, western Kenyans engaged in programs like the Lord's Acre project according to their individual circumstances. In so doing, they easily complicated the Friends' rural development agenda and frustrated the missionaries who in the post-1963 era expected to continue their services and to receive the same type of deference from their local converts that they had grown accustomed to under colonialism.

Local Maragoliland residents may have used the training they received from Morris and his stewardship team when they applied for the Lugari Settlement Scheme, which is the focus of chapter 6. The Lugari Settlement Scheme was part of the government's ambitious Million Acre Scheme project meant to address Kenya's landlessness and land-hunger problems. The Lugari settlement in particular was aimed initially at reducing the land pressure problem in places like North and South Maragoli. Like many of the agricultural development projects of this era, the land settlement schemes involved conditions that were too burdensome for its intended recipients. Thus, the Lugari Settlement Scheme faced a similar fate as the Chavakali Secondary school, 4-K program, and FAM projects, which failed to meet the goal of creating "modern" farmer citizens.

Chapter Six

"Home is Home": The Lugari Settlement Scheme and Maragoliland

> I was just willing to come. I looked back at my family, there were five of us. Five sons. So, looking at the piece of land that was there, I realized that it [my father's forty-one-acres of land] was kind of small [for everyone]. But, I realized that if I go to the settlement scheme and I get the fifteen-acres that means that I'll be there alone [but] I would be having these fifteen-acres, so I told myself that I should just go.[1]

On December 5, 1963, Nathan Molenje arrived to his assigned plot in the Lugari Settlement Scheme (LSS) to commence his new career as a full-time small-hold settler farmer. As his above comments suggest, Molenje was able to double the amount of land that his father was willing to provide him and his four brothers, which averaged about seven-acres for each son, by moving away from his family's homestead and onto his own fifteen-acre settlement plot in the Checkalini sub-location of Lugari. He had acquired this significant piece of property as a participant of the Million Acre Scheme's (MAS) high-density small-hold program. The Kenyan government had issued him a freehold title on which he was able to take out a mortgage for the property after he paid the required one hundred two shilling legal fee and stamp duty. Consequently, in the days leading up to Kenya's sovereignty from Great Britain on December 12, 1963, Molenje was benefiting from the government's ambitious project to develop the rural sector, especially its program for the people of Maragoliland.

The Ministry for Land Settlement and Water Development (LSWD), under the jurisdiction of the Kenya African Democratic Union (KADU) and Kenya African National Union (KANU) coalition government, began to plan the Lugari high-density small-hold project in May 1962. As a high-density settlement, LSS was to provide unemployed and landless Kenyans with land between ten and twenty-acres (depending on the soil quality) so that they could make a "decent" living in the post-colonial state.[2] The planners of the Lugari scheme specifically intended the participants to come from subsistence and small-hold homesteads in the Maragoli and Bunyore locations of western Kenya's North Nyanza district, a region that was predominately home to the people who identified as the Abaluhya.

As outlined in the Introduction, a subsistence holder within the Maragoliland region had access to roughly a quarter to two-acres of land while a small-hold farmer had between two and seven-acres of land. The community considered any Maragoli resident with more than five-acres of land a "big farmer." The majority of households in both Bunyore and Maragoli fell into the subsistence-holder category in the 1960s, because both locations were densely populated. The Maragoli area in particular was the most heavily populated region in Kenya, carrying more than one thousand people per square mile. Thus, the Kenyan government had intended for this particular high-density project to relieve the overcrowding in the two locations by relocating eligible Maragoli and Bunyore Luhya participants, meaning the junior sons from small-hold homesteads who likely had the capital and agricultural training, onto plots of land at the Lugari estate located fifty miles north of the district.[3]

Molenje, however, was from neither place at the time of his relocation to Lugari. Even though he identified as a Luhya and had no formal employment, he had moved to the settlement from North Nyanza's Kabras location. This fact was known to the scheme's local selection officers and in fact was the direct result of their actions. Under the direction of the Land Development and Settlement Board (LDSB) and its successor, the Central Land Board (CLB), which was the organization responsible for purchasing land and appointing settlers for the MAS program in the post-1963 era, the personnel responsible for selecting Lugari settlers ultimately found themselves having to redefine the selection criteria. They did so because they had difficulties persuading the LSS's intended recipients to relocate to the settlement site.

Specifically, a number of eligible Maragoliland residents presented challenges for the recruitment officers because they were suspicious of the MAS project and thus largely unsupportive of the Kenyan government's development program for the rural sector. Many in the Maragoli community who qualified decided to forgo the high-density scheme despite having little employment prospects or claim to more land on their father's homesteads. Put another way, participating in the Scheme was neither worth the huge risks and expensive fees nor were the terms appealing to a number of hopeful rural people in 1960s Kenya.

Although LSWD designed the high-density schemes with landless and unemployed people in mind, the land in the Lugari Settlement Scheme was not free. Kenyan officials like Bruce McKenzie, then the Minister for LSWD, fully anticipated that prospective settlers would be able to meet the required initial deposit of Shs.80/- either on their own or with the help of friends and family. By meeting this minimum financial requirement, participants could then acquire the title deeds needed to take out loans to develop their plots. The Minister presumed that settler farmers would be able to pay the Shs.1,600/- settlement fee in sixty half-yearly installments of Shs.61/- using the crops they grew on their assigned plots.[4] McKenzie was confident that the expenses would not inhibit cash-poor Maragoli and Bunyore residents from taking part in the settlement projects. He made his feelings clear on June 6, 1962 while responding (in a rather tongue-in-cheek manner) to questions from skeptical Members of the Legislative Council who inquired about what would happen if prospective settlers could not pay the required initial deposit. "I should think that his friends would rally round and help him," McKenzie quipped; "I might be one of the friends."[5]

However, for many rural Kenyans the decision either to accept or reject the high-density schemes involved more than whether or not they could garner the necessary deposit fee. Nineteen out of the twenty Maragoli smallhold residents in the study who qualified and had access to the start-up funds in the early 1960s, for example, were unwilling to use their limited funds to purchase land on the settlement site that was often of low-quality. More importantly, they were not prepared to follow the rigid guidelines that the LSWD established for the settler participants. While Maragoli residents expected their political leaders to make good on their campaign promises to provide land to the people, as *wananchi* (citizens) many Maragoliland people neither expected nor tolerated the government and international community's aims to dictate how they ought to live in an independent Kenya. Some of the eligible Maragoli residents, as a result, steered clear from the Lugari Settlement Scheme. In so doing, they challenged the development planners' assumptions that rural people at *uhuru* (independence) only wanted land, regardless of its soil quality, location, and strict regulations associated with the land settlement projects.

At the same time, both within and outside of Maragoliland, there were people like Molenje who willingly participated in the Scheme and who desperately wanted to become Lugari settlers. Christopher Leo, Colin Leys, and John Harbeson, who have argued that the Million Acre Scheme program was unsuccessful at redressing Kenya's land problem because it accommodated European settlers and allowed for the rural elite to accumulate more land at the expense of poor Kenyans, have essentially missed an important point.[6] The everyday Kenyans whom the MAS high-density projects intended to serve, in reality had options and were not all too desperate (or willing) to compromise their expectations at the time of independence to acquire land, especially if it was located far away and lacked the comforts of home. The choice to resettle or to remain behind, consequently hinged on the individual circumstances and particular expectations that rural people had for themselves and their families at Kenya's decolonization and during its independence era.

Historicizing the Lugari Settlement Scheme

As alluded to in the Introduction, the Lugari high-density settlement was part of a massive and ambitious land redistribution program that became known as the Million Acre Scheme (MAS). The MAS project began in the Spring of 1962 when the Kenyan government, via the Ministry for Land Settlement and Water Development, purchased 197,000 acres of land from departing European settlers for the purposes of creating high-density schemes for ordinary Kenyans in and around the "white highlands," a fertile region in the modern-day Rift Valley that was home to European settler farmers. The Lugari Settlement Scheme was the twenty-first project under the MAS program.[7] The British government was the main financier of the 1962 MAS project, which was estimated to cost £25 million. The Kenyan administration used the funds, much of which were loans, to buy land from European mixed farmers at favorable (and very generous) 1959 prices as this was the most recent year in which there was a strong market for land. McKenzie's ministry planned in 1962 to purchase two hundred thousand-acres of land for a period of five years for the sole purpose of developing high-density settlement projects.[8]

In all, the coalition KANU and KADU government and, subsequently, the Kenyatta regime purchased about 1.17 million acres of land within and around the highlands for African settlement by 1967. This amount was only a fraction of the extensive and coveted European territory. Since Kenyan authorities (both British and African) expected to continue the export-based economy at independence, they left much of the land in its original state. Namely, 1.5 million acres of plantations, 2.7 million acres of ranches, and 1.6 million large-scale farms remained intact and under European ownership in the 1960s.[9] Planners of the MAS therefore hoped that the high-density small-hold schemes would help them stabilize the land hunger problem while maintaining Kenya's agricultural economy that historically depended on the larger European farm estates and multinational plantations.

Although the term "million acre scheme" referred to the 1962 high-density schemes, it eventually encompassed the earlier land settlement projects that the interim hybrid government, consisting of British bureaucrats and KADU leaders, started in 1961. This government set into motion land transfer and settlement projects in the hopes that it would be able to control who would gain access to the highly desirable fertile land in the former white highlands. The 1961 government's Assisted Owner project, for example, was a willing-buyer-willing-seller scheme that allowed European landowners to sell their land as either whole or sub-divisions to rich Kenyan farmers who had the capital to obtain land in the highlands.

The LSWD discontinued the Assisted Owners projects in June 1962, which by then had settled 125 Kenyans on 34,000 acres of land in the highlands.[10] The highlands comprised about 21,000 of Kenya's 356,000 square-kilometer area in what is present-day Rift Valley Province. During the colonial period, this area was a racially exclusive farming enclave restricted to the European community. The settler farmers had access to six percent of Kenya's thirty-two percent arable land while the remaining productive land was shared by the indigenous population of about six million people who were forced to reside in "native" reserves. The imperial regime had established the reserves system in the early twentieth century in order to make colonial administration rational and practical in Kenya along with providing cheap labor for the settler community.[11]

In time, the "native" reserves created soil degradation and exacerbated social tensions for the more populous ethnic groups who had outgrown their specific reserves within a decade of its establishment. Western Kenya's provincial officials in the 1930s were already concerned with the region's growing population and the implications of this growth on the reserve system. By the 1950s, the local colonial administrators in the North Nyanza district were very much aware that the land in Maragoli and Bunyore locations within the Abaluhya reserve, could not adequately sustain the growing population. The Provincial Commissioner for Nyanza Province, C. H. Williams, for example, had written in 1952 to officials in Nairobi requesting that something be done about the overcrowding in the two locations.[12] Nonetheless, at the time, Nairobi officials could not grant Williams's request that a considerable number of ordinary Maragoli and Bunyore people be resettled elsewhere in order to relieve the land pressure in the reserve, because there was no land available.

After the passage of the 1959 Native Lands Registration Ordinance and the first Lancaster House talks of January 1960, the British government made it known that Kenya would be moving toward a speedy independence and the settlement projects became a reality. The events at the first Lancaster House resulted in the exodus of a number of white settlers as well as capital flight. European settler farmers and foreign investors were concerned about their status and financial interests in an independent Kenya, especially since Britain's decision to divest itself of colonial Kenya coincided with the 1960 turmoil in the Congo.[13] Consequently, as large numbers of British settlers left Kenya, land in the coveted white highlands became readily available for the government to address the major social problem and political threat it faced at decolonization: land hunger. The land, however, was sold rather than given back to the Kenyan government. This (controversial) system of land transfer—by sale, not nationalization—was part of the independence deal made between the British administration and the interim government that was formed after the general elections in April 1961, which was composed of KADU and the European Party, New Kenyan Group (NKG).[14]

By May 1961 the KADU and NKG government had implemented the previously mentioned Assisted Owner projects as well as the Colonial Development Corporation (CDC) and World Bank-funded low-density schemes, popularly known as the Yeoman and Peasant Schemes. This external financial support was crucial, according to Gary Wasserman, because it made the land transfer schemes less political, and linked independent Kenya's development project to international development agencies like the World Bank.[15] The original settlement projects, with the minor exception of the Peasant Scheme, largely catered to the influential and wealthy Kenyans who had also benefited from the 1955 Swynnerton Plan's land consolidation program discussed in the Introduction. Kenyan and British authorities hoped that this affluent group of Kenyans would take advantage of the Yeoman and Assisted Owner Schemes because they had the sufficient capital to purchase the land, and in theory had the "modern" farming background to prevent a drop in the estates' productivity.

The 1961 interim government initiated the original land transfer and settlement projects under the Land Development and Settlement Board (LDSB). Kenyan officials, with the backing of the European settler community, established the LDSB in 1961 "to prepare, approve, and carry out agricultural settlement schemes."[16] The LDSB had assumed all duties associated with the land settlement program until 1962 when the Ministry for Land Settlement displaced the organization. Although the LDSB intended to serve the interests of all communities, there was excessive European representation on its leadership board since its Chairman and Chief Executive Officer were both Europeans.[17] The LDSB, in other words, had the interest of the European community at heart rather than the land-poor and landless Africans. The European dominance of LDSB's leadership was problematic, especially for the international sponsors who did not want to seem as though they were supporting a particular group's agenda. The World Bank and CDC, for example, insisted that the LDSB be administered as an independent entity, and thus out of the jurisdiction of any future national African government.

Accordingly, by April 1962 the LDSB and its projects were undergoing significant modifications as the newly-formed coalition KADU and KANU government, which was formed following the second Lancaster House talks that were held earlier in the year, deemed the projects insufficient to solve the problem of land hunger.[18] The establishment of the Ministry for Land Settlement and Water Development and the Central Land Board (CLB) in 1962 and 1963 respectively, replaced the LDSB's functions. The Department of Settlement, which was part of the Ministry for Land Settlement, planned and operated the schemes while the CLB selected, valued, and purchased the land for settlement. The two institutions, in theory, were better at addressing the land question than the LDSB because they included African representatives from all seven of Kenya's regions, a governing system which the 1962 *majimbo* (regionalism) constitution created.

Specifically, the KADU-sponsored *majimbo* constitution provided that the CLB be independent of the central government with its leadership team consisting of representatives from each region and the Board's chairman coming from outside Kenya.[19] The CLB representatives were to reflect the interests of the smaller African minorities. This devolution of power to regional bodies, especially for the management of the land settlement and transfer program, was not popular with the KANU nationalist government under the leadership of Jomo Kenyatta, which ultimately won the independence elections in 1963. By the end of 1964, the Kenyatta regime had successfully turned Kenya into a Republic, thus ending regionalism through a series of constitutional amendments. In so doing, the central government retained more control over the CLB and allowed it more influence over the land purchases and selection of settlers.[20]

The fact that the Provincial Commissioners—politicians—rather than the Department of Settlement officers were responsible for selecting the settlers to relocate to the schemes created tension and problems at the local level. Department of Settlement officials were especially frustrated at not being able to choose the participants for the high-density projects since many of the participants were deemed to be inadequate farmers who lacked the skills to turn their small-hold plots into profitable enterprises.[21] A number of settlement officers therefore had no issues evicting plot holders if they could not maintain their land according to the standards set forth by the Ministry. Moreover, the selection process was problematic because the committees, which were made up of local Chiefs and District Commissioners, often decided on the settlers using unconventional metrics including whether or not the prospective settler was a known trouble maker.[22] Such tactics on behalf of all those involved with the MAS program, no doubt, led a number of ordinary Kenyans in the 1960s to thoroughly evaluate the high-density schemes and thus to be pragmatic in their decision to either join or refrain from the government's land settlement program.

High-Density and Low-Density Schemes: Contrasted

The new land settlement and transfer program that the coalition government began in the Spring of 1962 included the high-density projects and a modified low-density scheme program, both smallholder schemes became the basis of the MAS program. Whereas the former high-density projects catered to unemployed land-poor and landless participants who lacked commercial farming experience, the later CDC- and IBRD-funded settlement schemes targeted the semi-educated and financially stable Kenyans with "modern" agricultural training. The so-called low-density schemes aimed at promoting in the highlands the emergence of an African landed middle class whom European officials hoped would stabilize socioeconomic and political tensions during the transfer of power in Kenya.[23] These farmers were to diversify the racially exclusive "white highlands." More importantly, they had the capital to stimulate Kenya's land market and to protect settler investments in land on the eve of independence. The Yeoman and Peasant Schemes, in effect, continued the late colonial administration's rural economic program for developing African agriculture.

The LDSB officials responsible for facilitating the projects in 1961 planned to settle six thousand families on the peasant holdings and 1,800 families on the yeoman designated plots. Kenyan officials, due to pressure from the World Bank and CDC, specifically designed the low-density schemes to provide economic development in Kenya rather than to relieve land pressure.[24] Thus, the international developmental organizations had no intention of politicizing the land schemes and focused on making sure that the land plots and settlement participants in the low-density projects met specific quality standards: settlers on Yeoman plots were required to make £250 in yearly net income, while settlers on Peasant plots were required to make £100 in yearly net income.

Adhering to the CDC and IBRD agencies' stipulation that the land settlement program remain apolitical, however, was unrealistic for Kenya's national government in the 1960s. The land schemes were already under a great deal of scrutiny from leftwing KANU politicians like Bildad Kaggia and Oginga Odinga, who had expected the European lands to be returned to the Africans at no cost. Moreover, with the end of the Mau Mau emergency in 1960, the Kikuyu detainees were returning home landless. The detainees' status was largely the result of the Swynnerton Plan's consolidation program. As described previously, this controversial land reform program essentially allowed the pro-colonial "loyalists" to gain access to the fragmented pieces of land belonging to Kikuyu detainees, who had no real recourse to protect their holdings because of their detention.

Consequently, as both Christopher Leo and Garey Wasserman have argued in their respective works on Kenya's land resettlement programs, the low-density schemes failed to ease the major tensions dealing with land-hunger and the fears of land grabbing at independence. Kenyan politicians therefore found it necessary to modify the low-density projects in 1962 by doubling the original ninety-thousand-acres to be transferred and also lowering the income targets that settlers had to meet.[25] Furthermore, in the same year, the coalition KADU and KANU government implemented the MAS high-density plans because of pressure from the local administrators who were facing problems created by landless and land-poor Kenyans. These officials recognized that a land transfer and settlement program catering to the majority of ordinary people was a necessary political and social endeavor for the British administration and for Kenya's transition government.[26]

In contrast to the World Bank and Commonwealth land schemes, the British-financed MAS high-density plans were political in that they aimed to ease the land pressure of Kenya's most congested regions, including locations throughout central and western Kenya. Authorities feared that the overcrowded areas were (or had the potential to become) the most problematic because they had large concentrations of unemployed, desperate, and idle young people. The Kenyan government's anxiety therefore resulted in the high-density schemes representing the old "tribal" boundaries incorporated in colonial Kenya because each plan essentially accommodated a specific location and thus ethnic community.[27] The Lugari Settlement Scheme, for instance, predominately consisted of Abaluhya people because settlement officers recruited extensively from western Kenya's North Nyanza region—the "native reserve" for this ethnic community.

Britain had agreed to cover the expenses associated with pre-settlement and to fund one-third of the cost of the land to the MAS small-holders in the hopes to assuage the concerns of many European settlers and national corporations worrying that an African-dominated Kenyan government would either result in the complete confiscation of their properties (nationalization) or lead to a dramatic drop in land prices that would force them to abandon their farms without compensation.[28] The area that the Ministry for Land Settlement and Water Development demarcated for the Lugari Settlement Scheme, for example, had initially been a sisal estate managed by Mr. Edward Sargent. It is unclear if Sargent was the sole proprietor of the 19,000-acre estate located about fifty miles northeast of Maragoliland, but documents suggest that he was the main contact person at the Lugari estate who negotiated with Kenyan officials throughout the 1960s.[29]

At the start of 1962, the LDSB began talks with Sargent to purchase blocks of land from the Lugari sisal estate for the purpose of resettling farmers from western Kenya, especially individuals from the overcrowded Maragoli location. LDSB officials had planned the small-hold high-density project at Lugari to be completed in three phases. In the first phase, the LDSB officials purchased 640 acres of land from Sargent. The Land Ministry, which eventually took over the LDSB responsibilities in April 1962, intended to relocate the first fifty settlers on the acquired land throughout the long rain period beginning in May 1962. The Lugari sisal estate purchase was an ideal transaction for the pre-independence government as it was supposed to address two major concerns: ease land-pressure problems in western Kenya, and provide economic opportunities for the settler farmers, given that the plots were "full of established sisal."[30]

The economic prospect of the high-density projects, however, were less of a concern for Nairobi officials, who were preoccupied with keeping the land-hunger and soil degradation problems in check during the transfer-of-power period. The main objective that the Kenyan government had for the high-density projects was to provide some measure of relief for the landless and unemployed so that they would not become troublesome and threatening to the political establishment. For this specific reason, participants of the high-density projects received smaller plots compared to other MAS program participants.

Lugari participants each received on average twelve-acres of land. MacKenzie reasoned to Members of Kenya's Legislative Council in June 1962 that the smaller sized holdings his Ministry allocated for the high-density projects were more than fair given the target audience. "We do not intend giving too large an acreage," McKenzie declared, "but we intend giving him an acreage large enough for him to exert himself and to make a good living."[31] McKenzie and his administration, in particular, presumed that the targeted Maragoliland residents who were eligible and could meet the deposit fees for the Lugari Settlement Scheme would eagerly take up the government's offer to own land. The Minister, in other words, failed to grasp the motivations and expectations of rural Kenyans, especially those in Maragoliland, at independence. Land, though coveted, was not the only means of upward mobility for Maragoliland residents. Furthermore, ambitious agriculturalists who wanted to make a living on the land found the rigid government guidelines to be unappealing and constraining.

Lugari (High-Density) Settlement Scheme

On December 12, 1963, when Kenya became a sovereign nation, the Lugari Settlement Scheme was already in full-swing. The pioneering group of fifty settlers had relocated with the help of the Ministry for Land Settlement to their assigned plots and were in the process of setting up their new homes throughout the long rainy session of 1962. According to David Khatela, a settlement officer, and himself a Lugari small-hold plot holder, the settlers arrived at Lugari by government-charted lorry. Based on Khatela's recollections, along with several other Lugari participants' testimonies, it does not appear that any of the settlers actually visited their assigned plots prior to their arrival. They were simply assigned plots by settlement officers once on the scene.[32]

In establishing the land schemes, the Ministry for Land Settlement surveyed the site's topography, determined the water availability, and classified its soils. These procedures helped the LSDB and its replacement, the Central Land Board, value the land, and also enabled the Ministry for Land Settlement to demarcate scheme and plot boundaries.[33] Using this information, especially the soil classification data, the Lugari settlement officers placed the participants on their respective plots. Neither the participants nor the selection officers, it seemed, had the final say on where the settlers would establish their homes.

The first group of settlers were all married men between the ages of twenty-eight and fifty years old. More importantly, they all had previously resided in either Maragoli or Bunyore—the two most populated locations in the overcrowded North Nyanza district.[34] Alfred Machayo, who was an agricultural officer in 1962, insisted that potential settlers for the scheme were supposed to come from these two locations because the Lugari Settlement Scheme was meant to "ease land pressure."[35] While this first group of settlers may have met the specific location requirement, the majority of settlers were neither unemployed nor landless when their local LDSB selection committees approved their applications. Each of the original Lugari participants, for example, held plots of land in their home locations in North Nyanza district that averaged between half an acre to three acres in size. Seventeen of the fifty settlers listed their occupations, many of whom were teachers and drivers.[36]

Their status as landowners technically should have disqualified them from participating in the Scheme, since the government claimed that the MAS high-density projects were to serve the landless and unemployed Kenyans. The ideal MAS high-density project candidate was theoretically a junior son from a large household who did not have legitimate claim to his father's land. However, the transition government, especially officials from the Ministries of Agriculture and Land Settlement, were also worried that populating the settlement area with only landless individuals who had neither the interest nor the experience to turn their plots into a "payable proposition" would ultimately result in the settlement schemes facing the same "hardships" of the overcrowded African areas. Accordingly, the MAS program's local selection committees followed directions from their higher officials, who had expected the high-density projects like the one at Lugari to include individuals who had experience owning land and thus (officials assumed) had farming potential. These particular settler recruits theoretically were to ensure that the schemes would have some measure of success.[37] Hence, even though they were not landless, the first group of Maragoli and Buynore small-holders likely achieved plots in the Lugari Settlement Scheme because they demonstrated to their local selection committee that they were both enthusiastic about farming and committed to turning their assigned plots into viable economic holdings.[38]

The relocation of Lugari settlers happened in phases, allowing the former estate owners to close down business in an organized manner.[39] Moreover, it seemed that this strategy provided the local administration with time to adjust their eligibility requirements for the project, in the hopes of recruiting potential settlers outside of the Maragoli and Bunyore locations. Despite having the first group of Lugari settlers recruited directly from the two overcrowded locations, the selection committee officers encountered difficulties convincing more people to join. Rather than having too many applicants and therefore needing to turn away Maragoli and Bunyore people, the selection committee members quickly realized that they were being turned down by a number of residents from these communities.

Consequently, by late 1963, North Nyanza district residents such as Nathan Molenje had gained access onto the Lugari Scheme even though they resided outside of the two overcrowded locations. Molenje, who was born in the Kabras location of North Nyanza, had successfully acquired a fifteen-acre plot of land in the Checklaini location of the Lugari settlement site area by convincing his local selection committee that he was passionate about becoming a full-time farmer.[40] The requirement that Lugari settlers must come specifically from Maragoli and Bunyore was thus overlooked in the later phases of the project. What seemed to matter most to the Central Land Board, which by 1963 had replaced the LDSB's local selection committee, was that the Lugari settlers have no economic interests outside of agriculture.[41] That is, devoting oneself to full-time farming seemed to be the major condition to be awarded land in the project on the eve of decolonization. This requirement fell in line with the Kenyan government's development agenda for the rural sector, especially during the immediate years following colonial independence when idle young men posed a direct threat to the government.

While the original planners of the MAS high-density projects expected to ease land pressure in the African areas, the Lugari settlement project was also meant to motivate the settlers to take up small-scale commercial farming as an occupation. In so doing, officials hoped to put a check on the country's unemployment as well as to maintain Kenya's export economy. "We did three projects on the farm," Molenje explained; "one was to grow sisal on the five acres of land . . . the reason of growing this sisal was because it was to produce sisal sacks . . . then we also grew maize . . . and then we were also given cattle to get milk."[42] A 1963 correspondence by the Settler Controller in charge of the Lugari project provides vivid details as to what settler farmers were responsible for growing once they arrived at their new homes; it also reveals the micro (over) management of this development project. On their assigned farm plots, for example, settlers had to plant: "1⁄2 acres of fruit trees, 2-acres subsistence food crops, 2-acres cash crops (maize), 5 1⁄2-acres grass." This correspondence also corroborates Molenje's remarks about sisal cultivation because in this same notice the Controller advised the Lugari participants to make use of the "established sisal [plots left from the previous owner], which will give the holder a ready income."[43]

The Settler Controller's remarks underscore the fact that the Kenyan government was highly supportive of the MAS high-density projects, because they served the state's political and economic interests in the 1960s. As participants, the settlers received land, housing materials, a couple of dairy cows, and a small monthly allowance of Shs.30/- to feed the household until they could grow their own food crops. They were also eligible for the government development loans. In exchange for these resources, the settlers were to devote themselves to the land, becoming the "modern" small-hold farmers whom the Kenyan regime did not have to burden itself with in terms of providing employment and social services following complete political independence from Britain.[44]

The opening of the Lugari Farmers' Training Center in January 1964 supported the government's objectives. The Christian Council of Kenya (CCK) and the Department of Settlement, which had replaced the LDSB board, sponsored and jointly funded the Center. The grantees appointed the American Friends (Quaker) Africa Mission to run the Training Center. This was a convenient choice given that the Friends had a large influence throughout the Lugari settlement area as the majority of the Luhya settlers had been associated with the Friends Mission station back in their home villages.[45]

The Center's main purpose was to help train the first-time settlers in "better" farm practices and cash crop cultivation. It offered "a one-week course in specific agricultural and dairy management practices suitable to this settlement, to each settler soon after his arrival on his plot." This training was mandatory for the farmer *and* his spouse as the goal was to teach the entire household "advanced" farming practices. The Farmers' Training Center at Lugari also served the Kenyan government's intention of turning an ordinary farm man (along with his family members) into a practical small-hold commercial farmer who would help with the nation-building process by feeding the people and helping the nation maintain its export-economy.[46] By requiring that both husband and wife attend the training courses, settlement officers ensured that the family unit learned about the main responsibilities associated with being settlers of the project. Everyone in the household was to maintain the soil's fertility and to produce commodity crops such as sisal and sunflower seeds for the benefit of the family unit and the nation.[47]

Lugari Requirements and Maragoliland Reactions

The requirement that Lugari settlers must engage in farming full-time was certainly a deterrent for individuals who already had gainful employment but minimal or no access to any type of land whatsoever. It was especially unpopular for a number of Maragolis from small-hold households who understood the value of owning land yet were unwilling to compromise their expectations and, for some, to jeopardize their comfortable lifestyles. Joram Kaiga, for instance, refused to submit an application for the scheme due to this particular condition. Being a settler farmer was simply incompatible with his life circumstances at the moment of Kenya's decolonization. "I couldn't leave the job that I had been on for such a long time," he explained.[48] Kaiga worked as a meteorologist in Nairobi. He first learned about the Lugari project in 1962 from his father, who had demanded that Kaiga participate in the scheme. His father was adamant that Kaiga take an interest in the Lugari settlement because there was a total of seventeen children in the household. With his large family, Kaiga's father essentially was not able to provide him with a sizable piece of land, even though Kaiga was the first-born son of his first wife.

His father's request that Kaiga participate in the land resettlement program and thereby forsake his city job may seem unusual. After all, the appeal was made during a time when most people looked forward to acquiring non-manual jobs in towns away from the overcrowded "native reserves," which no longer existed after 1959. But, as Robert Bates has rightly pointed out, land is a fixed resource that was highly valued in the more crowded areas such as Maragoliland.[49] Accordingly, for Kaiga's father, landownership was analogous to having economic and societal wealth, particularly as there was no social security from the state. The coalition government, in fact, rejected a 1961 Committee on Social Security recommendation to initiate an old age pension system for wage-earning persons on the basis that it would be too costly to administer.[50] With no access to a formal retirement plan, Kaiga's father, naturally, assumed that his son's future security rested on owning land even if the ownership was attached to conditions. Thus, he insisted that his first-born son participate in the Lugari project, as a means to an end.

Kaiga, however, was unenthusiastic about quitting his job in Nairobi in order to farm full-time. Even though he was interested in acquiring land for retirement and had a penchant for horticulture, he did not imagine himself relocating to an area that was undeveloped and far from his family and friends. His decision was further solidified during a visit with his father to the Lugari scheme site. Unlike the pioneering group of settlers, Kaiga made the trip to the sisal estate suggesting that he was well connected and financially stable. In other words, he was an individual with options at independence. During this informational trip, Kaiga recalled, "I looked at the type of soil, the size of the land that they were giving at that time, which was ten acres . . . I [also] said if you have to uproot sisal then you start planting maize then you'll have to use a lot of inputs to get what you want." As a result of these concerns and because his real desire at the time was to "have a bigger plot than the ten acres," Kaiga never took part in the Lugari project.[51] Although he shared his father's sentiment for land ownership, he simply could not accept the Kenyan government's requirement that the Lugari settlers should only acquire monetary income from farming their settlement plots.

Kaiga was not alone in eschewing the Lugari scheme because it did not help him with his future goals and would have deprived him of a lifestyle to which he had grown accustomed on the eve of Kenya's independence. The Lugari project was unpopular with some of the educated and ambitious Maragoliland residents who did not envision themselves toiling on the soil as manual laborers at *uhuru*. Both Pierson Zavani and Gerishom Alukwri, for example, refrained from participating in the LSS because it promoted a career choice that neither they nor family members considered suitable to pursue because they had attended school. Unlike Kaiga, however, both Alukwri and Zavani did not reject the LSS on the basis that the soil and land allowances for Lugari settlers were insufficient. Their explanation for refusing the Scheme instead rested on the simple fact that they had obligations to family members and that they wanted to stay on their home plots where their ancestors were buried.

Zavani, for example, recalled that his father decided against relocating the family from their home in west Maragoli to the Lugari area because he did not want to leave his parents behind in the family homestead as there were neither pensions nor social security for the elderly. His father did not own a large piece of land because Zavani's grandfather only had access to a meager quarter-acre piece of property. Zavani's father was therefore eligible to take advantage of the Lugari Scheme if he desired and if he did not take his familial duties seriously. "You know Maragolians are very close as a family," Zavani explained; "so the idea of leaving ancestral land for a foreign land [was something] they didn't want . . . because like us, here, we are a family right from the road . . . It's just one family here, so we are used to it."[52] Alukwri echoed Zavani when explaining his own decision to remain behind on his modest half acre in the Maragoli location. "Well, it was just because we didn't want to leave our home . . . home is home . . . we didn't want to go to new places where we would go and start a new life because we already had settled this way."[53] Familial attachments might be a strong justification for not wanting to leave "home," but it does not adequately explain why Alukwri's and Zavani's fathers would knowingly give up the chance to acquire larger pieces of land, especially since they did not have sufficient land on their respective family homesteads. Rather, their decision to refrain from the LSS can be better understood by examining the kind of life the men had—Alukwri in particular—and the one they imagined they and their families would have under an African-ruled Kenya.

Born in 1938 at Chavakali in west Maragoli, Alukwri was fortunate enough to receive a good education. He started at Chavakali primary school in 1950, and in 1956 he continued at the prestigious Alliance High School for his secondary education. By 1959 he was training to become a teacher at Siriba College in Maseno, which trained local Kenyans to become agricultural officers and teachers. Accordingly, when local administrators advertised the Lugari Settlement Scheme through the chief's *barazas* (public meetings) in Maragoliland during the early 1960s, Alukwri was already on the path to becoming a teacher. Alukwri had also come to the conclusion that his parents placed more value on teaching than on farming. "When you've taken teaching, they'll know that you have at least taken something," he explained. Thus, Alukwri did not submit an application for the Lugari settlement even though his unemployment status and his residency in overcrowded Maragoli qualified him for a place in the Scheme. He simply had no intention to become a state-sponsored farmer within an independent Kenya because he saw a more promising future in teaching. He understood that his career choice would not only provide a higher and more stable income, but also elevate him to an esteemed position within his family and among the local society.[54]

Similarly, Zavani's father emphasized that educated people should not do farm work. Zavani, who was attending Masingo Quaker Boys Secondary school in 1962, fell into this category. His father insisted that he not touch a *jembe* (weeding hoe) after school, preferring his son only concentrate on academics while at home. Zavani's father went so far as to scold his son when he learned about his helping a neighbor prepare their land for harvest. Rather than work on his neighbor's farm, his father expected Zavani to use his expensive education to obtain the highly coveted "white-collar" jobs that were once restricted to the European community. He told me, "I took you to school, I didn't take you to go and dig for people," remembered Zavani.[55] Though his father's rebuke was harsh, his expectations for Zavani were reasonable because the "white collar" opportunities were within reach for educated Africans by 1961 when the transition government started Africanizing industries and government sectors in preparation for Kenya's independence.[56]

Despite being a peasant farmer himself, Zavani's father considered agriculture a "dirty job" that was unsuitable for his educated son. By refusing the scheme and thereby denying himself access to a large piece of land, his father demonstrated to Zavani that life in an independent Kenya did not have to be restricted to hard manual labor. In contrast to Kaiga, Zavani had a parent who believed that an education, rather than a larger piece of land, was the most valuable resource that he could ensure his children would own at independence. This did not mean that Zavani's father expected his son to remain landless, however. He simply wanted to ensure that his son had options. Thus, Zavani's father willingly avoided the land settlement opportunity because it promoted a lifestyle that was beneath the one that he imagined his son could have as a citizen in a free Kenya. Making sure that his son had access to schooling was likely the prime factor behind Zavani's father's decision to dismiss the Lugari project, especially since the settlement site was in an undeveloped area that was miles from any established school site.[57] Zavani eventually fulfilled his father's wishes by finding an office job after finishing school. He worked in a Nairobi bank until his retirement in early 2000.[58]

In addition to committing themselves to becoming small-scale commercial farmers, applicants for the Lugari settlement had to prove that they could provide the "necessary capital" to pay for the registration fee.[59] This fee was due in full once applicants received notice that they had been accepted into the scheme. In 1962, the first group of settlers were responsible for paying between Shs. 80/- to Shs.114/-. The fee amount was calculated according to the size of each assigned plot.[60] Indeed, the registration cost was a huge deterrent for prospective applicants, even for those individuals gainfully employed at the time of the recruitment process. The labor department, for example, reported that the average earnings for Kenyans in 1962 was

Shs.130/- per month with those employed in the agriculture sector making about 65/- per month.[61] Of course, these official figures do not reflect the occasional day laborer who was probably paid well below the national average. Considering these wage statistics, most rural Maragoli and Bunyore residents—the intended audience for the Lugari Settlement Scheme—would have thought twice about participating. Moreover, this kind of registration tax essentially put the Scheme out of reach for individuals who were unemployed and struggling to make ends meet.

Although such a fee may have undermined the MAS program's overall aim to provide land for ordinary Kenyans, the land settlement officials believed that the expense was necessary. The Kenyan government, in particular, expected the registration fee to dissuade individuals who neither had the capital nor the farming experience to turn their settlement plots into economically viable farm units that would benefit the small-hold farmer while providing exports for the Kenyan state. This initial registration cost essentially served as a screening device, allowing the transition government and then the *uhuru* regime to continue the rural development policies of the late colonial period. It ensured that the MAS high-density projects "be regarded as an economic proposition and not as a clearing house for the waifs and strays of the district."[62] For his part, Nathan Molenje was forced in 1963 to sell one of his father's cows in order to meet his registration fee of Shs.102/-. Some of his impoverished neighbors, however, were obliged to relinquish their spots in the Scheme, despite having successfully passed the interviewing stage, because they were unable to find the capital to pay the start-up expenses.[63]

The registration cost was intended to "cover the legal fees and stamp duty for the [settlers'] freehold title," and it was not the only financial obligation that the MAS high-density project participants had to accept when they received their plots in the settlement areas. Additionally, the Lugari settlers were required to pay a development fee for their piece of property, which basically functioned as a fixed mortgage. As previously mentioned, in 1962 this fee was set at Shs.1,600/- per household and payable over a thirty-year period. By 1963, it had increased to Shs.2,400/- per household and the Lugari settlers were eligible for start-up loans of up to Shs.2,000/- in order to assist them with their agricultural projects.[64] The development fee and loans were extremely important for Kenya's transition government to institute and thereby force upon the settlement participants, both in the high-density and low-density projects. These expenses assured the foreign investors, such as the British government, which was financing Kenya's land reform initiatives, that there were measures in place to compel settler farmers to pay for the land on which they resided. In other words, the British and the transition Kenyan governments did not necessarily trust that the more radical nationalist leaders, particularly Oginga Odinga, would actually hold the African settlers financially accountable for their plots once colonialism ceased.[65]

The financial expenses tied to the Lugari scheme, understandably, were discouraging for subsistence and small-hold Maragoli residents who were hopeful that their nationalist leaders would make good on their promises to "remove people from the burden of poverty . . . and the demoralizing lack of economic opportunity."[66] Maragoli Kenyans, like many throughout the country, had anticipated that an independent African government would at most provide land for the *wananchi* (citizens) without strings attached, least of all any type of registration fee. Hence, these financial conditions prompted several of the Maragoliland residents who barely managed to eke out a living on their subsistence plots to suspect that Kenya's independence did not mean much in terms of real change.

In particular, certain individuals in Maragoliland were doubtful that the Kenyan government would allow the Lugari participants to keep their land even if they managed to pay off the fees and loans affiliated with their relocation. This group of skeptics included Melice Onyango and Rachel Alunga both of whom had speculated that the Lugari settlement was a ruse by the government to remove people from their ancestral land and to get free manual labor from the Africans. Being rendered a squatter was a real concern for many ordinary people in the Maragoli community. It was most poignant amongst the elders in the community who had grown up with stories about *wazungus* (foreigners) evicting Africans from their land. Several informants, for example, referenced the Kikuyu community's situation, namely the way in which the Mau Mau detainees lost their land due to the land registration and titling program associated with the Swynnerton Plan of the mid-1950s. They also discussed the development of the so-called "white highlands" and its consequences for the indigenous communities. Their fears therefore convinced Onyango and Alunga to remain behind with their husbands in Maragoliland.

Onyango, who had moved from South Maragoli when she married in 1957, recalled that the Lugari scheme received a cautious welcome in her village. This reception, she maintained, was due in large part to the actions of the newly-elected African leaders. Specifically, Jomo Kenyatta and the KANU right-wing politicians were giving speeches in the years immediately following decolonization, in which they emphasized to the *wananchi* that "there's nothing for free" in an independent Kenya. These kinds of messages coincided with the local government's recruitment campaigns for the Lugari Scheme in the early 1960s. As a result, they prompted Onyango and her neighbors to question their official's real motives behind the land redistribution and settlement programs. The mixed messages from their political leaders, understandably made them suspicious of the Lugari Scheme, which seemed too good to be true for Maragoliland residents such as Onyango who historically had to endure Maragoliland's land pressure issue without any real assistance from the Kenyan government. "People now thought that this land is not for free . . . later on, we [thought the government] would snatched these pieces of land," she explained.[67]

This cynicism toward the Lugari scheme was also felt in Alunga's area of Chavakali in west Maragoli. Alunga, who was thirty-eight years-old when she first learned of the land resettlement project in 1962, remembers that many people in her area, herself included, presumed that the government would not provide secure land rights to the Maragoli transplants. Alunga and her neighbors inferred that the Lugari participants, who in theory had to relinquish all their rights to land in the Maragoli locations when they joined the Scheme, would eventually be made squatters and thus required to provide their labor in exchange for their property. "There was a rumor that spread all over, that if you go there [to Lugari] you'd end up being evicted. You'd be kicked out," she recalled, "either the government would kick you out or the white man would come and overturn the government and also take those pieces of land back."[68] These types of rumors and concerns influenced Alunga and her husband to decline the LSS when local settlement officials presented them with the opportunity to relocate. When explaining her family's decision to remain in Maragoli, Alunga emphasized that she did not trust the government to provide the Lugari settlers with secure land rights. She stated, "those who remained, myself included, we thought that those people [the settlers] had made the wrong decision . . . we thought that they would be forced to come back."[69] It is important, however, to note that Alunga and her husband's decision to turn down a spot in Lugari also may have been because they already had four-acres of land in a location where the average holding was less than two-acres. They were occupying what they believed to be sufficient land for their family, so they likely did not want to burden themselves by relocating to an unfamiliar environment, and they did not want to take on massive debt in the process.

Even so, the local Maragoli community's skepticism and concern over the government's land redistribution program seemed likely to have been influenced by the Kenyatta administration's 1964 economic development program in which the newly-elected KANU African leaders began to emphasize the "importance of land to the development of the Nation." In what become known as his "Return to Land" speech, Kenyatta had declared that all unemployed and land-poor able-bodied men—a group that was a serious threat to the nationalist government—ought to return to the countryside and "dirty their hands in the name of nation building."[70] While Kenyatta intended the speech to galvanize the unskilled and uneducated *wananchi* to take up farming as a viable career option, some Maragoli Kenyans interpreted this political rhetoric to mean that the *uhuru* government was reneging on its promise to provide non-manual jobs and opportunities for ordinary people.

For instance, as mentioned in the introduction, Maragoliland residents like Onyango and Keysia Mwasiagi were disappointed by the *uhuru* government's appeal to the *wananchi* to return to the countryside and to work the land. Both women were equally dismayed and annoyed at the fact that their leader, Kenyatta, expected rural Kenyans to contribute to the nation-building process through agriculture without much support. The Maragoliland residents were frustrated with how their urban, usually landholding nationalist leaders had changed their tune once in office, and thus were no longer espousing the notion of free land for poor Kenyans. "That was a mockery," recalled Mwasiagi.[71] Consequently, at the local level, the Lugari Settlement Scheme appeared highly suspect to people like Mwasiagi, Alunga, and Onyango, because it seemed a convenient way for the African government to backpedal on the grand promises of *uhuru* while at the same time projecting the image that it was trying to redress a major grievance of the people—landlessness.

A Welcomed Opportunity for Some

Even though the stipulation that Lugari settlers must be financially stable and full-time agriculturalists ultimately disappointed a number of local Maragoliland residents, not everyone in Maragoli rejected the Scheme, as evidenced by the pioneering group of settlers. Further, there were some people in the community who did not discount the fact that they could live a successful life in a "free" Kenya as (cash-crop) farmers. The junior sons from large Maragoli families, especially individuals from either subsistence or small-hold homesteads, wrote letters to their local selection committee officials hoping to secure a spot in the settlement projct. This group of sons were often land poor and had little educational training, since their parents usually had neither the means to afford extensive schooling, nor could they further subdivide the family's farm for them. These individuals lacked the proper training and, for some, the desire to go into towns to compete with their more educated peers and family members for the coveted white-collar jobs. Thus, the Lugari Settlement Scheme was a welcome opportunity.

Lawrence Mwanzi, for example, embraced the MAS high-density small-holder program because he was the youngest son in his family, who shared land with his father. In contrast to many of his peers who sought employment away from the countryside, Mwanzi wanted to remain on the land in the 1960s. Therefore, in his application letter to the Lugari selection committee, he made certain to express his interest in farming and to underscore that his position within his immediate family did not allow him any real prospects in Maragoliland. "I have been very much interested in farming," explained Mwanzi, "but my father who is only a simple peasant has four acres and has five sons . . . so, practically it is very hard for me."[72] In addition to stating his aspirations of becoming a full-time farmer, the twenty-four-year-old Mwanzi noted that he had temporary employment. This revelation was important as it demonstrated to the committee that he had the means to raise the capital to pay for the registration fee associated with the Scheme. Accordingly, rather than view the small-hold resettlement program as a malicious ploy, Mwanzi was glad for the government's initiative because he recognized the Lugari Scheme as a chance to gain access to land, which would enhance his economic and social status in the countryside and within an independent Kenyan state.

For this same reason, the more established landless farm laborers who had relocated from their homes in western Kenya throughout the colonial era to work on European estates were enthusiastic about the MAS program's high-density schemes. People such as Mteke Makhulo, Patrick Wawile, and Makokha Muchwingi, for example, associated the LSS as a perfect opportunity to which they wished to gain access. Accordingly, they sent application letters to the District Commissioners of North Nyanza district and Trans Nzoia district in August 1963—the latter place being their home district—to ask the settlement officials to take their candidacy for the Scheme seriously even though they resided outside the overpopulated region.

The letters from Makhulo, Wawile, and Muchwingi revealed that they were all affiliated with the same European farmer, Mr. Elmer, of Kitale in the Trans Nzoia District—located about eighty-one miles north of Maragoliland. Further, the identical handwriting and similar fashion in which the letters were organized suggest that each of the correspondences were written by the same individual. This particular individual was likely Wawile, a twenty-four-year-old primary school teacher who had been raised on the Elmer farm estate where the other two applicants worked as field laborers. Regardless of how their letters were produced, however, these ambitious men used it as a chance to sell themselves to the Lugari settlement selection committee. Each applicant stated that they were landless, referenced their connection to the North Nyanza region, emphasized their agricultural training and, more importantly, disclosed how much savings they had for the scheme. In so doing, they hoped to capture the sympathy of their letter readers and to secure a place in the Scheme.

Makhulo, for example, noted in his application letter that he had "Shs. 450/- in hand to enable me to start my work once I am given a plot." He had earned this fortune while working as a miller at the Elmer's farm. Not the typical Lugari applicant, Makhulo informed the committee that he had been living away from North Nyanza district for close to thirty-eight years due to his family not having sufficient land back on his homestead. Nevertheless, in his 1963 application, he identified himself as a landless Luhya from North Nyanza region. "I am a Mluhyia . . . I own no plot in my home District of North Nyanza . . . if you want proof, you can refer to the District Commissioner in Kakamega," his letter stated.[73]

By stating that he was a "Mluhyia," Makhulo essentially took advantage of the fact that the transition government and *uhuru* administration continued the colonial legacy of tying ethnic identity to specific localities, especially with respect to the planning and implementation of the MAS high-density projects. As discussed above, the 1962 Ministry for Land Settlement and Water Development (LSWD), had intended the Lugari settlement site to be "for the Abaluhya."[74] In other words, like the European colonialists, the Kenyan leadership supported and depended on local "tribal" identities to maintain their influence and to keep the state functioning. So, while Makhulo may have been aware that the scheme was for the Abaluhya who were presently residing in the North Nyanza district, he hoped to exploit his ethnic identity by stressing that he was, after all these years, still a landless Mluhyia regardless of his present location. This association, along with his financial assets, Makhulo expected would be enough for him to make a strong legitimate claim to a plot in the Scheme.[75]

In contrast, Muchwingi and Wawile emphasized in their application letters their agricultural experiences because both men were born in the Trans Nzoia district. Thus, they could not realistically claim any privileges for the Lugari Settlement Scheme as if they were displaced North Nyanza Abaluhyas. Regardless, in their appeals to the District Commissioner the men mentioned that they were Mluhyia and that their fathers were originally from the overcrowded North Nyanza district: "I am a Mluhyia from Trans Nzoia District at Mrs. Elmer and Elmer's farm . . . where I was born; and my father is still working . . . his former location is Bunyore in North Nyanza District" Wawile wrote.[76] Not surprisingly, assuming that Wawile helped write the application for him, Muchwingi's letter included an identical statement: "I am a Mluhyia born in Trans Nyzoia District. . . . My father's former location is Bunyore in North Nyanza District."[77] After briefly mentioning their loose connection to the overpopulated location of Bunyore, Wawile and Munchingi quickly directed their readers' attention to how their time on the Elmer farm estate had prepared them to become suitable candidates for the Lugari Scheme. Wawile, for example, revealed in his application that he was born at this particular estate where his parents had been squatters and laborers.[78] It was at this farm, Wawile noted, where he "gained a long experience in farming both theoretically and practically."[79] Similarly, Muchwingi explained that the agricultural training that he acquired as a worker on the Elmer farm would allow him "to work hard to keep [the settlement plot] up to date."[80]

Along with underscoring their agricultural experience, Muchwingi and Wawile made certain to note the amount of money that they had readily available to put toward the settlement expenses if they were fortunate enough to earn a place in the Scheme. Like Makhulo's letter, their correspondences listed the exact amount of savings the men had in 1963. This financial discloser was particularly important for the Kenyan government officials who were intent on keeping the MAS high-density small-hold projects from becoming a financial burden for the state.[81] It would appear that Makhulo, Wawile, and Muchwingi understood this message clearly as they each included their financial information in their letters. In fact, they were perhaps hopeful that their financial disclosures, along with farm experience, would give them an advantage over the humbler North Nyanza applicants.

It is unclear if the above applicants were actually successful in their pursuits. None of their names appeared on any Lugari settler roster dating from 1962 to 1965. The rosters, however, reveal that the Kenyan government could not win over all its critics in Maragoliland in particular and in North Nyanza district in general. The Lugari settlement officials eventually had to reevaluate their criteria for recruitment as they were having difficulty attracting settlers from this particular district. Thus, by 1965, the

Kenyatta administration had expanded the scheme to include other groups from across Kenya.[82]

Conclusion

In the early 1960s, the transitional Kenyan and British governments offered residents from the Maragoli location in the North Nyanza district the opportunity to take part in its land transfer and settlement program known as the Million Acre Scheme (MAS). The Lugari Scheme, in particular, was an MAS high-density project that was supposed to address the overpopulation and soil fertility problems plaguing this region of western Kenya. More importantly, British and Kenyan authorities had hoped that such a project would transform rural Maragoli family units into "modern" and profitable farmers who would be of little trouble for authorities. The state's objectives, however, were not easily met. Instead of having too many applicants, officials were having a difficult time persuading the local Maragoli community to take up residence in Lugari. The recruitment officers were often confronted with residents who believed that anyone who willingly relocated to the settlement site was "foolish." These individuals were neither particularly fond of the Scheme's intended purpose nor did they trust the government to provide land for the people without a substantial cost. However, while some eligible Maragoli residents from small-hold and large-hold homesteads declined to take part in the Scheme, others living in Maragoliland and elsewhere welcomed the Scheme as an opportunity to improve their status within an independent Kenya.

The decision to leave or stay ultimately rested on the type of lifestyle that Maragoliland residents wanted for themselves as *wananchi* in a sovereign Kenyan nation. The transition government and consequently the Kenyatta regime's efforts to address the problems lingering from the colonial era, such as landlessness and soil degradation, really did not matter much at the local and personal level. In this manner, ordinary Maragolis complicated the grand development plans of the decolonization and independence era.

Conclusion

Agricultural Production—The New (Old) Sexy

"Agriculture can create a million jobs for youth," was the title of Machel Waikenda's January 5, 2014 article in the *Standard Digital*, an online Kenyan media outlet. Writing over fifty-years after the independent Kenyan government initiated its development project of pragmatic agrarianism, Waikenda, a politician and youth activist, encouraged readers to embrace the Jubilee government's vision for the large number of unemployed young people living throughout Kenya's cities and townships. The Jubilee government, which assumed power in Spring 2013, had published its national economic program aimed at tackling the country's forty percent unemployment rate. Seventy percent of those unemployed were between the ages of fifteen and thirty-five. This statistic was of major concern for someone like Waikenda who also served as one of President Uhuru Kenyatta's trusted advisors on youth affairs.[1] Waikenda's piece in the *Standard Digital* lent support to his government's plan to reduce the nation's high level of unemployment by increasing Kenya's largest economic sector—agriculture.

At the time of Waikenda's article, Kenya's National Bureau of Statistics (KNBS) reported that agriculture was the fastest growing sector making up about twenty-five percent of the growth in Gross Domestic Product. This statistic convinced the Jubilee government that expanding agricultural output was a logical solution to employ in its effort to reduce the worsening unemployment rate among the growing urban youth population.[2] Like its predecessors, the current Kenyatta administration blamed this very group of individuals for escalating incidents of crime and insecurity in the country, and thus was a demographic the government sought to regulate. Waikenda, as a result, used the online news outlet to urge idle urban young Kenyans to consider the potential and "great opportunities" that working on the land and living in the countryside may offer them. "Over the years, we have seen millions of young people move to the cities searching for those elusive (white-collar) jobs," he writes; "it is time we encourage a reverse exodus (urban-to-rural migration) in an agricultural-based economy . . . yes, agricultural production can become the new sexy."[3]

Indeed, Waikenda's call for young people to explore agribusiness, a euphemism for tough manual labor, as a possible career path and his comments about the benefits of rural life are strikingly similar to the pleas made by elite politicians and their development partners during Kenya's decolonization period and early independence years. Waikenda's "urban-to-rural migration" appeal, in particular, echoes the 1964 speech made by Kenya's first president, Jomo Kenyatta, in which he urged all able-bodied and idle town dwellers to "go back to the land."[4] The Jubilee government's economic program recycled the agricultural-based development framework that the late colonial government and transition KADU and KANU administration implemented for Kenya, which the Kenyatta regime continued after it assumed complete power in December 1963.

More importantly, Waikenda's message suggests that the agrarian revolution that Kenya's nation-builders and development partners sponsored and promoted over fifty-years ago has yet to come to fruition. Hence, modern-day Developmentalists—among them the Gates Foundation, United States Agency for International Development (USAID), and Howard Buffett (son of Warren Buffet)—have invested billions in field research and projects meant to "improve" agriculture in present-day African countries. Notably, their efforts target turning local subsistence farmers into small-hold commercial agriculturalists who are knowledgeable of climate change and familiar with the latest seed technology.[5] The fact that contemporary development agents continue to fund and supervise such agricultural development initiatives suggests that Africans in places like Kenya have been reluctant to subscribe to the kind of economic development programs espoused by their government leaders in the decolonization and early independence era. The grand nation-building projects of the late 1950s and 1960s that gave priority to agricultural development neither transformed Kenya's agrarian economy into a modern industrial state nor persuaded local people to depend solely on the land for their prosperity. These "disappointing" outcomes were due in large part to the actions of different groups of historical actors, each of whose own experiences, expectations, and structural constraints influenced decisions and shaped the transfer of power.

Indeed, the agrarian-based development projects of the decolonization and national era such as the 4-K youth clubs, Lugari Settlement Scheme, Chavakali secondary school, and the Friends Africa Mission's Stewardship Rural Service Program did not provide lasting solutions to Kenya's economic and social problems. In theory, these programs and schemes were to help the political elites address the rampant landlessness and unemployment crises that the majority of rural Kenyans faced on the eve of colonial independence. Development projects were aimed at the well being of the vast majority of ordinary *wananchi*, as seen especially by initiatives aiming to improve the standard of living for residents living in the Maragoli region of western Kenya.

Kenyan officials and development practitioners anticipated that the various projects would encourage and provide incentive to young and able-bodied Maragoliland residents to recognize agriculture—particularly commercial farming—as a viable, lucrative, and beneficial career in the independence era. Practitioners and planners believed that a class of progressive African farmers would emerge as a result of the incentives provided by the government. The state expected that such farm men and women would sustain the national economy, which was predominantly agricultural, and at the same time would create jobs for the large number of unskilled and landless Kenyans in the countryside. This end goal, however, did not materialize. The planners could neither control the outcomes of the agricultural development initiatives and "betterment" schemes, nor were they able to successfully convince ambitious young Kenyans to remain on the land as full-time farmers. The movement of Kenyans from rural areas to urban centers, for instance, increased from 7.1 percent in the 1948–62 period to 10.1 percent between 1962 and 1969—the period when nation-builders focused on improving living conditions for the rural population.[6] The urban growth revealed that a considerable number of rural Kenyans were uninterested in the kind of development that their leaders had in mind for them throughout the independence era, and it also suggested that the promise of development was hollow.

Most rural Kenyans, regardless of economic and educational background, hoped for improvements in their living conditions at independence. Educated and land-poor rural Kenyans envisioned working in office buildings away from their fathers' overcrowded homesteads. At the same time, there were motivated Maragoliland residents who wanted to remain in the countryside but who had no desire to become small-hold farmers or skilled manual laborers for plantation estate owners. Rather, they envisioned themselves as large-scale farm owners and prominent agricultural officers. The career ambitions of young and determined farm men and women from places like Maragoliland were greater than the limited (and often unrealistic) opportunities that politicians and development experts predicted for this sector when creating Kenya's nation-building program. By glossing over such expectations and behaviors with one-size-fits-all rational actor theories, the development practitioners and policy makers at the local, national, and international levels had more to do with creating and perpetuating the lack of development in Kenya than the "traditional" and uncooperative rural communities.

Understandably, a number of ordinary Kenyans took advantage of the development programs and projects on their own terms and without much regard for how it would impact the foreign planners' objectives and the KANU government's nation-building goals. The 4-K program, a 1962 development initiative designed to "build a respect for the land" among the educated and landed young Kenyans, provided disadvantaged Maragoli youths with opportunities to explore towns outside of western Kenya while acquiring skills at the Farmers' Training Centers free of charge.[7] Maragoli farmers who utilized the Friends Africa Mission's Rural Service Program's services received access to hybrid maize seeds, as well as personal hands-on training from mission agriculturalists in the mid-1950s and throughout the 1960s. Chavakali high school had become a "beacon of hope" for Maragoliland parents by the start of the Kenyatta administration in 1963. Although this *harambee* project was a contentious enterprise for several local residents, the Maragoli Luhya community appreciated having a secondary school that was closer to home (and thus more affordable) for their children to receive the education necessary to garner a good job in an independent Kenya. At the same time, entrepreneurially-minded rural Maragolis who recognized the social and economic benefits of owning land, regardless of the land's condition and location, steadfastly applied for the Lugari Settlement Scheme.

Rural Kenyans, especially in Maragoliland, were therefore practical when approaching the developmentalist state's efforts to kick-start an agrarian revolution. Being pragmatic gave them access to coveted resources, which they willingly used to establish a standard of living that was comfortable for themselves and their family members. The agendas of nation-builders and the ulterior motives of developers mattered little to ordinary Maragolis because they, too, had their own unique reasons for partaking in and carrying out activities aimed at making "agribusiness" and farm living popular. Their choices were driven more by their own realities and immediate needs than by a desire to help the late colonial government or the newly-independent state ease social, economic, and political tensions.

However, while opportunistic rural Kenyans appropriated the agricultural development initiatives of the decolonization era, they were also keenly aware that their political leaders, along with Kenya's development planners, often championed and implemented unsustainable projects and schemes. In many ways this action was deliberate, especially on the part of elite politicians and development agents motivated to maintain special privileges and powers available to them resulting from Kenya's development decade. Due to the geopolitical climate of the Cold War, Kenya's decolonization era was marked by an unprecedented level of assistance from the international community, especially from Great Britain and the United States. Foreign powers expected that their benevolence, which came in the form of financial aid and technical "experts," would help transform Kenya into a politically stable and economically viable (Western) nation-state. As a result, Kenya's leaders and development partners had ample funds and resources to dedicate to national "development" throughout the 1950s and 1960s.

In theory, this international bolstering meant instituting policies and programs aiming to address the grievances that everyday Kenyans had at the twilight of colonial rule. In practice, however, this sponsorship often gave incentive to the developmentalists to implement schemes that protected their own interests while catering to the (economic) interests of their international development sponsors. For a number of elite politicians and their foreign allies (both secular and religious), the business of development ensured them well-paying, exciting, and morally gratifying careers. This particular outlook encouraged development specialists, along with national leaders, to brush aside the expectations and realities of the very groups of people they aimed to help with their projects and programs. This naiveté, in turn, led to the establishment of ineffective rural development projects that were nonstarters from the outset.

Not all of the Kenyan leaders who came to power during the Cold War era, to be clear, shared the economic values and practices of Kenya's Western donors. There were figures in the inaugural Kenyatta administration who were vocal about the fact that the *uhuru* government needed to create development policies that seriously addressed ordinary peoples' grievances rather than satisfying the expectations of the British government and the Cold War superpowers. Oginga Odinga, then Vice President, along with Bildad Kaggia, then Assistant Minister for Education, were among the top officials within the first government of independent Kenya to publicly question the validity of their administration's positive non-alignment stance vis-à-vis the country's position in the Cold War conflict. In fact, in April 1966, Odinga forcibly resigned from the KANU government because he had become completely dissociated from the pro-West and pro-capitalist leanings of his parliamentary colleagues.[8]

While Kenya's leaders politicized the process of development on the national and international stage, the men and women at the local level who were tasked by developmental organizations and agencies (both secular and religious) with "improving" the conditions of ordinary Kenyans continued their work into the post-independence era. Like the elite politicians and foreign governments, these development practitioners often established programs requiring their long-term service and guidance. In this manner, some were able to safeguard their careers and positions within the local communities in which they assisted, long after Kenya had achieved its sovereignty from Britain. Through its Stewardship Rural Service Program, for instance, the Friends Africa Mission (FAM) missionaries were able to maintain a strong presence in western Kenya during the decolonization and early independence years. It was not until the mid-1970s that FAM finally completed its Kenyanization process, which it adopted after World War II by appointing a local church member to direct its Rural Service Program. As a result, despite the number of agricultural technicians on the ground and the immense financial assistance from the international community devoted to reforming the local farming communities, Kenya's agrarian revolution hardly materialized because of self-serving individuals who understood that development was simply a business venture.

Development planners in particular seemed not to consider (or perhaps care) that poor and unskilled farmers lacked the same degree of access to abundant fertile plots of land as their more affluent and influential neighbors. Instead, the nation-builders and their development industry partners devised and implemented schemes predicated on suitable land being readily accessible to all landless Kenyans on the eve of independence. In an article written for the East African Standard newspaper's special *Uhuru* Day edition on December 12, 1963, the Minister of Agriculture, Bruce McKenzie, for instance, noted that his Ministry's newly-adopted Cash Crop Policy Plan required all rural Kenyans to take advantage of the "vast tracts of good and fertile land" that were "virtually empty and unused." McKenzie argued that the majority of Kenya's subsistence farmers would benefit greatly if they embraced his advice, because they would have the necessary resource—land—to be able to double their agricultural exports and thus increase their annual household income by £35.[9] McKenzie's comments demonstrate the lack of facts and, more importantly, the lack of empathy some government officials showed regarding the problems facing the majority of rural Kenyans at independence for which the colonial government was largely responsible; namely, the inequalities related to accessing arable (and reasonable size) plots of land.

Access to productive land had been problematic for ordinary Kenyans, especially the residents of Maragoliland, since the establishment of the colonial state at the beginning of the twentieth century. Encouraged by the influential European settler community, the colonial administration instituted unfair legislation and practices in order to provide settlers with secure and stable access to land. As chapter 2 noted, the establishment of the "native reserves" in the 1920s allowed British immigrants, such as McKenzie, to expropriate and alienate large tracts of fertile land from the indigenous communities. This imperial construct tied ethnicity to land by confining Kenya's "tribes" to their specific "home lands," which were relatively non-productive and congested areas with little room to absorb the population growth. Moreover, under the "native reserves" system, colonial administrators overlooked individual property rights of local famers by self-servingly upholding the pretense that the "natives" observed collective land tenure practices. Unsurprisingly, under this land policy, Kenya's colonial administration faced a growing African population that was frustrated with the congestion and infertile soil in their respective reserves, along with dissatisfied with their status as communal land holders.

It was not until 1951, with pressure from the Colonial Office, that Nairobi officials began to shift their attitudes about African private land ownership.[10] By 1955, the colonial regime officially reversed its policy on individual land tenure in the "native" reserves as a way to ensure a rural support base against the Mau Mau insurgents. The colonial administration's attitude changed with the adoption of the Swynnerton Plan, which stipulated that the colonial regime must endorse land consolidation and encourage individual land tenure, specifically among the Kikuyu community that was mostly involved in the Mau Mau crisis.[11] The consolidation of land and thus the registration of individual legal title was a means by which the colonial regime aimed to economically develop while also politically stabilizing the rural sector. Colonial officials hypothesized that land consolidation and registration would create a conservative middle class of cash-crop farmers empowered to increase agricultural exports and to provide employment for the landless.

However, the administration's encouragement of individual land tenure exacerbated Kenya's land issue at the local level and created tensions within households. Families often disagreed about whose name would go on the deed, and therefore who would have complete access to the loans and resources associated with having a legal title to the family's consolidated landholding.[12] In this manner, the colonial regime contributed to the land grievances keenly felt by poor Kenyans, who at independence had found it nearly impossible to acquire productive land because of its scarcity and cost.

While Kenya's land crisis had its roots in the colonial period, the transition government of 1961–63, and eventually the 1963 *uhuru* administration, intensified the issue by implementing a land resettlement and transfer program in the early 1960s. The ambitious Million Acre Scheme program, which was a national and international undertaking, was supposed to provide the overwhelming number of landless and unemployed Kenyans with access to planned farm units on former European settler estates. Yet, as shown in chapter 6, the architects of the MAS program created a development project that catered largely to landed rural Kenyans with capital and farming experience. The high-density Lugari Settlement Scheme in particular did little to support the majority of subsistence farm households in Maragoliland. Individuals from these homesteads, that is households with holdings that were less than two acres, often could not afford the Scheme's expenses. To be considered for the LSS, applicants had to pay registration fees that ranged between Shs.80/- to Shs.114/-.[13] These costs made joining the Scheme nearly impossible for poor Maragoliland residents who on average made Shs. 2/- per day as farm laborers.

Nonetheless, politicians, primarily from the ruling KANU party, upheld this problematic land settlement and transfer Scheme. They did so because it allowed them to showcase to constituencies and, more importantly, to international donors like the World Bank, that the government was taking steps to develop the country. Put simply, like many of the agrarian-focused projects of the development decade, the Lugari Settlement Scheme met the needs of the developers and the political elite more than it resolved the problems facing ordinary Kenyans. Consequently, the agricultural revolution that was supposed to have taken off in 1960s sub-Saharan Africa in general and in western Kenya in particular did not do so because of the international, national, and local sectors' interests all simultaneously at play.

Contemporary policy makers, practitioners, and scholars of development have overlooked that "development" constituted different things to different groups of people, especially to the "underdeveloped" local communities. Instead, the conversations about development and aid in Africa have largely been presentist and focused too heavily on how agricultural development in sub-Saharan Africa has "failed." Yet, when development is viewed as a form of historical change, then it becomes noticeable that this particular "change" is never entirely "good" or "bad." The actions, experiences, and motivations of rural Maragoliland residents during the decolonization and early independence era reveal that the development process was anything but unilateral and straightforward. Hence, the outcomes of Africa's development decade should not be measured using generalizations and metrics like GDP that reveal little about who was helped, who was hurt, and who may have found opportunities in programs intended for economic and social change.

Moreover, to see the lack of an agricultural revolution and rural development solely in terms of failed state production or as the result of "gate-keepers," ignores other dynamics at work, especially at the local level, which also shaped plans and projects. Observing the ways in which the farm schemes of the 1950s and 1960s actually played out "on the ground" reveals that rural development was a malleable process with several end results and possibilities. Opportunistic individuals, governments, and organizations (secular and religious) complicated development projects with their own experiences, motivations, and expectations for Kenya's independence era. The development table was crowded with multiple parties, each with very different understandings of the nature and purpose of development at *uhuru*.

If contemporary development specialists and nation-builders such as Waikenda, along with aid organizations such as the Gates Foundation, want to meet their own objectives, they have a far more likely chance of doing so if they pay closer attention to the various interpretations and notions of "development" that exist, and if they listen to local communities and incorporate the local people's agendas into their projects and policies that aim to bring about an agrarian revolution. Furthermore, it is worthwhile for the participants of the development industry to explore the following questions: What exactly is the purpose of development in the global South? Is development a project specifically aiming to reduce poverty and improve the lives of the poor? Is it a project that ultimately allows for national governmental elites, international agencies, and outside "specialists" and technocrats to sustain their particular interests and to maintain their comfortable lifestyles? To do so would require a more nuanced understanding of the underlying factors perpetuating the "underdevelopment" of Africa and would encourage honest introspection about their own agendas for the people of the global South.

Appendix

Interviewee Information

Name (Males)	Land in Maragoli	Occupation in 1963	Name (Females)	Land in Maragoli	Occupation in 1963
Alfred Machyo	>5	Senior Ag. Officer	Trofosa Kaneri	<5	Tailor (rural)
Andrew Mukulu	3	Teacher (rural)	Teresa Lukalo	>5	Tailor (rural)
Gerisom Alukwri	<5	Teacher (rural)	Salina Kenyani	>5	Supermarket Clerk (Nairobi)
David Khatela	2	Ag. Field Officer	Rachel Sabwa	6	Community Leader (rural)
David Sagala	<5	Police Officer/ Farmer	Rachel Zavani	<5	Student
Ellam Kitambaya	>5	Security Guard (Nairobi)	Rachel Amudava	>5	Farmer
Herbert Abwogi	1	Bank/Teacher (Nairobi/ Rural)	Melice Onyango	0.37	Farmer
Jethro Luseno	2	Dental Tech	Mary Ganira	<5	Student
Joram Chvasuh	0.29	Teacher (rural)	Kesyia Mwasiagi	2.5	Farmer

(continued)

Name (Males)	Land in Maragoli	Occupation in 1963	Name (Females)	Land in Maragoli	Occupation in 1963
Joseph Edalia	0	FAM field Officer	Keran Magunamu	3.25	Farmer
Joram Kaiga	>5	Meteorologist (Nairobi)	Julia Awinjah	2	Teacher
Joseph Otiende	20	MP (Nairobi)	Jones Ndagadwa	<5	Farmer
Nicholas Ganira	>5	Teacher (rural)	Jescar Chanyisa	2	Farmer
Peter Amalamba	>5	FAM Farm Manager	Febe Chagira	1.25	Farmer
Peter Joshua	0.8	Clerk/Asst. Ag. Officer	Febe Alumasa	1	Farmer
Pierson Zavani	>5	Student	Fanice Amaheno	4	Farmer
Robert Endusa	8	Teacher	Ester Alyo	>5	Trained Nurse
Sammy Akifuma	<5	Accountant (Nairobi)	Erastus Asithua	1.1	Student
Timuna Mido	7	"Progressive Farmer"	Epharina Esabu	2	Farmer
Zakaria Esabu	>5	Migrant Laborer	Betty Alukwri	<5	Student
William Onyango	0.37	Farmer	Dina Esolio	>5	Nursing Student

Notes

Introduction

1. The independent government was under the control of the dominant political party, Kenya African National Union (KANU), which was headed by Jomo Kenyatta who served as the first Prime Minister until December 12, 1964 when Kenya effectively became a Republic, with Kenyatta as its first President.
2. Kenyatta, "Back to the land," 60.
3. Swynnerton, *A Plan to Intensify the Development of African Agriculture in Kenya*, 7–15; Kenya Government, *African Socialism and Its Applications to Planning Kenya*, 36–39.
4. World Bank, *The Economic Development of Kenya*, 2.
5. Agriculture and economic development was intricately linked by nationalist leaders and development economists steeped in modernization theory during the 1950s and 1960s. Modernization theorists, such as Walt Rostow, emphasized that capital accumulation via commercial agriculture was the launching pad for industrialization, and thus encouraged the newly-independent African governments to support the economic viability of progressive cash farmers and to preserve existing large-scale commercial farms rather than build industry. Increasing the country's production of export crops would allow "traditional" societies to supply more food to their growing populations, expand markets, as well as provide funds to support a modern industrial sector. See Rostow, *The Stages of Economic Growth*, 1–17.
6. Mwasiagi, interview with the author.
7. Onyango, interview with the author.
8. District Officials, "Village Surveys: Bunyore, Nyangori, Maragoli, Tiriki, Boholo, January 30, 1960."
9. Luseno, interview with the author.
10. Kenyatta, *Harambee!*, "Speech in Machakos District," 62.
11. Kenya African National Union and Jomo Kenyatta, *The K.A.N.U. Manifesto*, 18.
12. Bates, *Markets and States in Tropical Africa*; Lal, *The Poverty of Development Economics*; Sachs, *The End of Poverty*; Easterly, "Africa's Growth Tragedy," 1203–50; Moyo, *Dead Aid: Why Aid Is Not Working and How There Is a Better*

Way for Africa; Henly, "Rural Development in South-East Asia and sub-Saharan Africa," 25–47.

13. Mkandawire, "Running While Others Walk," 4; Thomas, "Development as Practice in a Liberal Capitalist World," 773–87.
14. Cooper, "Writing the History of Development," 10.
15. Seers, "The Meaning of Development," 2.
16. Owen, *English Philanthropy,* 1–7.
17. Bourdillon, "Colonial Development and Welfare," 369–80; CT. "The Economic Development of the British Colonial Empire," 139–45.
18. Wicker, "Colonial Development and Welfare, 1929–1957: The Evolution of a Policy," 174.
19. Milburn, "The Fabian Society and the British Labour Party," 338–39.
20. Creech-Jones, "The British Experiment in Colonial Development and Welfare," 559.
21. Low and Lonsdale, "Introduction," 12–16.
22. Wicker, "Colonial Development and Welfare, 1929–1957: The Evolution of a Policy," 185.
23. Spulber, *Foundations of Soviet Strategy for Economic Growth*; Bagchi, "Developing Planning," 98.
24. Robinson, *African Development Planning*; Todaro, Development Planning, 1–5; Hira and Parfitt, *Development Projects for a New Millennium*, 2–5.
25. Rostow, *The Stages of Economic Growth,* 20–22.
26. Kenya's concept of African Socialism, for example, was in direct contrast to Tanzania's understanding of African Socialism or *Ujamaa*, which was a moral philosophy rather than an economic and socio-political theory. See Nyerere, "Ujamma," 238–48; *African Socialism and its Application to Planning in Kenya*, 26–27.
27. Kierman, "Economic Planning Becomes Fashionable in Kenya, July 23, 1962."
28. Mboya, "The Future of Kenya," 6–12.
29. "New Settlers Face Problems of Squatters," *East Africa Standard*, September 10, 1963; "Stock market Gloom Remains," *East African Standard*, February 2, 1962; "Kenya's Vast Army of Unemployed People," *East African Standard*, July 26, 1963.
30. Packard and Cooper, "Introduction," 10.
31. Lewis, *The Theory of Economic Growth*, 5; Seers, "The Congruence of Marxism and other Neoclassical Doctrines," 37–8.
32. Streeten, "Development Ideas in Historical Perspective," 26–7; Sen, "The Concept of Development," 10–24.
33. Seers, "The Meaning of Development," 2.
34. Singer and Jolly, "Employment, Incomes and Equality: Lessons of the ILO Employment Strategy Mission to Kenya," 121–34.
35. Bauer, *Equality, the Third World, and Economic Delusion.*

36. African Strategy Review Group, *Accelerated Development in sub-Saharan Africa*, 24–45.
37. Sachs, *Investing in Development*, 1–19.
38. Grubbs, *Secular Missionaries*; Ekbladh, *The Great American Mission;* Escobar, *Encountering Development.*
39. Ferguson, *The Anti-Politics Machine.*
40. Scott, *Seeing like a State.*
41. Bowman, "Mass Production or Production by the Masses?," 201–21.
42. Hyden, *Beyond Ujamaa in Tanzania*; Berry, *Fathers Work for their Sons*; Mandala, *Work and Control in a Peasant Economy.*
43. Aerni-Flessner, "Self-Help Development Projects and Conceptions of Independence in Lesotho, 1950s–1970s," 11–33.
44. McCullers, "Like Biscuits in Wrappers: Apartheid Development and Decolonization in South West Africa, 1962–1968," 59–78.
45. Lal, *African Socialism in Postcolonial Tanzania.*
46. Isaacman and Isaacman, *Dams, Displacement and the Delusion of Development.*
47. Hodgkin, *Nationalism in Colonial Africa*; Anderson, *Issues of Political Development.*
48. Ranger, *Peasant Consciousness and Guerrilla War in Zimbabwe;* Kanogo, *Squatters and the Roots of Mau Mau*; Furedi, *The Mau Mau War in Perspective*; Geiger, *TANU Women.*
49. Haugerud, *The Culture of Politics in Modern Kenya*; Parsons, "The Limits of Sisterhood," 143–58.
50. Schler, *Nations on Board*; Tague, "Displaced Agents of Development," 121–45.
51. Anderson, *Imagined Communities.*
52. Hastings, *A History of African Christianity*; examples from the edited collection include: Tuma, "Major Changes and Development in Christian Leadership in Busoga Province, Uganda 1960–74," 60–78; Stuart, *British Missionaries and the End of Empire: East, Central, and Southern Africa, 1939–1964*; Stanley, *The Bible and the Flag.*
53. See Western Kenya Map.
54. District Officials, "North Nyanza District Statistics, 1951 Census."
55. See Appendix.
56. Morris, "Friends Africa Mission Report."
57. Russell, "Oral History Methodology."

Chapter One

1. Mwasiagi, interview with the author.
2. Anderson, "Depression, Dust Bowl, Demography and Drought," 321–43.

3. Tiffen, *More People, Less Erosion*; Maxon, *Going Their Separate Ways*; Shanguhyia, *Population, Tradition, and Environmental Control in Colonial Kenya.*
4. Anderson, *Histories of the Hanged*, 119–81.
5. Swynnerton, *A Plan to Intensify the Development of African Agriculture in Kenya*, 10.
6. Harbenson, *Nation-Building in Kenya*, 32; Parsons, "Being Kikuyu in Meru," 45–64.
7. Swynnerton, *A Plan to Intensify the Development of African Agriculture in Kenya*, 1.
8. Elkins, *Imperial Reckoning: The Untold Story of Britain's Gulag in Kenya*, 91–121; Sorrenson, Land Reform in Kikuyu Country, 113.
9. Ongoli, "Land Consolidation, January 16, 1958."
10. Machayo, interview with the author.
11. Jones, "The Decolonization of the White Highlands of Kenya," 188; Machayo, interview with the author.
12. Director of Intelligence and Security, "Land Consolidation—North Nyanza, March 21, 1957."
13. Berry, *No Condition is Permanent*, 86.
14. Sorrenson, Land Reform in Kikuyu Country, 227.
15. Ogot, "The Decisive Years 1956–63," 48.
16. Anderson, "'Yours in Struggle for Majimbo,'" 550.
17. North Nyanza District Commissioner, "Synopsis of North Nyanza District." Otiende, interview with the author.
18. Gertzel, *The Politics of Independent Kenya*, 1–48; Anderson, "'Yours in Struggle for Majimbo'"
19. "East Africa Royal Commission," 19, quoted in Harbenson, *Nation-Building in Kenya*, 54.
20. Kenya African National Union, *The KANU. Manifesto for Independence, Social Democracy, and Stability*, 1.
21. Ibid, 10–11.
22. Wandibba, *Masinde Muliro*, 16.
23. Odinga, *Not Yet Uhuru.*
24. Wasserman, *Politics of Decolonization*, 157–59.
25. KADU's political ideology of *majimboism* (regionalism) rested on having Kenya administered under a federal system of government whereby six regional assemblies and a capital territory were to be given equal power. KADU politicians hoped that this arrangement would protect the interests of smaller minority groups, including those of the European settlers, from being dominated by the larger Luo and Kikuyu ethnic communities that constituted the KANU party. See Anderson, "'Yours in Struggle for Majimbo,'" 547; Arnold, *Kenyatta and the Politics of Kenya*, 25.
26. Jones, *The Decolonization of the White Highlands of Kenya,* 192.

27. Ibid, 190; Wasserman, *Politics of Decolonization*, 155–57.
28. Odinga, *Not Yet Uhuru*, 300–305; Branch, *Kenya,* 60.
29. Widner, *The Rise of a Party-State in Kenya*, 39–72.
30. "Draft Sessional Paper, I.B.R.D. Report, Chapter 4—Agriculture," 58.
31. Republic of Kenya, *Kenya Development Plan, 1965/66 to 1969/70.*
32. Hodge, *Triumph of the Expert.*
33. MacKenzie, "Betterment and the Gendered Politics of Maize Production, Murang'a District, Central Province, Kenya, 1880–1952," 73–74; Anderson, *Eroding the Commons.*
34. Spencer, "Settler Dominance, Agricultural Production and the Second World War in Kenya," 497–514.

Chapter Two

1. Fearn, *An African Economy*; Ogot, "British Administration in the Central Nyanza District of Kenya, 1900–60," 249–73.
2. Kenya Regional Boundaries Commission, *Report of the Regional Boundaries Commission.*
3. District Officials, "North Nyanza District Statistics, 1951 Census."
4. Were, *A History of the Abaluyia of Western Kenya*, 56–60.
5. MacArthur, *Cartography and The Political Imagination,* 87–110.
6. Spear, "Neo-Traditionalism and the Limits of Invention in British Colonial Africa," 3–27; Berman & Lonsdale, *Unhappy Valley*, 267–68.
7. Were, *A History of the Abaluyia of Western Kenya*, 60.
8. MacArthur, "The Making and Unmaking of African Languages," 172.
9. North Nyanza District Commissioner, "Synopsis of North Nyanza District, November 23, 1961."
10. MacArthur, *Cartography and The Political Imagination,* 110–34.
11. Williams, "Memorandum on the Subject of Over Population in the Maragoli and Bunyore Locations, 1952."
12. For more on the Mau Mau civil war see Branch, *Defeating Mau Mau, Creating Kenya*; Anderson, *Histories of the Hanged.*
13. Wagner, "Maragoli Land Tenure."
14. Brown, "Maragoli 10 Year Plan, 1956–1966"; District Officials, "North Nyanza District Statistics, 1951 Census."
15. Brown, "Maragoli 10-Year Plan, 1956–1966."
16. Zavani, Rachel and Pierson, interview with the author.
17. Miller and Yeager, *Kenya,* 14–15.
18. Ominde, *Land and Population Movements in Kenya*, 27.
19. Berry, "Hegemony on a Shoestring," *Africa*, 62, 327–55.
20. Mamdani, *Citizen and Subject,* 62–109.

21. Carter, *Report of the Kenya Land Commission*, 287.
22. Parsons, "Local Responses to the Ethnic Geography of Colonialism in the Gusii Highlands of British-Ruled Kenya," 58, 491–523.
23. Kanogo, *Squatters and the Roots of Mau Mau.*
24. Carter, *Report of the Kenya Land Commission*, 287–88.
25. United Nations, "Declaration Regarding Non-Self Governing Territories."
26. Low and Lonsdale, "Introduction," 12–16.
27. Berry, *No Condition Is Permanent,* 48–49; MacKenzie, "Betterment and the Gendered Politics of Maize Production, Murang'a District, Central Province, Kenya, 1880–1952," 73–74.
28. Saccio, "ICA Paper on U.S. Assistance to Tropical Africa for Mr. Dillon"; Withers, "U.S. Aid to East Africa"; Dan Beane, interview with the author.
29. Kay, "The Southern Abaluyia, The Friends Africa Mission, and the Development of Education in Western Kenya 1902–1965," 78.
30. Ibid, 64–65.
31. Ibid, 79; Rasmussen, *A History of the Quaker Movement in Africa*, 39.
32. Kay, "The Southern Abaluyia, The Friends Africa Mission, and the Development of Education in Western Kenya 1902–1965," 64.
33. Hotchkiss, *Sketches from the Dark Continent.*
34. "Friends Africa Industrial Mission First Report, 1903," in Printer, *The Hill of Vision,* 24.
35. Chilson, "Friends Africa Industrial Report, October 16, 1904."
36. Simkin, interview with the author.
37. Rasmussen, *A History of the Quaker Movement in Africa*, 108–10.
38. Kay, "The Southern Abaluyia, The Friends Africa Mission, and the Development of Education in Western Kenya 1902–1965," 95.
39. Parsons, *Race, Resistance, and the Boy Scout Movement in British Colonial Africa*, 15.
40. Rasmussen, *A History of the Quaker Movement in Africa*, 102.
41. Ibid., 102.
42. Friends Africa Mission Board, "Letter to Rodney and Joan Morris, February 18, 1955."
43. Rice, "Location Statistics Table."

Chapter Three

1. Maxwell, "The Relationship of Social Differentiation to Academic Success in Secondary School and Occupational Patterns in Kenya," 166.
2. Chavasuh, interview with the author; Ngala, "KADU," *East African Standard*, July 6, 1962; "Mr. Odinga is quoted: Oust Colonialists," *East African* Standard, February 7, 1962.

3. Morris, "Letter from Rodney Morris, American Friends (Quaker) Mission Board, 1958."
4. Macris, "Kenya and East Africa," 1.
5. Cooper, *Africa Since 1940*, 4.
6. Mutongi, *Worries of the Heart,* 1–6. As others have shown elsewhere, ethnic patriots and cultural brokers in the post-World War II era "invented" the Abaluhya (or Luyia) ethnicity as a means to actively participate in the imperial project of charting African communities and identities. See MacArthur, *Cartography and the Political Imagination*; Spear, "Neo-Traditionalism and the Limits of Invention in British Colonial Africa," 3–27.
7. Rice, "Location Statistics Table, 1951."
8. Morris, "Transcript of Tape Correspondence to Mildred White."
9. "Project Proposal and Approval—Explanation—Short—North Nyanza Education Department."
10. "Minutes of the 1st Meeting of the AD Hoc Board of Governors of Chavakali High School."
11. "Minutes of a Meeting to Discuss the Proposed Establishment of a Day Secondary School at Chavakali."
12. Morris, "Letter from Rodney Morris, American Friends (Quaker) Mission Board, 1958."
13. Alunga, interview with the author.
14. "Letter from Matthew Mwenesis to Mr. C. O. Kilasi, Kyavakali Day Secondary School."
15. Esabu, interview with the author.
16. Ibid.
17. Magunamu, interview with the author.
18. Ibid.
19. "Letter from James Mage Aluda to Chief of North Maragoli, 'RE: Claim of My Table'"
20. Magunamu, interview with the author.
21. "Memorandum on the Proposal to establish a Day Secondary School, Chavakali, North Maragoli."
22. Chavasuh, interview with the author.
23. Hoskins, *Chavakali*, 3.
24. Jones and Phelps-Stokes Fund, *African Education Commission.*
25. Peterson, *Creative Writing*, 139–63.
26. Marcis, "Kenya and East Africa," 1.
27. Mulinidi, "Day Secondary School Development in North Maragoli, Delegation."
28. Ibid.
29. Brown, "A straight Look at Some Hard Facts, Appendix III"; Leys, *Underdevelopment in Kenya: The Political Economy of Underdevelopment 1964–71*, 28–62.

30. Macris, "Kenya and East Africa—Agricultural Courses in Secondary Schools," 1.
31. Republic of Kenya, *Kenya Development Plan.*
32. Dalgleish and Kenya, *Survey of Unemployment*; Williams, "Memorandum on the Subject of Over Population in the Maragoli and Bunyore Locations 1952."
33. For more on the urban employment and youth crisis in colonial Kenya, see Cooper, *On the African Waterfront*; Willis, *Mombasa, the Swahili, and the Making of the Mijikenda.* British Colonial concerns over African urbanization and migration was not unique to Kenya. See Sheldon, "Urban African Women Courtyards, Markets, City Streets"; Burton, *African Underclass.*
34. Anderson, "The Kenya Education Commission Report."
35. Ogot, "The Decisive Years 1956–63," 48–79; Mboya, *Legislative Council Debates*, 84; Alexander, *Legislative Council Debates*, 79–80.
36. Republic of Kenya, *Kenya Development Plan.*
37. Kay, "The Southern Abaluyia, The Friends Africa Mission, and the Development of Education in Western Kenya 1902–1965," 78.
38. By 1960, the Friends Africa Mission was in charge of approximately 300 schools, the majority being primary schools, with 30 intermediate schools, a nurse training school, two teacher training schools, along with a secondary boarding school for boys. See Hoskins, *Chavakali: An Experiment in Practical Education in Kenya*, 3–4.
39. For a discussion of the establishment of the Friends Africa Mission in western Kenya, see Rasmussen, *A History of the Quaker Movement in Africa.*
40. Rasmussen, *A History of the Quaker Movement in Africa.* 2.
41. Indire, "A Comprehensive High School Curriculum Proposal for Reviewing and Revising the Program of Chavakali Secondary School, Maragoli, Kenya," 45.
42. Printer, "Opportunities for Friends in Kenya," 200; Marcis, "Kenya and East Africa," 2.
43. Morris, "Letter to Family, April 2, 1960."
44. Maxwell, "The Relationship of Social Differentiation to Academic Success in Secondary School," 12.
45. Beane, interview with the author.
46. Chavakali School's opening, for example, occurred on the heels of the 1958 national elections that brought to power vocal nationalists like Tom Mboya and Oginga Odinga. Moreover, within the school's first few years of operation, events like Harold MacMillan's famous "winds of change" speech to the South African Parliament in 1960 ultimately led Kenya into the 1960, 1962, and the 1963 Lancaster House Conferences in London. Such events allowed Kenya to achieve its political independence from Great Britain faster than previously envisioned by the Colonial Office. See Ogot, "The Decisive Years 1956–63."

47. Magunamu, interview with the author.
48. Morris, "Letter to Family, April 2, 1960."
49. Maxwell, "The Relationship of Social Differentiation to Academic Success in Secondary School," 70–75.
50. Luseno, interview with the author.
51. *Legislative Council Debates* 86, "The Egerton Agricultural College (Amendment) Bill, December 7, 1960," 910.
52. Ganira, interview with the author.
53. Magunamu, interview with the author.
54. Akifuma, interview with the author.
55. Luseno, interview with the author.
56. Chavasuh, interview with the author.

Chapter Four

1. Zavani, interview with the author.
2. Ibid.
3. "Kenya 4-K Clubs Constitution and Rules."
4. Porter, "Recommendations on Rural Education Arising out of a Tour of Nyanza and Central Provinces, August 22–26, 1956."
5. Litwiller, "Proceedings of the Third Annual National 4-K Program Planning Meeting, January 12–15, 1965."
6. Cooper, *Africa Since 1940*, 91–98.
7. "Kenya 4-K Clubs Constitution and Rules."
8. Odinga, *Not Yet Uhuru*, 283–84; Withers, "U.S. Aid to East Africa."
9. "Kenya Agricultural Projects 615–11–008 and 615–11–002: A Synopsis"; Saccio, "FY 1961 Economic Aid Program for fund for Cooperative Assistance to Africa."
10. Finkelstein, *United States Policy with Respect to Economic Development of Non-Self-Governing Territories*; "US–UK 115 (K) Economic Cooperation Act, June 25, 1953"; Withers, "U.S. Aid to East Africa." For more insights on the extensive aid programs offered by the American and British governments to emerging nation-states in sub-Saharan Africa, see Percox, *Britain, Kenya and the Cold War*; Grubbs, *Secular Missionaries.*
11. Skiles, "Memorandum on AID," National Archives at College Park.
12. "All Foreign Aid is Welcome: KANU Seminar," *East African Standard*, June 30, 1962; Odinga, *Not Yet Uhuru*, 257–58.
13. "Department Conference on Rural Youth Clubs, Held November 7 to 9, 1962 in Conjunction with A.I.D. Extension Team."
14. Wessel and Wessel, *4-H, an American Idea, 1900–1980,* 1–25; Rosenberg, *The 4-H Harvest*, chapter 1.

15. "Department Conference on Rural Youth Clubs, Held November 7 to 9, 1962 in Conjunction with A.I.D. Extension Team."
16. Dalgleish and Kenya, *Survey of Unemployment*, 8; "Survey of Unemployment, Secretary of North Nyanza African District Council."
17. Mboya, "The future of Kenya," 6–12.
18. "Kenya 4-K Clubs Constitution and Rules."
19. Swynnerton, *A Plan to Intensify the Development of African Agriculture in Kenya*, 10; Juma, "Unemployment," *East African Standard*, February 11, 1960.
20. Litwiller, "Proceedings of the Third Annual National 4-K Program Planning Meeting, January 12–15, 1965."
21. Wagema, "Proceedings of the Third Annual National 4-K Program Planning Meeting, January 12, 1965."
22. "Principles of Extension Rural Youth Work Applied to Africa."
23. Porter, "Recommendations on Rural Education Arising out of a Tour of Nyanza and Central Provinces, August 22–26, 1956."
24. Office of the District Officer, "Comments to Unemployment Survey."
25. Morris, "Letter from Rodney Morris to Fred Reeve, September 1, 1958."
26. Morris, "Letter to Family, April 2, 1960." For more on the Young Farmers' Club Movement in the United Kingdom see Hirsch, *Young Farmers' Clubs*, 1–22; Shields and National Federation of Young Farmers' Clubs, *Youthful Forward Thinking*, 1–50.
27. "Correspondence from Bob Mills to American Friends Board of Missions Executive Committee, July 1960"; Morris, "Letter to Family, April 2, 1960."
28. Morris, "Christmas letter from Rodney Morris to Morris Family, December 1959."
29. "Minutes from Departmental Conference on Rural Youth Clubs in Conjunction with A.I.D. Extension Team."
30. "4-K Clubs: What They Do."
31. Parsons, "The Consequences of Uniformity," 363.
32. Litwiller, "Proceedings of the Third Annual National 4-K Program Planning Meeting, January 12–15, 1965."
33. Pierson Zavani, interview with the author; Ganira, interview with the author.
34. "Department Conference on Rural Youth Clubs, Held November 7 to 9 1962 in Conjunction with A.I.D. Extension Team."
35. Swynnerton, *A Plan to Intensify the Development of African Agriculture in Kenya,* 214.
36. "Principles of Extension Rural Youth Work Applied to Africa."
37. "4-K Clubs: What They Do."
38. "Minutes from Departmental Conference on Rural Youth Clubs in Conjunction with A.I.D. Extension Team."
39. Rachel Zavani, interview with the author.
40. Magunamu, interview with the author.

41. "Proceedings of Third Annual National 4-K Program Meeting."
42. "Minutes from Departmental Conference on Rural Youth Clubs in Conjunction with A.I.D. Extension Team."
43. Kaneri, interview with the author.
44. Department of Agriculture, "Annual Report."
45. Kaneri, interview with the author.
46. Litwiller, "Proceedings of the Third Annual National 4-K Program Planning Meeting, 12–15 January 1965."
47. Rachel and Pierson Zavani, interview with the author.
48. "Learning by Doing in Western Kenya, July 12, 1968."
49. Chavasuh, interview with the author.
50. Ibid.
51. Rachel Zavani, interview with the author.
52. Pierson Zavani, interview with the author.
53. Litwiller, "Proceedings of the Third Annual National 4-K Program Planning Meeting, January 12–15, 1965."
54. "Learning by Doing in Western Kenya, July 12, 1968."
55. Litwiller, "Proceedings of the Third Annual National 4-K Program Planning Meeting, January 12–15, 1965."
56. Chavasuh, interview with the author.
57. Chanyisa, interview with the author.
58. Awinjah, interview with the author.
59. Machayo, interview with the author.
60. Ibid.
61. Ganira, interview with the author.
62. "Kenya 4-K Clubs Constitution and Rules."
63. "Bukura Farmers' Training Center Policy Notes."
64. "District Jeanes Schools, November 29, 1956."
65. "Bukura Farm Institute & District Jeanes School May 1957."
66. "Bukura Group Courses, May 12, 1960."
67. Agricultural Director, "Report of the Director of Agriculture, 1963."
68. Litwiller, "Proceedings of the Third Annual National 4-K Program Planning Meeting, January 12–15, 1965."
69. Ganira, interview with the author.
70. "Lugari Settlement Schemes Selection of Settlers, December 14, 1962"; Alfred Machayo, interview with the author.
71. K. H. Winter, "Bukura Training Certificates, August 24, 1956."
72. Ibid.
73. Ganira, interview with author.
74. Litwiller, "Proceedings of the Third Annual National 4-K Program Planning Meeting, January 12–15, 1965."

Chapter Five

1. Morris, "Memorandum to Members of EAYM Board and Monthly Meeting Clerks, May 31, 1962."
2. "Rural Service Program Objective."
3. Morris, "Proposal with EAYM and World Neighbors, March 1962."
4. Morris, "Memorandum to Members of EAYM Board and Monthly Meeting Clerks, May 31, 1962."
5. Young, "Letter to Rodney Morris RE: Minutes Concerning Stewardship Program, April 27, 1961."
6. "Stated Mission of Friends African Mission, October 1954."
7. Morris, "Letter to Norman E. Young, American Friends Board of Missions, May 13, 1962."
8. Morris, "Memorandum to Members of EAYM Board and Monthly Meeting Clerks, May 31, 1962."
9. Morris, "Report of Agricultural Worker to EAYM, 15 September to October 30, 1960."
10. Morris, "Proposal with EAYM and World Neighbors, March 1962."
11. Morris, "Letter to Family, October 8, 1955."
12. Ibid.
13. Simkin, interview with the author.
14. Morris, "Letter to Norman E. Young, American Friends Board of Missions, May 13, 1962."
15. Morris, "Personal Information Page, 1959."
16. Reeve, "Memo to George Scherer RE: Rod Morris Concern, February 20, 1958."
17. Tubesing, "Letter to I. W. Moomaw RE: Rodney Morris, June 22, 1961."
18. Morris, "Agricultural Development Proposal, March 2, 1958."
19. Reeve, "Memo to George Scherer RE: Rod Morris Concern, February 20, 1958."
20. Bolling, Thorp, and Hoskins, "Land Use at Kaimosi, 1958."
21. Ibid.
22. Thorp, "Discussion of Land Usage, March 6, 1959."
23. Tubesing, "Letter to I. W. Moomaw RE: Rodney Morris, June 22, 1961."
24. Morris, "Report of Agricultural Worker to EAYM, September 15 to 30 October 1960."
25. Ibid.
26. Morris, "Letter to Norman E. Young, American Friends Board of Mission, May 13, 1961."
27. World Neighbors, "Records of the World Neighbors, 1962–1980." For a thorough history of the World Neighbor's Association see Peters, *Cry Dignity!*
28. Morris, "Memorandum to Members of EAYM Board and Monthly Meeting Clerks, May 31, 1962."

29. Morris, "Stewardship Report to the East Africa Yearly Meeting of Friends for 1963–1964."
30. Morris, "Letter to Family, May 6, 1962."
31. Morris, "Proposal with EAYM and World Neighbors, March 1962."
32. Morris, "Report of the East Africa Yearly Meeting Stewardship Advisor: Submitted to Yearly Meeting Conference at Lugulu, August 1962."
33. Morris, "Memorandum to Members of EAYM Board and Monthly Meeting Clerks, May 31, 1962."
34. Morris, "Proposal with EAYM and World Neighbors, March 1962."
35. Swynnerton, *A Plan to Intensify the Development of African Agriculture in Kenya*; Ochieng', "Structural and Political Changes," 83–89.
36. Morris, "Stewardship Report to the East Africa Yearly Meeting of Friends for 1963–1964."
37. Lonsdale, Booth-Clibborn and Hake, "The Emerging Pattern of Church and State Cooperation in Kenya," 267–84.
38. Young, "Letter to Rodney Morris RE: Minutes Concerning Stewardship Program, April 27, 1961."
39. Ibid.
40. Morris, "Letter to Family, October 20, 1961."
41. Morris, "Letter to Norman E. Young, American Friends Board of Mission, May 13, 1961."
42. Morris, "Letter to Family, May 6, 1962."
43. Onyango, interview with the author.
44. Magunamu, interview with the author.
45. "More Acres for the Lord," *Time* (1941), 44.
46. For a nuanced discussion about the growth of the Lord's Acre Project in the United States and abroad, see Lowe, *Baptized with the Soil,* 96–137.
47. "More Acres for the Lord," *Time* (1941), 44.
48. Edalia, interview with the author.
49. Ombwara, "Handing Over Report Western Region, 1965."
50. Morris, "Memorandum to Members of EAYM Board and Monthly Meeting Clerks."
51. Morris, "Report of Agricultural Worker to E.A.Y.M., September 15 to October 30, 1960."
52. Morris, "Memorandum to Members of EAYM Board and Monthly Meeting Clerks."
53. Sagala, interview with the author.
54. Esabu, interview with the author.
55. Morris, "Letter to Family, February 28, 1962."
56. Morris, "Letter to Family, April 14, 1959."
57. Edalia, interview with the author.

58. Brown, "Maragoli 10 Year Plan"; "North Nyanza District Statistics, 1951 Census."
59. Ndagadwa, interview with the author.
60. Sagala, interview with the author.
61. Ndagadwa, interview with the author.
62. Sagala, interview with the author.
63. Ibid.
64. Morris, "Stewardship Report to East Africa Yearly Meeting of Friends for 1963–1964."
65. Ibid.
66. Esabu, interview with the author.
67. Magunamu, interview with the author.
68. Tiffen, *More People, Less Erosion*; Maxon, *Going Their Separate Ways,* 40.
69. Morris, "Proposal with EAYM and World Neighbors."
70. Morris, "Letter to Family, May 6, 1962."
71. Magunamu, interview with the author.
72. Esabu, interview with the author.
73. Magunamu, interview with the author.
74. "Survey of Unemployment, Secretary of North Nyanza African District Council, January 30, 1960"; Sagala, interview with the author.
75. Ndagadwa, interview with the author.
76. Morris, "Letter to Family, May 6, 1962."
77. Ndagadwa, interview with the author.
78. Magunamu, interview with the author.
79. Morris, "East Africa Yearly Meeting: Future of Stewardship Program, July 2, 1963."
80. Morris, "Letter to Family, October 30, 1966."
81. Simkin, interview with the author.

Chapter Six

1. Molenje, interview with the author.
2. Kenya National Assembly, "Vote 15—Ministry of Land Settlement and Water Resources," 705.
3. Walker, "Settlement Meeting."
4. Land Development and Settlement Board, "High Density Settlement Scheme, May 25, 1962."
5. Kenya National Assembly, *Oral Answers to Questions.*
6. Leo, "Who Benefited from the Million-Acre Scheme?" 201–22; Leys, Underdevelopment in Kenya; Harbeson, "Land Reforms and Politics in Kenya, 1954–70," 231–51.

7. Nottidge, "High Density Smallholder Settlement Scheme, July 22, 1963."
8. Nottidge and Goldsack, *The Million-Acre Settlement Scheme*, 7–12.
9. Mbithi and Barnes, *The Spontaneous Settlement Problem in Kenya*; Bradshaw, "Perpetuating Underdevelopment in Kenya," 1–28; Anderson & Lochery, "Violence and Exodus in Kenya's Rift Valley," 328–43.
10. Nottidge and Goldsack, *The Million-Acre Settlement Scheme*, 10.
11. Berman, "Ethnicity, Patronage and the African State," 26; Lonsdale, "The Moral Economy of Mau Mau"; Lonsdale, "Moral Ethnicity and Political Tribalism"; Spear, "Neo-Traditionalism and the Limits of Invention in British Colonial Africa."
12. Williams, "Memorandum on the Subject of Over Population in the Maragoli and Bunyore Locations, 1952."
13. "Talks on Kenya Bring Cautious Attitude on Stock Market," *East African Standard*, January 29, 1960; Reuters, "Terror Ends in Congo City," New York Times, July 9, 1960; "First Killing of Europeans," New York Times, July 10, 1960.
14. Anderson, "'Yours in Struggle for Majimbo,'" 553.
15. Wasserman, *Politics of Decolonization,* 157–59.
16. Chairman of the Land Development and Settlement Board, *The Land and Settlement Board*; Leo, "Who Benefited from the Million-Acre Scheme?"
17. Harbeson, *Nation-Building in Kenya*, 210–11.
18. Nottidge and Goldsack, *The Million-Acre Settlement Scheme*, 3.
19. Harbeson, *Nation-Building in Kenya*, 154.
20. J. H. A., "Proposed Legislation to Effect Changes in the Procedure for Selection of Settlers on Land Settlement Schemes, March 1965."
21. Walker, "Settlement Meeting."
22. Babu, interview with the author; Asituha, interview with the author; Machayo, interview with the author.
23. Jones, "Land Settlement in the Scheduled Areas, April 2, 1964."
24. Nottidge and Goldsack, *The Million-Acre Settlement Scheme.*
25. Kenya Legislative Council, "Vote 15-Ministry of Land Settlement and Water Resources," 705.
26. Wasserman, "Continuity and Counter-Insurgency," 210; Harbeson, Nation-Building in Kenya, 136; Leo, "Who Benefited from the Million-Acre Scheme?"
27. Chairman of the Land Development and Settlement Board, *The Land and Settlement Board,* 5.
28. Oates, "Case for Speed in Farm Take-Over," *East African Standard*, August 3, 1962.
29. Hartley, "Smallholder Scheme Lugari"; Sargent, "Letter to Mr. David H. McVey, November 24, 1966."
30. Hartley, "Smallholder Scheme Lugari."

31. Kenya Legislative Council, "Vote 15—Ministry of Land Settlement and Water Resources," 705.
32. Khatela, interview with the author; Molenje, interview with the author; Machayo, interview with the author.
33. Nottidge and Goldsack, *The Million-Acre Settlement Scheme*, 16–20.
34. District Officer, "Lugare Settlers."
35. Machayo, interview with the author.
36. District Officer, "Lugare Settlers."
37. Walker, "Settlement Meeting."
38. Nottidge, "High Density Smallholder Settlement Scheme."
39. Hartley, "Smallholder Scheme Lugari."
40. Molenje, interview with the author.
41. Walker, "Settlement Meeting."
42. Molenje, interview with the author.
43. Nottidge, "High Density Smallholder Settlement Scheme."
44. Kaiga, interview with the author; Khatela, interview with the author.
45. "Lugari Rural Christian Training Center, May 25, 1967."
46. Babu, interview with the author.
47. "Lugari Rural Christian Training Center, May 25, 1967."
48. Kaiga, interview with the author.
49. Bates, *Beyond the Miracle of the Market,* 49.
50. Republic of Kenya, *Labor Department Annual Report,* 20.
51. Kaiga, interview with the author.
52. Rachel and Pierson Zavani, interview with the author.
53. Alukwri, interview with the author.
54. Ibid.
55. Rachel and Pierson Zavani, interview with the author.
56. "Provincial General Hospital Nakuru, to Gavaghan, May 18, 1962."
57. Harbeson, *Nation-Building in Kenya*, 264.
58. Rachel and Pierson Zavani, interview with the author.
59. Walker, "Settlement Meeting."
60. Kaiga, interview with the author; Nottidge, "High Density Smallholder Settlement Scheme."
61. Republic of Kenya, *Labor Department Annual Report,* 6.
62. Walker, "Settlement Meeting."
63. Molenje, interview with the author.
64. Land Development and Settlement Board, "High Density Settlement Scheme."
65. Odinga, *Not Yet Uhuru*, 22–23; Harbeson, *Nation-Building in Kenya,* 312–13.
66. Kenya African National Union and Jomo Kenyatta. *The KANU Manifesto for Independence, Social Democracy and Stability.* 2.
67. Onyango, interview with the author.
68. Alunga, interview with the author.

69. Ibid.
70. Kenyatta, *Harambee! The Prime Minister of Kenya's Speeches,* 70.
71. Mwasiagi, interview with the author.
72. Mwanzi, "Application for a Plot in the Lugari Settlement Scheme."
73. Makhulo, "Application for a Plot in Lugari Settlement Scheme."
74. Machayo, interview with the author; Kaiga, interview with the author; Nalianya, "Settlement, February 11, 1964."
75. Nalianya, "Settlement, February 11, 1964."
76. Wawile, "Application for a Plot in Lugari Settlement Scheme."
77. Muchwingi, "Application for a Plot in Lugari Settlement Scheme."
78. Wawile, "Application for a Plot in Lugari Settlement Scheme."
79. Ibid.
80. Muchwingi, "Application for a Plot in Lugari Settlement Scheme, August 31, 1963."
81. Walker, "Settlement Metting, August 7, 1963."
82. "Constitution Chapter XII Part I."

Conclusion

1. Ministry of Development and Planning, *Economic Survey 2013 Highlights*, 41–42.
2. Ministry of Development and Planning, *Economic Survey 2014 Highlights*, 6.
3. Waikenda, "Agriculture Can Create a Million Jobs for Youth," News Outlet, January 5, 2014.
4. Kenyatta, "Back to the Land."
5. Munk, "How Warren Buffet's Son Would Feed the World," *The Atlantic*, May 2016; Harman and Williams, "International Development in Transition," *Affairs* 90 (2014), 925–41; Rosenberg, "A Green Revolution, This Time for Africa," *New York Times*, April 9, 2014; Bill and Melinda Gates Foundation, "2012 Annual Letter," January 2012, 1–10; Juma, *The New Harvest Agricultural Innovation in Africa; Christiansen and Demery, Down to Earth.*
6. Kaplan (with) Dobert et al. Area Handbook for Kenya, 77.
7. "Kenya 4-K Clubs Constitution and Rules."
8. "Mr. Odinga's Resignation Accepted," East African Standard.
9. McKenzie, "Using the Land with Care and with Wisdom."
10. Mitchell, "Land and Population in East Africa."
11. Swynnerton, *A Plan to Intensify the Development of African Agriculture in Kenya.*
12. Machayo, interview with the author.
13. Hartley, "Smallholder Scheme Lugari."

Bibliography

Archival Sources

Arthur and Kathleen Postle Archives and Friends Collection. Earlham College, Richmond, IN.

FRG 37. East Africa Yearly Meeting General Collection.
FPG1. Friends United Meeting Wider Ministries Records.

Carnegie Corporation of New York Records. Grant Files.

Columbia Rare Books and Manuscript Library. Columbia University, New York, NY.

Kenya National Archives [KNA]. Nairobi, Kenya. The file numbers listed below reflect the classification system used from 2010–16:

AB. Ministry of Community Development.
ACW. Ministry of Finance.
AK. North Nyanza.
AVS. Department of Land Adjudication. Ministry of Lands and Settlement.
AVT. Western Province.
AV. Friends Africa Mission (General).
BC. 4-K Clubs.
BV. Ministry of Agriculture.
DC/KMG. District Commissioner, Kakamega.
DC/NN. North Nyanza.
DX. Ministry of Lands and Settlement.
HB. Provincial Commissioner, Western Province.
HD. Agriculture, North Nyanza.

HP. Community Groups.
KPC/NZA. Land Consolidation, Nyanza.
MOH. Ministry of Health.

Library of the Religious Society of Friends. London, England.

East Africa Yearly Meeting Records.

Rodney Morris Family Personal Archives [RMFPA]. Cortland, NY.

Morris Family Kenya Letter Collection, 1955–1968.

HILA: The Hoover Institute Library and Archives. Stanford University, Stanford, CA:

N30: Mfilm: East African Standard Series. Kenya Country Files. KANU Series.

NACP: The National Archives at College Park, Maryland.

469: Records of the U.S. Foreign Assistance Agencies, 1948–1961.
286: Department of State.

TNA. The National Archives of the U.K.

CO 1045: Colonial Office and other Departments: Papers of Sir Christopher Cox, Educational Adviser.
CO 822: Colonial Office: East Africa: Original Correspondence, 1927–64.
FCO 141: Foreign and Commonwealth Office and Predecessors: Records of Former Colonial Administrations: Migrated Archives, 1835–2012.
M.A.F. 184: Ministry of Agriculture and Fisheries and Ministry of Agriculture, Fisheries and Food: Establishment Divisions: Registered Files, Personnel (EP Series).
OD 26: Department of Technical Co-operation and Successors: East Africa Department, 1964–75.
OD 2: Records of African and Mediterranean Departments. 1963–2006.
PREM 11: Prime Minister's Office: Correspondence and Papers, 1951–1964.
PRO 57: Public Record Office: Accessions of Records, Registered Files (Case Files).
T 236: Treasury: Overseas Finance Division.

RAC: The Rockefeller Foundation Archive Center, Sleepy Hollow, New York.

476 D: Kenya Series, National Science and Agriculture Sub Series.

RHL: University of Oxford, Bodleian Library of Commonwealth and African Studies at Rhodes House, Oxford.

MSS Afr s 746: Papers of Sir. Michael Blundell.
MSS Afr s 2282: Report by J. S. S. Rowlands.
MSS Afr s 1699: Papers of William Crawford Heaney.
MSS Afr s 531: Papers of T. Hughes Rice.
MSS Afr s 1426: Papers of Sir. Roger Swynnerton.
MSS Brit s 476: Food and Cash Crops.
MSS Brit s 478: Papers of Terence Gavaghan.

WPRC: Western Provincial Record Center, Kakamega.

ARC: Marketing Boards.
BV: Ministry of Agriculture.
DC/KMG: District Commissioner, Kakamega.
DX: Ministry of Lands and Settlement.
HA: Cash Crops.
HB: Provincial Commissioner, Western Province.
HD: Western Province Agriculture.
HN: Western Provincial Agricultural Board, District.
HP: Community Groups.
HY: African Education.
MG: Co-operative Societies.
MOH: Ministry of Health.
WD: Land Consolidation.

Oral Interviews

Interviews were conducted by author, translator noted if present, and mainly done throughout rural western Kenya from 2010 to 2016.

Abwogi, Herbert. Lugari, Kenya. April 12, 2011.
Akifuma, Sammy. Nairobi, Kenya. December 5, 2010.
Alukwri, Betty. Chavakali Location, West Maragoli, Kenya. March 28, 2011.
Alukwri, Gerishom. Chavakali Location, West Maragoli, Kenya. March 28, 2011.

Alumasa, Febe. Chavakali Location, West Maragoli, Kenya. April 20, 2011. Nicholas Lagoswa.
Alunga, Rachel Amudava. Chavakali Location, West Maragoli, Kenya. April 18, 2011. Nicholas Lagoswa.
Alyo, Ester. Chavakali Location, West Maragoli, Kenya. March 31, 2011. Nicholas Lagoswa.
Amaheno, Fanice. Chavakali Location, West Maragoli, Kenya. April 18, 2011. Nicholas Lagoswa.
Amalamba, Peter. Idaho, Kenya. March 11, 2011.
Amatangu, Zablon. Emsire, Bunyore, Kenya. April 6, 2011.
Amudava, Rachel. Chavakali Location, West Maragoli, Kenya. April 18, 2011. Nicholas Lagoswa.
Anyoso, Juliana. Chavakali Location, West Maragoli, Kenya. April 7, 2011. Nicholas Lagoswa.
Asituha, Erastus. Lugari, Kenya. April 12, 2011. Richard Amwayi.
Awinjah, Julia. Chavakali Location, West Maragoli, Kenya. March 14, 2011; May 27, 2016. Nicholas Lagoswa.
Babu, Peter. Lugari, Kenya. April 11, 2011.
Beane, Dan. Phone Interview, November 18, 2010.
Chagira, Febe Saya. Chavakali Location, West Maragoli, Kenya. April 20, 2011. Nicholas Lagoswa.
Chanyisa, Jescar Lumire. Chavakali Location, West Maragoli, Kenya. April 28, 2011. Nicholas Lagoswa.
Chavasuh, Joram. Chavakali Location, West Maragoli, Kenya. April 18, 2011; June 1, 2016.
Edalia, Joseph Omega. Chavakali Location, West Maragoli, Kenya. March 31, 2011.
Endusa, Robert. Chavakali Location, West Maragoli, Kenya. March 14, 2011. Richard Amwayi, June 1, 2016.
Esabu, Epharina. Chavakali Location, West Maragoli, Kenya. April 27, 2011.
Esolio, Dina Elizabeth. Chavakali Location, West Maragoli, Kenya. March 28, 2011.
Ganira, Mary. Kaimosi, Kenya. April 8, 2011.
Ganira, Nicholas Ben. Kaimosi, Kenya. March 9, 2011.
Kaiga, Joram. Kaimosi, Kenya. March 10, 2011.
Kaneri, Trofosa. Chavakali Location, West Maragoli, Kenya. March 28, 2011. Nicholas Lagoswa.
Kenyani, Salina. Chavakali Location, West Maragoli, Kenya. March 28, 2011. Nicholas Lagoswa.
Khatela, Agnus. Lugari, Kenya. March 11, 2011.
Khatela, Daniel. Lugari, Kenya. March 11, 2011.
Kitambaya, Ellam. Kiritui, Central Maragoli, Kenya. March 23, 2011. Richard Amwayi.
Lukalo, Teresa. Chavakali Location, West Maragoli, Kenya. March 25, 2011.

Lumire, Jescar. Chavakali Location, West Maragoli, Kenya. April 28, 2011. Nicholas Lagoswa.
Luseno, Jethro. Chavakali Location, West Maragoli, Kenya. March 17, 2011.
Machayo, Alfred. Lugari, Kenya. March 10, 2011.
Magomere, John. Emsire, Bunyore, Kenya. April 7, 2011. Richard Amwayi.
Magunamu, Keran. Chavakali Location, West Maragoli, Kenya. April 21, 2011. Nicholas Lagoswa.
Mido, Timuna. Lugari, Kenya. April 11, 2011. Richard Amwayi.
Molenje, Nathan. Lugari, Kenya. April 13, 2011. Richard Amwayi.
Mukulu, Andrew. Chavakali Location, West Maragoli, Kenya. April 20, 2011. Nicholas Lagoswa.
Musera, Zipurah. Lugari, Kenya. April 13, 2011. Richard Amwayi.
Musiewze, Zakaria Esabu. Chavakali Location, West Maragoli, Kenya. April 28, 2011. Nicholas Lagoswa.
Mwasiagi, Kesyia. Chavakali Location, West Maragoli, Kenya. April 19, 2011. Nicholas Lagoswa.
Namoro, Zablon Andoyi. Emsire, Bunyore, Kenya. April 7, 2011. Richard Amwayi.
Ndagadwa, Jones. Chavakali Location, West Maragoli, Kenya. April 28, 2011. Nicholas Lagoswa.
Onyango, Melice. Chavakali Location, West Maragoli, Kenya. April 21, 2011. Nicholas Lagoswa.
Onyango, William. Chavakali Location, West Maragoli, Kenya. April 21, 2011, Nicholas Lagoswa.
Otiende, Joseph. Mbale, Kenya. March 21, 2011.
Sabwa, Rachel. Chavakali Location, West Maragoli, Kenya. March 15, 2011. Richard Amwayi.
Sagala, David. Chavakali Location, West Maragoli, Kenya. April 27, 2011. Nicholas Lagoswa.
Simkin, Michael E. Ithaca, New York. October 30, 2008.
Thomas, Donald. Nairobi, Kenya. November 15, 2010.
Zablon, Selpha Esmire. Bunyore, Kenya. April 7, 2011. Richard Amwayi.
Zavani, Rachel. Chavakali Location, West Maragoli, Kenya. March 26, 2011.
Zavani, Pierson. Chavakali Location, West Maragoli, Kenya. March 26, 2011.

Primary Sources

Government Publications and Reports

African Strategy Review Group. *Accelerated Development in sub-Saharan Africa: An Agenda for Action*. Washington, D.C.: International Bank for Reconstruction and Development, 1981.

Alexander, R. S. "Kenya's Economic Situation." *Legislative Council Debates* 84. 24 March 1960.

Chairman of the Land Development and Settlement Board. *The Land and Settlement Board: How the Board* Operates. Nairobi: Government Printer, 1962.

Dalgleish, A. G., and Kenya. *Survey of Unemployment*. Nairobi: Government Printer, 1960.

District Officials. "North Nyanza District Statistics, 1951 Census."

District Officials. "Village Surveys: Bunyore, Nyangori, Maragoli, Tiriki, Boholo, January 30, 1960."

District Officials. *Proceedings of Third Annual National 4-K Program Meeting*, January 12–15.

Finkelstein, Lawrence S. *United States Policy with Respect to Economic Development of Non-Self-Governing Territories*.

International Labour Office. *Employment, Incomes and Equality: A Strategy for Increasing Productive Employment in Kenya*. Geneva: International Labour Office, 1972.

Kaplan, Irving and Margarita K. Dobert. *Area Handbook for Kenya*. Second Edition. Washington, DC: American University, 1976.

Kenya African National Union and Jomo Kenyatta. *The KANU Manifesto for Independence, Social Democracy and Stability*. Cairo: Dar El-Hana, Press 1960.

Kenya Ministry of Economic Planning and Community Affairs. *Motion [on] Sessional Paper No. 10 of 1963/65, African Socialism and Its Application to Planning in Kenya*.

Kenya National Assembly. *Kenya Legislative Council Debates*.

Kenya Regional Boundaries Commission. *Report of the Regional Boundaries Commission*. Nairobi: Government Printer, 1962.

Mboya, Tom. "The Future of Kenya." *African Affairs* 63, no. 250 (January 1964): 6–12.

Ministry of Agriculture and Animal Husbandry. "4-K Clubs: What They Do."

———. "Department Conference on Rural Youth Clubs, Held November 7 to 9, 1962 in Conjunction with A.I.D. Extension Team," n.d.

———. "District Jeanes School, July 23, 1957."

Ministry of Development and Planning. *Economic Survey 2013 Highlights*. Nairobi, Kenya: Kenya National Bureau of Statistics, December 2013.

———. *Economic Survey 2014 Highlights*. Nairobi, Kenya: Kenya National Bureau of Statistics, April 29, 2014.

Republic of Kenya. Kenya Agricultural Projects 615-11-008 and 615-11-002: A Synopsis. Nairobi: Government Printer, 1960.

Republic of Kenya. *Kenya Development Plan, 1965/66 to 1969/70*. Nairobi: Ministry of Economic Planning and Development, 1966.

Republic of Kenya. *Education Commission Report II*. Nairobi: Government Printer, 1965.

Republic of Kenya. *Kenya 4-K Clubs Constitution and Rules*. Nairobi: Government Printer, 1962.

Republic of Kenya, *Labor Department Annual Report*. Nairobi: Government Printer.

United Kingdom. *Hansard Parliamentary Debates*, 1960–1962.

United Nations. "Declaration Regarding Non-Self Governing Territories." In *Charter of the United Nations*. Washington, DC: US Government Print Office, 1945.

United States Agency for International Development. *Program and Project Date Related to Proposed Programs-FY 1965*, 1965.

World Bank. *The Economic Development of Kenya*. Baltimore: Johns Hopkins Press, 1963.

Periodicals

The East African Standard (Nairobi)
The New York Times
Kenya Weekly News (Nairobi)
Standard Digital (Nairobi)
Time

Friends Africa Mission Documents

Bolling, Landrum, James Thorp, and Lewis Hoskins. "Land Use at Kaimosi, 1958."

Chilson, Arthur. "Friends Africa Industiral Report. October 16, 1904."

Friends Africa Mission Board. "Letter to Rodney and Joan Morris, February 18, 1955."

Kirck, Morris L. "Fees for 1961, January 9, 1960."

Mills, Bob. *Correspondence with American Friends Board of Missions Executive Committee*. July 1960.

Morris, Rodney. "Agricultural Development Proposal, March 2, 1958."

———. "Christmas Letter to Family, December 1959."

———. "East Africa Yearly Meeting: Future of Stewardship Program, July 2, 1963."

———. "Letter to American Friends (Quaker) Mission Board, 1958."

———. "Letter to Family, April 14, 1959."

———. "Letter to Family, April 2, 1960."

———. "Letter to Family, October 20, 1961."

———. "Letter to Family, February 28, 1962."

———. "Letter to Family, May 6, 1962."

———. "Letter to Family, October 30, 1966."

———. "Letter to Family, October 1960."

———. "Letter to Fred Reeve, September 11, 1958."

———. "Letter to Fred Reeve, July 15, 1958."

———. "Letter to Friends Board, October 1960."
———. "Letter to Norman E. Young, American Friends Board of Missions, May 13, 1961."
———. "Memorandum to Members of EAYM Board and Monthly Meeting Clerks, May 31, 1962."
———. "Personal Information Page, 1959."
———. "Proposal with EAYM and World Neighbors, March 1962."
———. "Friends Africa Mission Report, October 10, 1955."
———. "Report of Agricultural Worker to E.A.Y.M. September 15–October 30, 1960."
———. "Report of the East Africa Yearly Meeting Stewardship Advisor: Submitted to Yearly Meeting Conference at Lugulu, August 1962."
———. "Stewardship Report to the East Africa Yearly Meeting of Friends for 1963–1964."
———. "Transcript of Tape Correspondence to Mildred White."
Reeve, Fred. "Memo to George Scherer RE: Rod Morris Concern." February 20, 1958.
———. "Rod Morris Concern, February 20, 1958."
"Rural Service Program Objective."
"Stated Mission of Friends African Mission, October 1954."
Thorp, James. "Discussion of Land Usage, March 6, 1959."
Tubesing, Martha K. "Letter to I. W. Moomaw RE: Rodney Morris, June 22, 1961."
World Neighbors. "Records of the World Neighbors, 1962–1980."
Young, Norman E. "Letter to Rodney Morris RE: Minutes Concerning Stewardship Program, April 27, 1961."

Documents

A, J. H. "Proposed Legislation to Effect Changes in the Procedure for Selection of Settlers on Land Settlement Schemes, March 1965."
Agricultural Secretary for African Affairs. "District Jeanes Schools, November 29, 1956."
Barwell, C. W. "Bukura Farmers' Training Center Progress Report, June 23, 1961."
Barrow, J. R. "Five-Point Program for a Strong U.S. Policy in East Africa, December 7, 1954."
Bergey, Chester. "Report on Industrial Arts Curriculum, March 1961."
Bill and Melinda Gates Foundation. "2012 Annual Letter, January 2012."
"Bukura Farmers' Training Center Policy Notes, 1959–1968."
"Bukura Farm Institute & District Jeanes School, May 1957."
"Bukura Group Courses, May 12, 1960."
"Bukura Training Certificates, August 24, 1956."
Brown, Leslie H. "Maragoli 10 Year Plan 1956–1966."

———. "A Straight Look at Some Hard Facts, Appendix III."
Carey Jones, N. S. "Land Settlement in the Scheduled Areas, April 2, 1964."
"Chavakali Secondary School Student Roster, 1959."
"Comments to Unemployment Survey, March 9, 1960."
"Constitution Chapter XII Part I: The Central Land Board, March 30, 1965."
"Department Conference on Rural Youth Clubs, Held November 7 to 9, 1962 in Conjunction with A.I.D. Extension Team."
District Officer. "Lugare Settlers, May 25, 1962."
Director of Intelligence and Security. "Land Consolidation—North Nyanza, March 21, 1957."
"Draft Sessional Paper, I.B.R.D. Report, Chapter 4." Finkelstein, Lawrence S. "United States Policy With Respect to Economic Development of Non-Self-Governing Territories, December 29, 1949."
Friedmann, Wolfgang G. "Public International Development Financing in East Africa (Kenya, Tanganyika, Uganda), January 1962."
Hartley, W. P. "Smallholder Scheme Lugari, April 2, 1962."
"I.C.A. Agricultural Education." Kierman, Frank A. "Economic Planning Becomes Fashionable in Kenya, July 23, 1962."
Land Development and Settlement Board. "High Density Settlement Scheme, May 25, 1962."
"Letter from James Mage Aluda to Chief of North Maragoli, 'RE: Claim of My Table, January 11, 1960."
"Letter from Matthew Mwenesis to Mr. C. O. Kilasi, 'Kyavakali Day Secondary School' October 16, 1958."
Litwiller, William F. "Proceedings of the Third Annual National 4-K Program Planning Meeting, January 12–15, 1965."
"Lugari Rural Christian Training Center, May 25, 1967."
"Lugari Settlement Schemes Selection of Settlers, December 14, 1962."
Marcis, A. J. "Kenya and East Africa—Agricultural Courses in Secondary Schools."
Makhulo, Mteke. "Application for a Plot in Lugari Settlement Scheme, August 28, 1963."
McKenzie, Hon. B. R. "Using the Land with Care and with Wisdom, December 12, 1963."
Melville, A. R. "Report of the Director of Agriculture, 1963."
"Memorandum on AID to Congressman Silvio O. Conte, November 17, 1961."
"Memorandum on the Proposal to establish a Day Secondary School, Chavakali, North Maragoli, May 23, 1958."
"Minutes of the 1st Meeting of the AD Doc Board of Governors of Chavakali High School, November 26, 1958."
"Minutes of a Meeting to Discuss the Proposed Establishment of a Day Secondary School at Chavakli, October 10, 1958."

Mitchell, P. E. "Land and Population in East Africa, November 16, 1951," Her Majesty's Stationery Office, 1952.

Muchwingi. Makokha. "Application for a Plot in Lugari Settlement Scheme, August 31, 1963."

Mwanzi, Lawrence. "Application for a Plot in the Lugari Settlement Scheme, September 19, 1964."

Nalianya, P. N. "Settlement, February 11, 1964."

North Nyanza District Commissioner. "Synopsis of North Nyanza District, November 23, 1961."

Nottidge, C. P. R. "High Density Smallholder Settlement Scheme, July 22, 1963."

Office of the District Officer, Vihiga, North Nyanza. "Comments to Unemployment Survey 9, March 9, 1960."

Okinda, James. "Letter to District Commissioner, September 11, 1975."

———. "Letter to Ministry of State, November 13, 1975."

———. "Letter to Provincial Commissioner, September 25, 1975."

———. "Ministry of State, November 13, 1975."

Ombwara, C. J. "Handing Over Report Western Region, 1965."

Ongoli, A. O. "Land Consolidation, January 16, 1958."

Opwondi Opanga, Jonston. "Letter to Ministry of State, January 16, 1976."

"Outline of Proposed A.I.D. Projects for Fiscal Year 1963: Revision 1: July 11, 1962," July 11, 1962.

Penwill, D. J. "Instructions on Tea Planting in North Nyanza District, August 24, 1961."

———. "Tea in Maragoli, January 17, 1962."

Porter, J. L. "Recommendations on Rural Education Arising out of a Tour of Nyanza and Central Provinces, August 22–26, 1956."

"Principals of Extension Rural Youth Work Applied to Africa."

"Project Proposal and Approval—Explanation—Short—North Nyanza Education Department."

"Provincial General Hospital Nakuru, to Gavaghan, May 18, 1962."

R, A. P. "A Summary of the Present Position in Regard to the Availability of New Capital for Investment in Kenya, June 23 1960."

Rice, T. Hughes. "Location Statistics Table, 1951."

Rimington, G. P. "Coffee Policy, March 9, 1957."

"Rural Service Program Objective." Saccio, L. S. "ICA Paper on U.S. Assistance to Tropical Africa for Mr. Dillon, March 25, 1960."

———. "FY 1961 Economic Aid Program for fund for Cooperative Assistance to Africa, October 26, 1959."

Sargent, Edward. "Letter to Mr. David H. McVey, November 24, 1966."

Sauli, A. H. "The Need for Adult Education in Agriculture, October 4, 1956." "Secondary Schools, 1963."

Scott, Richard D. "Coffee General, March 2, 1957."

Stern, G. "Accelerated Tea Development: Nyanza Province, February 11, 1963."
"Survey of Unemployment, Secretary of North Nyanza African District Council, January 30, 1960."
Tobler, John H. "Statement of U.S. Policy toward Africa South of the Sahara Prior to Calendar Year 1960, October 28, 1957."
"The U.S. International Cooperation Administration Program in East Africa, July 3, 1961."
"Tea Development: North Nyanza, October 2, 1959."
"US-UK 115 (K) Economic Cooperation Act, June 25, 1953."
"U.S. Aid to East Africa: Memo to Robert W. Powers, June 16, 1960."
"US-UK 115 (K) Economic Cooperation Act, June 25, 1953."
"Village Surveys: Bunyore, Nyangori, Maragoli, Tiriki, Boholo, January 30, 1960."
Wagema, Grace. "Proceedings of the Third Annual National 4-K Program Planning Meeting, January 12, 1965."
Wagner, Gunter. "Maragoli Land Tenure, December 1946."
Walker, James. "Settlement Meeting, August 7, 1963."
Wawile, Patrick. "Application for a Plot in Lugari Settlement Scheme, August 28, 1963."
Williams, C. H. "Memorandum on the Subject of Over Population in the Maragoli and Bunyore Locations, 1952."
Wilson, Dr. G. "Village Survey: Bunyore, Nyangori, Maragoli, Tiriki, and Boholo, 1956."
Winter, K. H. "Bukura Trainees Certificates, August 24, 1956."
Withers, Charles D. "U.S. Aid to East Africa: Memo to Robert W. Powers, June 16, 1960."

Published Sources

Aerni-Flessner, John. "Self-Help Development Projects and Conceptions of Independence in Lesotho, 1950s–1970s." *International Journal of African Historical Studies* 50, no. 1 (2017): 11–33.
———. *Dreams for Lesotho: Independence, Foreign Assistance, and Development.* Notre Dame: University of Norte Dame Press, 2018.
Anderson, Benedict. *Imagined Communities*. New York: Verso, 1991.
Anderson, Charles W. *Issues of Political Development.* New Jersey: Prentice-Hall, 1967.
Anderson, David M. and Emma Lochery. "Violence and Exodus in Kenya's Rift Valley, 2008: Predictable and Preventable?" *Journal of Eastern African Studies* 2, no. 2 (July 2008): 328–43.
———. *Histories of the Hanged: The Dirty War in Kenya and the End of Empire*. New York: W. W. Norton, 2005.

———. "'Yours in Struggle for Majimbo.' Nationalism and the Party Politics of Decolonization in Kenya, 1955–64." *Journal of Contemporary History* 40, no. 3 (July 1, 2005): 547–64.

———. "Depression, Dust Bowl, Demography, and Drought: The Colonial State and Soil Conservation in East Africa during the 1930s." *African Affairs* 83, no. 332 (July 1984): 321–43.

———. *Eroding the Commons: The Politics of Ecology in Baringo, Kenya, 1890s–1963*. Athens: Ohio University Press, 2003.

Anderson, J. E. "The Kenya Education Commission Report: An African View of Educational Planning." *Comparative Education Review* 9 (June 1965).

Arnold, Guy. *Kenyatta and the Politics of Kenya*. West Sussex: Littlehampton Book Services, Ltd., 1974.

Askwith, Tom. *From Mau Mau to Harambee*. Edited by Joanna Lewis. Cambridge: African Studies Center, University of Cambridge, 1995.

Bagchi, Amiya Kumar. "Development Planning." In *New Palgrave: Economic Development*. New York: W. W. Norton & Company, 1989.

Bak Rasmussen, Ane Marie. *A History of the Quaker Movement in Africa*. New York: I. B. Tauris & Co Ltd., 1995.

Bates, Robert H. *Beyond the Miracle of the Market: The Political Economy of Agrarian Development in Kenya*. New York: Cambridge University Press, 2005.

———. *Markets and States in Tropical Africa: The Political Basis of Agriculture Policies*. 2nd Edition. Berkeley: University of California Press, 2005.

Bauer, Peter Thomas. *Equality, the Third World, and Economic Delusion*. Cambridge: Harvard University Press, 1981.

Berry, Sara. "Debating the Land Question in Africa." *Comparative Studies in Society and History* 44, no. 4 (2002): 638–68.

———. *No Condition is Permanent: The Social Dynamics of Agrarian Change in Sub-Saharan Africa*. Madison: The University of Wisconsin Press, 1993.

———. *Fathers Work for Their Sons: Accumulation, Mobility, and Class Formation in an Extended Yorùbá Community*. Berkeley: University of California Press, 1985.

———. "Hegemony on a Shoestring: Indirect Rule and Access to Agricultural Land." *Africa: Journal of the International African Institute* 62, no. 3 (1992): 327–55.

Berman, Bruce. "Ethnicity, Patronage and the African State: The Politics of Uncivil Nationalism." *African Affairs* 97, no. 388 (July 1998): 305–41.

———, and John Lonsdale. *Unhappy Valley: Conflict in Kenya & Africa*. Vol. 1. Athens: Ohio University Press, 1992.

———, and John Lonsdale. *Violence & Ethnicity*. Vol. 2. Athens: Ohio University Press, 1992.

Benson, T. G. "The Jeanes School and the Education of the East African Native." *Journal of the Royal African Society* 35, no. 141 (October 1936): 418–31.

Bourdillon, Bernard H. "Colonial Development and Welfare." *International Affairs (Royal Institute of International Affairs 1944–)* 20, no. 3 (July 1944): 369–80.

Bowman, Andrew. "Mass Production Or Production by the Masses? Tractors, Cooperatives, and the Politics of Rural Development in Post-Independence Zambia." *The Journal of African History* 52, no. 2 (July 2011): 201–21.

Burton, Andrew. *African Underclass: Urbanization, Crime and Colonial Order in Dar Es Salaam*. Oxford: James Currey, 2005.

———. "Urchins, Loafers and the Cult of the Cowboy: Urbanization and Delinquency in Dar-Es-Salaam, 1919–1961." *The Journal of African History* 42, no. 2001 (n.d.): 199–216.

Bradshaw, York W. "Perpetuating Underdevelopment in Kenya: The Link between Agriculture, Class, and State." *African Studies Review* 33, no. 1 (April 1990): 1–28.

Branch, Daniel. *Kenya: Between Hope and Despair, 1963–2011*. New Haven: Yale University Press, 2011.

———. *Defeating Mau Mau, Creating Kenya: Counterinsurgency, Civil War, and Decolonization*. Cambridge: Cambridge Unviersity Press, 2009.

C. T. "The Economic Development of the British Colonial Empire." *Bulletin of International News* 20, no. 4 (February 1943): 139–45.

Calderisi, Robert. *The Trouble with Africa: Why Foreign Aid Isn't Working*. London: Palgrave MacMillan, 2006.

Carter, William Morris. *Report of the Kenya Land Commission*. London: His Majesty's Stationary Office, 1933.

Christiansen, Luc and Lionel Demery. *Down to Earth: Agriculture and Poverty Reduction in Africa*. Washington, DC: The World Bank, 2007.

Collier, Paul. *The Bottom Billion*. Oxford: Oxford University Press, 2008.

Comaroff, John and Jean. *Of Revelation and Revolution: Christianity, Colonialism and Consciousness in South Africa*. Chicago: University of Chicago Press, 1991.

Cooper, Frederick. "Writing the History of Development." *Journal of Modern Europe History* 8 no. 1 (2010): 5–23.

———. *Africa Since 1940: The Past of the Present*. Cambridge: Cambridge University Press, 2002.

———. "Modernizing Bureaucrats, Backward Africans, and the Development Concept." In *International Development and the Social Sciences*. Berkeley: University of California Press, 1997.

———. *On the African Waterfront: Urban Disorder and the Transformation of Work in Colonial Mombasa*. New Haven: Yale University Press, 1987.

Cullen, Anthony, ed. *Harambee! The Prime Minister of Kenya's Speeches 1963–1964*. New York: Oxford University Press, 1964.

Creech-Jones, Arthur. "The British Experiment in Colonial Development and Welfare." *Civilizations* 6, no. 4 (January 1956); 557–64.

Davidson, Basil. *The Black Man's Burden: Africa and the Curse of the Nation-State*. New York: Times Books, 1992.

De Jong, Albert. *Mission and Politics in Eastern Africa: Dutch Missionaries and African Nationalism in Kenya, Tanzania and Malawi, 1945–1965*. Nairobi, Kenya: Paulines Publications Africa, 2000.

Dobb, Maurice. *Papers on Capitalism, Development and Planning*. New York: Routledge & K. Paul, 1967.

Easterly, William. *The White's Man's Burden: Why the West's Efforts to Aid the Rest Have Done so Much Ill and so Little Good*. New York: Penguin Books, 2009.

———. "Africa's Growth Tragedy: Policies and Ethnic Divisions." *Quarterly Journal of Economics*, no. 4 (1997): 1203–50.

Ekbladh, David. *The Great American Mission: Modernization and the Construction of an American World Order*. Princeton: Princeton University Press, 2010.

Elkins, Caroline. *Imperial Reckoning: The Untold Story of Britain's Gulag in Kenya*. New York: Henry Holt and Company, 2005.

Elliott, Kendall, R. *The End of an Era: Africa and the Missionary*. London: S.P.C.K., 1978.

Escobar, Arturo. *Encountering Development: The Making and Unmaking of the Third World*. Princeton: Princeton University Press, 1995.

Fearn, Hugh. *An African Economy: A Study of the Economic Development of the Nyanza Province of Kenya, 1903–1953*. Oxford: Oxford University Press, 1961.

Ferguson, James. *The Anti-Politics Machine: "Development," Depoliticization, and Bureaucratic Power in Lesotho*. Cambridge: Cambridge University Press, 1990.

Furedi, Frank. *The Mau Mau War in Perspective*. Athens: Ohio University Press, 1989.

Geiger, Susan. *TANU Women: Gender and Culture in the Making of Tanganyikan Nationalism, 1955–1965*. Portsmouth: Heinemann, 1997.

Gertzel, Cherry. *The Politics of Independent Kenya, 1963–8*. Evanston: Northwestern University Press, 1970.

Grubbs, Larry. *Secular Missionaries: Americans and African Development in the 1960s*. Boston: University of Massachusetts Press, 2009.

Hamer, John H. "Preconditions and Limits in the Formation of Associations: The Self-Help and Cooperative Movement in Sub-Saharan Africa." *African Studies Review* 24, no. 1 (1981).

Harbenson, John W. *Nation-Building in Kenya: The Role of Land Reform*. Evanston: Northwestern University Press, 1973.

———. "Land Reforms and Politics in Kenya, 1954–70." *Journal of Modern African Studies* 9, no. 2 (August 1971): 231–51.

Harman, Sophie and David Williams. "International Development in Transition." *Affairs* 90 (2014): 925–41.

Hastings, Adrian. *A History of African Christianity, 1950–1975*. New York: Cambridge University Press, 1979.

Haugerud, Angelique. *The Culture of Politics in Modern Kenya*. New York: Cambridge University Press, 1997.

Hearn, Julie. "The 'Invisible' Ngo: Us Evangelical Missions in Kenya." *Journal of Religion in Africa* 32, no. 1 (February 2002): 32–60. https://doi.org/10.1163/15700660260048465.

Henly, David. "Rural Development in South-East Asia and sub-Saharan Africa." *Development Policy Review* no. 30 (2012): 25–47.

Hira, Anil and Trevor Parfitt. *Development Projects for a New Millennium*. Westport: Praeger Publishers, 2004.

Hirsch, Guenther Paul. *Young Farmers' Clubs: A Report on a Survey in England and Wales of Their History, Organisation and Activities with Recommendations for Their Future Development*. London: National Federation of Farmers' Clubs, 1952.

Hotchkiss, Willis Ray. *Sketches from the Dark Continent*. Cleveland: Friends Bible Institute and Training School, 1901.

Hodge, Joseph. "British Colonial Expertise, Post-Colonial Careering and the Early History of International Development." *Journal of Modern European History* 8, no. 1 (2010): 24–44.

———. *Triumph of the Expert: Agrarian Doctrines of Development and the Legacies of British Colonialism*. Athens, OH: Ohio University Press, 2007.

Hodgkin, Thomas. *Nationalism in Colonial Africa*. New York: New York University Press, 1957.

Holmquist, Frank. "Self-Help: The State and Peasant Leverage in Kenya." *Africa: Journal of the International African Institute* 54, no. 3 (1984): 72–91.

Hoskins, Lewis M. *Chavakali: An Experiment in Practical Education in Kenya Directed by Earlham College, 1960–64*. Richmond, 1964.

Hyden, Goran. *Beyond Ujamaa in Tanzania: Underdevelopment and an Uncaptured Peasantry*. Berkeley: University of California Press, 1980.

Indire, Filemona Fundi. "A Comprehensive High School Curriculum Proposal for Reviewing and Revising the Program of Chavakali Secondary School, Maragoli, Kenya." PhD Dissertation. Indiana University, 1962.

Isaacman, Allen and Barbara Isaacman. *Damns, Displacement and the Delusion of Development: Cahora Bassa and Its Legacies in Mozambique, 1965–2007*. Athens: Ohio University Press, 2013.

Jennings, Michael. "We Must Run While Others Walk: Popular Participation and Development Crisis in Tanzania, 1961–69." *The Journal of Modern African Studies* 41, no. 2 (June 2003): 163–87.

Jolly, Richard, ed. *Milestone and Turning Points in Development Thinking*. London: Palgrave MacMillan, 2012.

Jones, N. S. Carey. "The Decolonization of the White Highlands of Kenya." *The Geographic Journal* 131, no. 2 (June 1965): 140–55.

Jones, Thomas Jesse and Phelps-Stokes Fund. *African Education Commission*. New York, 1922.

Juma, Calestous. *The New Harvest Agricultural Innovation in Africa.* New York: Oxford University Press, 2011.

Kalilombe, P. A. "The African Local Churches and the World-Wide Roman Catholic Communion." In *Christianity in Independent Africa*, 79–95. Bloomington: Indiana University Press, 1978.

Kanogo, Tabitha. *Squatters and the Roots of Mau Mau, 1905–63.* Athens: Ohio University Press, 1987.

Kaplan, Irving and Margarita K. Dobert et al. *Area Handbook for Kenya.* Second Edition. Washington, DC: U.S. Govt. Print Office, 1976.

Kasfir, N. *The Shrinking Political Arena: Participation and Ethnicity in African Politics, with a Case Study of Uganda.* Berkeley: University of California Press, 1976.

Kay, Stafford. "The Southern Abaluyia, The Friends Africa Mission, and the Development of Education in Western Kenya, 1902–1965." PhD Dissertation. University of Wisconsin, 1973.

Kirk-Greene, Anthony. "Towards a Retrospective Record: Part I—What Became of Us?" *The Overseas Pensioner* 82 (2002): 30–34.

Kilemi Mwiria. "Kenya's Harambee Secondary School Movement: The Contradictions of Public Policy." *Comparative Education Review* 34, no. 3 (August 1990).

Kitching, Gavin. *Class and Economic Change in Kenya: The Making of an African Petite Bourgeoisie 1905–1970.* New Haven: Yale University Press, 1980.

Kendall, R. Elliott. "The Missionary Factor in Africa." In *Christianity in Independent Africa.* Bloomington, IN: Indiana University Press, 1978. 16–25.

Kenyatta, Jomo. *Harambee! The Prime Minister of Kenya's Speeches, 1963–1964.* New York: Oxford University Press, 1964.

Komba, Donatus. "Contributions to Rural Development: Ujamaa and Villagization." In *Mwalimu: The Influence of Nyerere.* London: James Currey, 1995.

Lal, Deepak. *The Poverty of Development Economics.* London: Institute of Economic Affairs, 1983.

Lal, Priya. *African Socialism in Postcolonial Tanzania: Between the Village and the World.* New York: Cambridge, 2015.

Landau, Paul. *The Realm of the World: Language, Gender, and Christianity in a Southern African Kingdom.* Portsmouth: Heinemann, 1995.

Leonard, David, and Scott Straus. *Africa's Stalled Development: International Causes and Cures.* Boulder: Lynne Rienner, 2003.

Leo, Christopher. "Who Benefited from the Million-Acre Scheme? Toward a Class Analysis of Kenya's Transition to Independence." *Canadian Journal of African Studies* 15, no. 2 (1981): 201–22.

Lewis, W. R. *The Theory of Economic Growth.* Homewood: Richard D. Irwin, 1955.

Leys, Colin. *Underdevelopment in Kenya: The Political Economy of Underdevelopment 1964–71.* London: Heinemann, 1975.

Lonsdale, John. "Moral Ethnicity and Political Tribalism." In *Inventions and Boundaries: Historical and Anthropological Approaches to the Study of Ethnicity*. Roskilde, Denmark: International Development Studies, Roskilde University, 1994.

———. "The Moral Economy of Mau Mau: Wealth, Poverty and Civic Virtue in Kikuyu Political Thought." In *Unhappy Valley, Book Two: Violence and Ethnicity*. Athens, OH: Ohio University Press, 1992. 315–461.

———, Stanley Booth-Clibborn, and Andrew Hake. "The Emerging Pattern of Co-Operation in Kenya." In *Christianity in Independent Africa*, 267–84. Bloomington: Indiana University Press, 1978.

Lowe, Kevin. *Baptized with the Soil: Christian Agrarians and the Crusade for Rural America*. New York: Oxford University Press, 2015.

Low, D. A., and John Lonsdale, "Introduction: Towards the New Order 1945–63." In *History of East* Africa. Vol. III. Oxford: Oxford University Press, 1976.

MacArthur, Julie. "The Making and Unmaking of African Languages: Oral Communities and Competitive Linguistic Work in Western Kenya." *Journal of African History*, no. 53 (2012): 151–72.

———. *Cartography and the Political Imagination: Mapping Community in Colonial Kenya*. Athens: Ohio University Press, 2016.

MacKenzie, A. Fiona D. "Betterment and the Gendered Politics of Maize Production, Murang'a District, Central Province, Kenya 1880–1952." *Canadian Journal of African Studies* 33, no. 1 (1999): 64–97.

Mamdani, Mahmood. *Citizen and Subject: Contemporary Africa and the Legacy of Late Colonialism*. Princeton, NJ: Princeton University Press, 1996.

Mandala, Elias. *Work and Control in a Peasant Economy: A History of the Lower Tchiri Valley in Malawi, 1859–1960*. Madison: University of Wisconsin Press, 1990.

Manji, Firoze, and Carl O'Coill. "The Missionaries Position: NGOs and Development in Africa." *International Affairs (Royal Institute of International Affairs 1944–)* 78, no. 3 (July 2002): 567–83.

Maxon, Robert. *Going Their Separate Ways: Agrarian Transformation in Kenya, 1930–1950*. Cranbury, NJ: Associated Univeristy Presses, 2010.

Maxwell, Robert. "The Relationship of Social Differentiation to Academic Success in Secondary School and Occupational Patterns in Kenya: The Chavakali Case." PhD Dissertation. Cornell University, 1970.

Maxwell, David. "Decolonization." In *Missions and Empire*. The Oxford History of the British Empire. New York: Oxford University Press, 2005. 285–305.

Mbithi, Philip M., and Carolyn Barnes. *The Spontaneous Settlement Problem in Kenya*. Nairobi, Kenya: East African Literature Bureau, 1975.

———, and Rasmus Rasmusson. *Self-Reliance in Kenya: The Case of Harambee*. Stockholm: Alqvist & Wickseel, 1977.

McCullers, Molly. "Like Biscuits in Wrappers: Apartheid Development and Decolonization in South West Africa, 1962–1968." *International Journal of African Historical Studies* 50, no. 1 (2017): 59–78.

Milburn, Josephine Fishel. "The Fabian Society and the British Labour Party." *The Western Political Quarterly* 11, no. 2 (July 1958): 319–39.

Miller, Norman and Rodger Yeager. *Kenya: The Quest for Prosperity*. Second Edition. Boulder: Westview Press, 1994.

Mkandawire, Thandika. "Running While Others Walk: Knowledge and the Challenge of Africa's Development." *African Development*, no. 2 (2011): 1–36.

Moyo, Dambisa. *Dead Aid: Why Aid Is Not Working and How There Is a Better Way for Africa*. New York: Farrar, Straus and Giroux, 2009.

Munk, Nina. "How Warren Buffet's Son Would Feed the World." *The Atlantic*. May 2016.

Mutongi, Kenda. *Worries of the Heart: Widows, Family, and Community in Kenya*. Chicago: University of Chicago Press, 2007.

Ngau, Peter. "Tensions in Empowerment: The Experience of the 'Harambee' (Self-Help) Movement in Kenya." *Economic Development and Cultural Change* 35, no. 3 (n.d.): 523–38.

Nolte, Insa. "Religion, Development and Politics in Nigeria." In *Handbook of Research on Development and Religion*. Northampton: Edward Elger Publishing, 2013.

Nottidge, C. P. R. and J. R. Goldsack. *The Million-Acre Settlement Scheme, 1962–1965*. Nairobi: Government Printer, 1967.

Nyerere, Julius. "Freedom and Development, 16 October 1968." In *Freedom and Development: Uhuru Na Maendeleo. A Selection from Writings and Speeches 1968–1973*. New York: Oxford University Press, 1973.

———. "'Ujamma': The Basis of African Socialism, April 1962." In *African Socialism*. Stanford: Stanford University Press, 1992. 238–48.

Ochieng', William R. "Structural and Political Changes." In *Decolonization and Independence in Kenya 1940–1993, edited by B. A. Ogot and W. R. Ochieng'*. Athens, OH: Ohio University Press, 1995.

Odinga, Ajuma Oginga. *Net Yet Uhuru*. London: Heinemann, 1967.

Ogot, B. A. "The Decisive Years 1956–63." In *Decolonization and Independence in Kenya 1940–1993, edited by B. A. Ogot and W. R. Ochieng'*. Athens, OH: Ohio University Press, 1995. 48–79.

———. "British Administration in the Central Nyanza District of Kenya, 1900–60. *Journal of African History* 4, no. 2 (1963): 249–73.

Osogo, John. *A History of the Baluyia*. New York: Oxford University Press, 1966.

Ominde, S. H. *Land and Population Movements in Kenya*. Evanston: Northwestern University Press, 1968.

Owen, David E. *English Philanthropy, 1660–1960*. Cambridge, MA: Belknap Press of Harvard University Press, 1964.

Packard, Randall and Frederick Cooper. *International Development and the Social Sciences: Essays in the History of the British West Indies, British Colonial Africa, South Africa, Cuba, and Brazil*. Pittsburgh, PA: University of Pittsburgh Press, 2007.

Parpart, Jane. "Where Is Your Mother?' Gender, Urban Marriage, and Colonial Discourse on the Zambian Copperbelt, 1924–1945." *The International Journal of African Historical Studies* 27, no. 2 (1994): 241–71.

Parsons, Timothy H. "Being Kikuyu in Meru: Challenging the Tribal Geography of Colonial Kenya." *The Journal of African History* 53, no. 1 (March 2012): 45–64.

———. "The Limits of Sisterhood: The Evolution of Guide Movement in Colonial Kenya." In *Scouting Frontiers: Youth and the Scout Movement's First Century*. London: Cambridge Scholars Publishing, 2009.

———. "The Consequences of Uniformity: The Struggle for the Boy Scout Uniform in Colonial Kenya." *Journal of Social History* 40, no. 2 (Winter 2006), 361–83.

Pearse, A., and M. Stiefel. *Inquiry into Participation: A Research Approach*. Geneva: UN Research Institute for Social Development, 1979.

———. "Local Responses to the Ethnic Geography of Colonialism in the Gusii Highlands of Brith-Ruled Kenya." *Ethnohistory* 58, no. 3 (2011): 491–23.

———. *Race, Resistance, and the Boy Scout Movement in British Colonia Africa*. Athens: Ohio University Press, 2004.

Peel, J. D. Y. *Religious Encounter and the Making of the Yoruba*. Bloomington: Indiana University Press, 2003.

Percox, David. *Britain, Kenya, and the Cold War: Imperial Defense, Colonial Security, and Decolonization*. New York: Tauris Academic Studies, 2004.

Peters, John L. *Cry Dignity!*. World Neighbors, Inc., 1976.

Peterson, Derek. *Creative Writing: Translation, Bookkeeping, and the Work of Imagination in Colonial Kenya*. Portsmouth: Heinemann, 2004.

Porter, Andrew. *Religion versus Empire? British Protestant Missionaries and Overseas Expansion, 1700–1914*. Manchester: Manchester University Press, 2004.

Printer, Levinus King. *The Hill of Vision: The Story of the Quaker Movement in East Africa, 1902–1965*. Nairobi: East Africa Yearly Meeting of Friends, 1966.

———. "Opportunities for Friends in Kenya." *Friends Journal: Quaker Thought and Life Today* 12, no. 8 (April 1966): 200–201.

Ranger, Terence O. *Peasant Consciousness and Guerrilla War in Zimbabwe: A Comparative Study*. Berkeley: University of California Press, 1985.

Robinson, Ronald. *African Development Planning: Impressions and Papers of the Cambridge Conference on Development Planning, 22 September–5 October 1963 at Queens' College, Cambridge*. London: The Whitefriars Press, Ltd., 1963.

Rodney, Walter. *How Europe Underdeveloped Africa*. Washington, DC: Howard University Press, 1972.

Rosenberg, Gabriel N. *The 4-H Harvest: Sexuality and the State in Rural America*. Philadelphia: University of Pennsylvania Press, 2015.

Rostow, W. W. *The Stages of Economic Growth*. Cambridge, MA: University Press, 1962.

Russell, David E. "Oral History Methodology, The Art of Interviewing." Ohio History Workshop, University of California, Santa Barbara. https://www.library.ucsb.edu/special-collections/oral-history/oralhlec (accessed January 2018).

Sachs, Jeffrey. *The End of Poverty*. New York: Penguin Books, 2005.

———. *Investing in Development: A Practical Plan to Achieve the Millennium Development Goals, Overview*. New York: United Nations Development Programme, 2005.

Schneider, Leander. "Freedom and Unfreedom in Rural Development: Julius Nyerere, Ujamaa Vijijini, and Villagization." *Canadian Journal of African Studies* 38, no. 2 (2004): 344–92.

Schler, Lynn. *Nations on Board: Becoming Nigerian at Sea*. Athens: Ohio University Press, 2016.

Scott, James. *Seeing like a State: How Certain Schemes to Improve the Human Condition Have Failed*. New Haven: Yale University Press, 1999.

Seers, Dudley. "The Congruence of Marxism and Other Neoclassical Doctrines." In *Toward a New Strategy for Development, A Rothko Chapel Colloquium*. New York: Pergamon Press, 1979.

———. "The Meaning of Development." *Institute of Development Studies*. Communication Series 44 (1969): 1–28.

Segers, Kaatje, Joost Dessein, Sten Hagberg, Patrick Develtere, Mitiku Haile, and Jozef Deckers. "Be Like Bees: The Politics of Mobilizing Farmers for Development in Tigray, Ethiopia." *African Affairs* 108, no. 430 (January 1, 2009): 91–109.

Sen, Amartya. "The Concept of Development." In *Handbook of Development Economics*. Vol. 1. New York: Elsevier Science Publishers, 1988.

Sorrenson, M. P. K. *Land Reform in Kikuyu Country*. Nairobi, Kenya: Oxford University Press, 1967.

Spear, Thomas. *Mountain Farmers: Moral Economics of Land and Agricultural Development in Arusha and Meru*. Berkeley: University of California Press, 1997.

———. "Neo-Traditionalism and the Limits of Invention in British Colonial Africa." *The Journal of African History* 44, no. 1 (2003): 3–27.

Spencer, Ian. "Settler Dominance, Agricultural Production and the Second World War in Kenya." *Journal of African History* 21, no. 4 (1980): 497–514.

Spulber, Nicholas. *Foundations of Soviet Strategy for Economic Growth*. Bloomington: Indiana University Press, 1964.

Shanguhyia, Martin S. *Population, Tradition, and Environmental Control in Colonial Kenya*. Rochester: University of Rochester Press, 2015.

Sheldon, Kathleen. "Urban African Women Courtyards, Markets, City Streets." In *Countryside, Markets, City Streets: Urban Women in Africa*. Boulder: Westview Press, 1996.

Shields, Tanner and National Federation of Young Farmers' Clubs. *Youthful Forward Thinking: Young Farmers Clubs of England and Walesg: Their Past, Present and Future*. [Kenilworth]: National Federation of Young Farmers' Clubs, 1980.

Stanley, Brian. "Christianity and the End of Empire." In *Missions, Nationalism, and the End of Empire*. Cambridge: Wm. B. Eerdmans Publishing Co., 2003.

———. *The Bible and the Flag: Protestant Missions and British Imperialism in the Nineteenth and Twentieth Century*. Leicester: Apollos, 1990.

Streeten, Paul. "Development Ideas in Historical Perspective." In *Toward a New Strategy for Development*. New York: Pergamon Press, 1979.

Stuart, John. *British Missionaries and the End of Empire: East, Central, and South Africa, 1939–1964*. Grand Rapids, Michigan: William B. Eerdmans Publishing Company, 2011.

Swynnerton, R. J. M. *A Plan to Intensify the Development of African Agriculture in Kenya*. Nairobi: Government Printer, 1954.

Tague, Joanna T. "Displaced Agents of Development: Mozambican Refugees and Tanzanian Nation-Building Projects, 1964–1975." *International Journal of African Historical Studies* 50, no. 1 (2017): 121–45.

Thabo, David. "The Jeanes School in Kenya, 1924–1964: A Social Experiment to Train Teachers for Rural Education and Community Development." PhD Dissertation. Syracuse University, 1984.

Thomas, Allen. "Development as Practice in a Liberal Capitalist World." *Journal of International Development* 12, no. 6 (2000): 773–87.

Throup, David. *Economic & Social Origins of Mau Mau 1945–53*. Eastern African Studies. London & Athens, OH: Ohio University Press; Nairobi, Kenya: J. Currey, 1988.

Tiffen, Mary. *More People, Less Erosion: Environmental Recovery in Kenya*. John Wiley & Sons Ltd., 1994.

Todaro, Michael. *Development Planning; Models and Methods*. Nairobi, Kenya: Oxford University Press, 1971.

Tuma, Tom. "Major Changes and Developments in Christian Leadership in Busoga Province, Uganda 1960–74." In *Christianity in Independent Africa*, 60–78. Bloomington, IN: Indiana University Press, 1978.

Van Beusekom, Monica M. and Dorthy L. Hodgson. "Lesson Learned? Development Experiences in the Late Colonial Period." *Journal of African History* 41, no. 1 (2000): 29–33.

Verma, Ritu, and International Development Research Centre (Canada). *Gender, Land and Livelihoods in East Africa through Farmers' Eyes*. Ottawa: International Development Research Centre, 2001. http://public.eblib.com/choice/publicfull record.aspx?p=295143.

Waikenda, Machel. "Agriculture Can Create a Million Jobs for Youth." News Outlet. *Standard Digital*, January 5, 2014. http://www.standardmedia.co.ke/?articleID=2000101477.

Waller, Richard. "Rebellious Youth in Colonial Africa." *The Journal of African History* 47, no. 1 (2006): 77–92.

Wandibba, Simiyu. *Masinde Muliro: A Biography*. Nairobi: East African Educational Publishers, 1997.

Wasserman, Gary. *Politics of Decolonization: Kenya Europeans and the Land Issue, 1960–1965*. New York: Cambridge University Press, 1976.

———. "Continuity and Counter-Insurgency: The Role of Land Reform in Decolonizing Kenya, 1962–70." *Canadian Journal of African Studies / Revue Canadienne Des Études Africaines* 7, no. 1 (January 1, 1973): 133–48.

Were, Gideon S. *A History of the Abaluyia of Western Kenya*. Nairobi: East Africa Publishing House, 1967.

Wessel, Thomas R., and Marilyn. Wessel. *4-H, an American Idea, 1900–1980: A History of 4-H*. Chevy Chase, MD (7100 Connecticut ave., Chevy Chase 20815): National 4-H Council, 1982.

Wicker, E. W. "Colonial Development and Welfare, 1929–1957: The Evolution of a Policy." *Social and Economic Studies* 7, no. 4 (December 1958): 170–92.

Widner, Jennifer A. *The Rise of a Party-State in Kenya: From "Harambee!" To "Nyayo!"* Berkeley: University of California Press, 1992.

Williams, Gavin. "Studying Development and Explaining Policies." *Oxford Development Studies* 31, no. 1 (2003): 37–58.

Willis, Justin. *Mombasa, the Swahili, and the Making of the Mijikenda*. Oxford Studies in African Affairs. Oxford: Oxford University Press, 1993.

White, Luise. *The Comforts of Home: Prostitution in Colonial Nairobi*. Chicago: University of Chicago Press, 1990.

Young, Crawford. "Evolving Modes of Consciousness and Ideology: Nationalism and Ethnicity." In *Political Development and the New Realism in sub-Saharan Africa*. Charlottesville: University of Virginia Press, 1994.

Index

Page numbers in italics indicate illustrations.

www.ingramcontent.com/pod-product-compliance
Ingram Content Group UK Ltd.
Pitfield, Milton Keynes, MK11 3LW, UK
UKHW020841290926
15470UKWH00004B/1478

9 781580 469791